THE LOST CAUSE

JAMES P. MUEHLBERGER

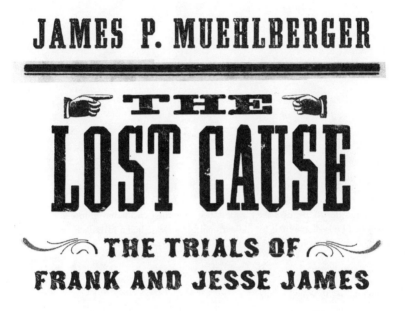

THE
LOST CAUSE
THE TRIALS OF
FRANK AND JESSE JAMES

WESTHOLME
Yardley

Frontispiece: A rare tintype featuring, from left to right, Jesse James, Frank James, and an unknown accomplice. The James brothers grew beards in order to disguise their appearance after their clean-shaven like-nesses had been distributed by the national press. Jesse had a full black beard when he was murdered in 1882. (*Courtesy Steve Crowley*)

Westholme Publishing, LLC
904 Edgewood Road
Yardley, Pennsylvania 19067
Visit our Web site at www.westholmepublishing.com

First Printing May 2013
10 9 8 7 6 5 4 3 2 1
ISBN: 978-1-59416-173-5
Also available as an eBook.

Printed in the United States of America.

To my "Dream Team," Jayme, Alex, and Max

CONTENTS

List of Maps

A gallery of illustrations follows page 102

PROLOGUE

As America lurched into civil war during the winter and spring of 1860–61, the cause of the crisis was foremost in the minds of the nation's political leaders. The slave states stated in their declarations of secession that they were leaving the Union to preserve slavery—what Confederate vice president Alexander Stephens called "the cornerstone of the Confederacy." Four years later, in his second inaugural address, just about a month before he was killed, President Abraham Lincoln pronounced the institution of slavery to be the inextricable cause of the war that would soon grind to an end, a war that would leave over six hundred thousand Americans dead. "These slaves," who made up "[o]ne eighth of the whole population . . . constituted a peculiar and powerful interest," he wrote. "All knew that this interest was, somehow, the cause of the war."[1]

Adding to his burden of attempting to manage "the fiery crucible" of America's Civil War, "in which the old nation was melted down and out of which modern America poured," Lincoln was at the center of a political, societal, and human storm, deciding the fate of tens of thousands of slaves who had escaped to the North during the war, planning for African-Americans to serve in the Union army, freeing slaves in the Confederacy through the Emancipation Proclamation, and then steering the tumultuous passage of the 13th Amendment, making slavery illegal. Lincoln, perhaps more than any man in the nation, knew well the cause of the Civil War. What was self-evident then, however, has purposely been obscured by some ever since the guns fell silent.

White Southerners emerged from the war beaten, but many were largely unrepentant. Following the surrender at Appomattox Courthouse, Virginia, they nurtured a public memory of the Confederacy that placed their wartime sacrifice and defeat in the best possible light. Widely known then and now as the "Lost Cause" explanation of the Confederate experience, they sought to justify their actions and find something positive in failure. They also wanted to provide their children and future generations of white Southerners with a "correct" narrative of the war.[2]

Generally, the Lost Cause legend claims that the war was an essentially heroic and romantic melodrama, an honorable sectional dual, fought over states' rights, not slavery, and a time of martial glory on both sides. In the myth of the Lost Cause, the South's culture and way of life are portrayed as superior.[3] The South is blessed as peopled by aristocrats displaying grace and gentility, and the human beings they held in bondage happy and content. The cause was allegedly lost because of massive Union resources and manpower.[4]

Beginning in 1870, after learning about Jesse James's first brush with the law, former Confederate major John Newman Edwards, the editor of the *Kansas City Times* newspaper, decided that he may be able to recast the emerging outlaw as a postwar extension and embodiment of the Lost Cause, an American Robin Hood, a former Confederate guerrilla and "noble robber" turned into a political criminal. Jesse was a defender of the Southern tradition of honor, family, and friendship, while his pursuers were faceless corporate cowards representing banking and railroad interests. Edwards was largely successful in his effort to spin an alternative, more grandiose "history."

Edwards was assisted in his effort by sensational dime pulp novels and largely fictional books containing overblown rhetoric, in which accuracy is sometimes hard to find. Writers wasted no time in capitalizing on the popular myth of Jesse James. Only one month after Jesse's death in 1882, St. Louis author Frank Triplett published a sensational and largely fictional account, *The Life, Times and Treacherous Death of Jesse James*, based almost exclusively on interviews of Jesse's widow and mother. Not surprisingly, all murders attributed to Jesse and his brother Frank, and most of the robberies, are denied. Almost all of the "history" of Frank and Jesse that followed for the next eighty years was carelessly written and romanticized their crimes.

Hollywood has for decades also glorified the Lost Cause through the myth of Jesse's "noble robber" exploits. Seventy-five years ago, actors Henry Fonda and Tyrone Power immortalized the James brothers in the movie *Jesse James,* an entertaining but seriously flawed film in its historical content. In the movie, the Pinkerton Detective Agency's "bombing" of Jesse's home leads to his life of crime against corporate greed. In truth, Frank and Jesse James had been robbing and murdering for almost a decade at the time of the attack. The rationalization of Jesse James's crimes as protecting the former Confederate states from Northern exploitation is an appendage to the Southern argument that the Civil War was about states' rights, not slavery.

This book brings a new perspective to research and interpretation of Jesse James by exploring the sworn testimony contained in the criminal trials and legal proceedings against the James brothers, in an effort to strip myth from fact. If reporting is the first rough draft of history, sworn testimony is the second. Did Jesse James rob and murder for politics or for profit? Was he the last great rebel of the Civil War, or the first notorious robber after the Civil War?

Trial lawyers are storytellers, and we piece together a narrative based on small pieces of evidence. During my over thirty years as a prosecutor and trial lawyer, I have sifted through thousands of pages of documents looking for the "smoking gun" that will make my case. I have spent months, sometimes years, tracking down leads to find a witness—sometimes when they don't want to be found—

who may know key facts about the case. I have used the same approach here, analyzing and arranging the facts as a lawyer might do in presenting a case to the jury. Generally, the legal papers, personal papers, and sworn testimony I uncovered and rely on tend to be fact-based, uncolored by the partisan politics of late nineteenth-century Missouri.

I started on this journey ten years ago because I was told that Henry McDougal, one of the founders of my law firm, had successfully sued Frank and Jesse James, although no one had been able to find any record of the prosecution. This intrigued me. I knew little of Jesse James other than what I'd seen in movies, read in the occasional newspaper or magazine article, or learned from living for over fifty years in the same area where he lived and rode 140 years ago.

I began by travelling northwest Missouri searching court files. At the Daviess County clerk's office, I spent nearly a week during a sabbatical from my law firm in 2007 carefully paging through a wall of file drawers of lawsuits, each drawer containing about one hundred cases. Finally in drawer No. 145 I found what I was looking for: the long-forgotten, dusty documents titled *Daniel Smoote v. Frank and Jesse James*. These papers proved that the legendary prosecution had indeed taken place. What I discovered bore little resemblance to what I'd seen, heard, or read. In fact, much of the "history" of Jesse James is as firm as gun smoke. I also interviewed descendants of participants in the events recounted here. I read over five hundred original sources, including legal records, newspapers, personal papers, letters, memoirs, and army reports in order to prepare the manuscript.

While Jesse James has been the subject of thousands of books, articles, movies, and songs, the prosecutions of Frank and Jesse and their gang members are little known, but important, historical facts. One surprise that came from the documents I discovered was that it was a female who was first responsible for bringing Jesse James to national attention: she had long slender legs, wide shoulders, and a graceful neck—her name was Kate, and she was a thoroughbred racehorse. What ignited Jesse James's meteoric rise to fame was the loss of Kate after the murder of a bank cashier in Gallatin, Missouri, in 1869. The new evidence also reveals that the Gallatin bank cashier was not murdered during a bank robbery, but that he was mistaken for another Union officer who was targeted for assassination because of his ambush of a Confederate guerrilla fighter during the Civil War. It also turns out that it was unlikely that Frank James, who was charged with murder along with Jesse, had participated in the homicide. The murder turned out to be an intriguing whodunit.

Evidence also suggested that the letters attributed to Jesse denying responsibility for the murder were likely not written by him. And I found records of the little known first jury trial of a member of what became known as the James-Younger Gang, and a second trial of another gang member, who unexpectedly was found guilty by a Missouri jury, the first wedge in the destruction of the gang.

It was of paramount importance that the James Gang and other outlaws be brought to justice: America was in the midst of a revolution in railroads, communications, and industry, and states like Missouri could not afford to be bypassed in this transformation due to any perception of lawlessness and risk to communities, companies, or investors.

An infuriated Jesse James twice tried to murder Henry McDougal for prosecuting him for the Gallatin killing. As a result of Jesse's threats and assassination attempts, McDougal began secretly collaborating with the Pinkerton agency in its efforts to put a stop to Jesse and his gang. McDougal's law partner, on behalf of his railroad client, offered Missouri's governor up to $10,000 in reward money for Jesse, dead or alive. Following Jesse's death, McDougal prosecuted Frank James for murder, a story missing from the well-known tales of the James brothers.

McDougal was intensely ambitious, and he loved the rough-and-tumble of courtrooms and smoke-filled political backrooms. He became the youngest judge in Missouri state court history, one of the first presidents of the Missouri bar, and one of the state's leading railroad lawyers. He argued and won cases before the U.S. Supreme Court, and he was one of the founders of what became the internationally known law firm of Shook, Hardy & Bacon, LLP. But his success stems from the unknown story of his pursuit and prosecution of some of America's most notorious outlaws, told here for the first time.

THE LOST CAUSE

ONE

GRAND RIVER COUNTRY

ON DECEMBER 7, 1869, Gallatin, Missouri, came to life shortly before daybreak. A fog hung over the town like a thick, sprawling ghost, and drifted in gray wraiths lurking among the old oak and hickory trees in the surrounding forest. Stone chimneys belched smoke from freshly stoked fires that had died to embers during the cold night. Lights from lamps began to appear in house windows.

Located on the northwest Missouri frontier, Gallatin was a hilltop hamlet that sheltered three hundred adventurous souls. The Grand River flowed through a valley east of town, so the settlers referred to the hilly, tree-covered area as the Grand River Country. The first white settlers had followed the Grand River up from the Missouri River in the early 1830s, attracted by the abundance of wild game, such as turkeys, elk, deer, fox, panthers, and black bear. In the spring and fall, geese and ducks darkened the river. By 1869, Gallatin's few merchants had located their businesses in gray-fronted buildings on a hill west of the river in a square, in the center of which was a two-story courthouse. In the northwest corner of the yard surrounding the courthouse was a small stone jail.

The courthouse and offices located inside served the surrounding 570-square-mile Daviess County, named after Colonel Joseph Hamilton Daviess, a Kentucky lawyer and Indian fighter who had been killed at the Battle of Tippecanoe.[1] The county was inhabited mostly by plain-mannered and plainspoken Kentucky farmers who had little or no formal education, many of whom were illiterate. The courthouse yard was enclosed by a wooden fence and a worn and polished hitching rail for horses. Around the square were rutted roads.

The optimistically named Grand Street ran east/west along the south side of the square, where the newly constructed dance hall dominated the northwest corner of the block directly south of the square. Market Street formed the western border of the square, along which, across from the dance hall, stood a small brick building, barely twenty feet wide and twice as deep. The little building was eight feet high, with a pitched roof, and had two windows on the north side, a door in front, and a window on the south. The structure was home to the newly formed Daviess County Savings Association, known locally as the "bank." Within its narrow walls, farmers and tradesmen came to deposit their earnings or draw upon their credit from the iron safe in the back room. South of the bank stood an old two-story log bunkhouse that called itself a hotel.[2]

Virginia native John W. Sheets was the 51-year-old cashier of the bank. In spring 1838, when Martin Van Buren was president, Sheets's father, Henry, a Virginia gunsmith, and his wife, Mary, packed their belongings and, with 19-year-old John, started for the far West. They had decided to stake their future in the unseen, unfamiliar prairie of northwest Missouri, which was then the extreme frontier of the United States. The Sheets family, like the majority of Gallatin's residents, were of Scotch-Irish descent. They were Baptists and Democrats, and their idol was Andrew Jackson, Old Hickory of Tennessee. Along with their Bibles, rifles, farm tools, corn whiskey, and black slaves, they brought from Virginia and Kentucky a loathing for taxes and government.[3]

John Sheets was one of the earliest occupants of Gallatin, and he drafted handwritten deeds for its first residents. He had seen bloodshed since the town's beginning. In October 1838, Sheets watched as Mormons from a nearby settlement, acting under the direction of Joseph Smith Jr., drove the people away and burned the town to the ground following earlier attacks on the Mormons by Missourians. In response, Governor Lilburn Boggs ordered the state militia to "exterminate" the Mormons, who were ultimately forcibly driven from Missouri to neighboring Illinois.[4]

Gallatin was rebuilt, and in 1846, John Sheets enlisted in the army and rode one thousand miles from the bluegrass sod of the Grand River Country with Colonel Alexander W. Doniphan to fight in the Mexican War. They were victorious in two important battles and several skirmishes. Upon his triumphant return to Gallatin, Sheets was elected sheriff of Daviess County, a position he held until 1856, when he was elected circuit clerk and county recorder of deeds. He married and had two children.[5]

At the start of the Civil War in 1861, Gallatin was a divided town in a divided state. Missouri was a border state during the Civil War. Although it was a slave state, most of its citizens were not slaveholders. For instance, St. Louis was largely populated by Germans and other immigrants who had no ties to the South. On the other hand, in Daviess County, Abraham Lincoln received only sixteen out of several hundred votes cast in the 1860 presidential election. The Union largely retained control of Missouri's major cities and vital resources during the war; Confederate guerrillas generally controlled the rural areas south of the Missouri River, particularly after sundown.

Only eight Gallatin men openly declared for the Union after the fall of Fort Sumter. Rebel supporters harassed the Unionists as "goddamn abolitionists," and before long the verbal abuse turned into threats of murder. Missouri governor Hamilton Gamble soon received permission from President Lincoln to raise ten cavalry regiments. John Sheets commanded Company D of one of the regiments, and he would be known as Captain Sheets for the rest of his short life. After a skirmish with Union soldiers, rebel troops fled Daviess County.[6]

Missouri citizens suffered cruelly as a result of fierce warfare between the Union soldiers and Southern guerrillas. In fact, Missouri was the third most fought over state during the war, as measured by the number of battles and skirmishes. The Missouri River town of Lexington, from which Gallatin received most of it supplies, was the scene of several fierce battles. Lexington was the seat of Lafayette County, and the city occupied a position of considerable importance on the Missouri River. Hemp (used for rope), tobacco, coal, and cattle contributed to the town's wealth, as did the river trade. Many of Lexington's residents were slave owners; in fact, slaves made up almost one-third of the population of Lafayette County. A bloody three-day battle occurred in Lexington in September 1861, as Major General Sterling "Old Pap" Price's forces overran Union troops before being driven out of town. A second battle occurred there as part of Price's Missouri Expedition of 1864, which also resulted in a Confederate victory. After the war, the once beautiful town was in ruins.

Major Samuel P. Cox, a Gallatin resident, had won considerable fame during the war when his Daviess County Union cavalry ambushed and killed the notorious Confederate guerrilla leader William T. "Bloody Bill" Anderson, who had been terrorizing northwest Missouri. Anderson's trademark was to scalp his victims and tie the bloody trophies to his bridle. In 1864, seventeen-year-old Jesse James was one of Bloody Bill's guerrillas. Jesse and others in Anderson's band, including Jim Anderson, Bloody Bill's younger brother, swore they would kill Cox for slaying Anderson.

The Civil War made Gallatin more dangerous than ever. Soldiers and their supporters on both sides committed assassinations and reprisal killings. Captain Sheet's wife had two relatives murdered. In 1863, John D. Casey, a notorious rebel sympathizer and recruiter, tried to cut the throat

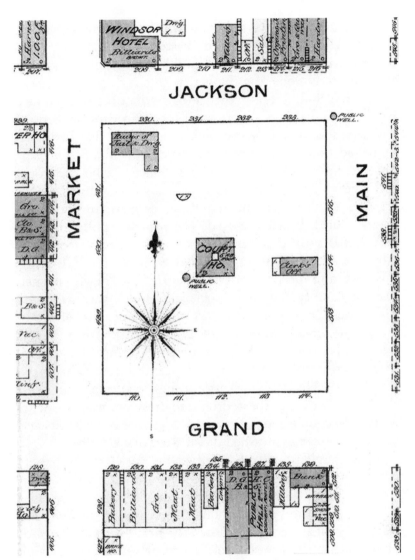

Detail from an 1886 map of Gallatin, Missouri, showing the town square with the court house in the center and the jail to its northwest. At the southwest corner of Grand and Market is the small dwelling occupied by a boot and shoe maker that was originally the Daviess County Savings Association building. The dance hall that existed in 1869 was across Market Street from the association but was occupied by a bakery in 1886. The darker shaded buildings were constructed of stone or brick, such as the old Association building and the court house, while the lighter shade indicates buildings built of wood. (*Daviess County Historical Association*)

of a Union man, William Bristow, while in a saloon. Passing Union soldiers heard Bristow's cries and ran into the bar, where they shot Casey and his son, John Jr., killing them both. No one was charged with the deaths.[7]

In late 1864, Sheets returned to civilian life to become a partner in a dry-goods store with Jonathan Brosius. Brosius had sent several wagons to pick up supplies that had been delivered to a nearby town. He paid four dollars per wagonload and offered the same to a teamster who had come into the store for payment. The teamster wanted $4.50, arguing that he had hauled more cargo than the other wagon teams. Brosius refused. The teamster pulled a pistol and shot Brosius dead, as Sheets stood just a few feet away. After seeing this, Sheets decided to leave the dry-goods business and become the cashier at the newly formed Daviess County Savings Association, which was owned by his former Union commander, Colonel James McFerran.[8]

On the dreary morning of December 7, 1869, Sheets woke before dawn. In his long underwear and heavy socks, he went into the kitchen, lit a lamp, and started a fire in the wood stove. He put on a kettle to heat water for coffee and then went back into the bedroom to dress and wake his wife, Mary. The couple and their two children ate hot biscuits and gravy for breakfast, washed down with black coffee.

After breakfast, Sheets combed his dark hair and short beard, and dressed as warmly as he could in his vest, coat, trousers, heavy socks, hat, and gloves. At the door, he kissed Mary goodbye and left the house. She stood in the door and watched him as he walked down the brick path to the road. His breath misted in the cold morning air. He did not go directly to the bank, as his daily ritual was to walk around the public square and greet and visit with the merchants and townspeople on the gray, warped wooden boardwalk.

Shopkeepers were opening their stores, and the air was full of the sounds of stamping and snorting horses, wagons lurching and banging. A hammer clanged on an anvil at Jacobs's blacksmith shop, where he was shoeing a horse. Two black men pushed carts in the road, shoveling up manure from the day before. Children walked to the log schoolhouse. Shop windows were decorated for Christmas with pinecones and evergreen wreaths. Miller's general store offered wooden sleds, along with dry goods, gun oil, and ammunition. The grocery store had spices, freshly ground coffee, and small barrels of hard candy and ingredients for holiday baking. A fresh hog's head hung from a hook outside the butcher's shop, dripping blood into sawdust below.[9]

Between 8:30 and 9 a.m., Sheets arrived at the bank. Throughout the morning, he and the bank clerk and notary public, William A. McDowell, were busy taking care of bank business and customers. Sheets had recently taken out a $5,000 life insurance policy. He had reason to be nervous. A few months earlier, he had received some disturbing news from Gallatin's Civil War hero, Samuel Cox. In December 1869, Cox was the circuit clerk and county recorder, positions to which he had been elected and which he had assumed from Sheets.[10]

Cox told Sheets that he had received a letter from Jim Anderson, delivered by a Gallatin citizen, who said that Anderson had given him the letter in battle-scarred Lexington, Missouri. The letter contained a bank draft for fifty dollars and told Cox to send Anderson the two revolvers taken from Bloody Bill's body, which had been given to Cox after Anderson's death. The letter threatened that if Cox failed to send the revolvers, Anderson would ride to Gallatin and take them. Cox told Sheets that he had sent the bank draft back to Anderson, with an answer that the only way Jim Anderson was going to get the pistols was to "come and take them." Sheets knew that gun-toting Confederate bushwhackers had been suspected of recent bank robberies at Liberty, Lexington, and Richmond, Missouri, in which four civilians had been murdered. If they rode into Gallatin looking for Cox, the bank would be an attractive target to the robbers.[11]

As the hour approached noon, Gallatin merchants began closing their shops for dinner, and the trickle of bank customers stopped. Sheets told McDowell that he was going to step outside. As Sheets did so, he saw Cox crossing the rutted road toward the bank. The men could have been brothers: they were of the same height and build, wore short, dark beards, and strongly resembled each other.[12]

Outside of town, two Gallatin residents, Mr. and Mrs. Josiah Y. Powell, were driving their buggy along a little-used side road when they were stopped by two riders who asked them the way to Gallatin. A light snow had fallen, and Mr. Powell suggested they follow their tracks in the snow back toward town. Soon after, a couple of miles south of town, Solomon McBryer and a hired hand were mending a fence when they heard the rumble of hooves on the frozen ground. The mist was particularly thick in the wooded hollows and low areas along the Grand River, and they could barely make out a couple of horses and riders on the horizon galloping through the gray wraiths of drifting fog. As the riders sped through the clearing below, McBryer remarked with surprise, "They're sure ridin' hard."[13]

TWO

THE MURDER OF
CAPTAIN JOHN W. SHEETS

IT WAS SHORTLY BEFORE NOON when the two strangers rode into Gallatin. The men attracted little attention as they hitched their horses in an alley off of Market Street. One man was tall, with sand-colored hair, and clad in a dark overcoat. The other was shorter, with a light beard and mustache, wearing a fur cap and a blue overcoat. Captain John Sheets and Major Samuel Cox were talking in front of the Daviess County Savings Association building on the corner of Market and Grand streets, on the southwest corner of the public square. Unnoticed, the two strangers stood at the edge of the boardwalk not far off. Cox turned and walked toward the courthouse. Sheets went inside the two-room bank where the clerk, William McDowell, was sitting at his rough wooden desk in the front room, which also contained a wood-burning, potbellied stove, a crudely made chair for visitors, and a wooden counter. The back room held the iron safe.[1]

A few minutes later, the man with the fur cap pushed open the bank door. The dusty-booted and long-spurred riders clanked noisily into the bank. The first man's blue eyes stared unflinching at Sheets. "Can I get change fer a note?" asked the stranger, as he took out a banknote and placed it on the counter. His voice had a harsh, unused sound. Although he was in his early twenties, his lean brown face was crossed with the wear lines of one much older. Sheets said that he could get the man change, and he turned to walk into the bank's smaller inner office behind the counter toward the safe. As he did so, the taller stranger asked McDowell for some paper and ink so that he could write a receipt. The impression that the two men conveyed to the clerk was that the first man owed the second money and wanted change to pay him. McDowell pushed a piece of paper and an ink quill toward the second man.[2]

As Sheets came out of the little inner office with the money, the first man reached inside his open overcoat and pulled out a long-barreled revolver. "This is for the death of Bill Anderson!" Flame stabbed from the muzzle of the gun as the deafening report thundered, booming off the walls of the tiny room. Sheets was jerked backward with the slam of the .44. Although he died instantly as the bullet tore through his heart, the gunman pointed his revolver at the side of Sheets's head as he lay on the floor, blood oozing from his chest, and fired again.[3]

McDowell, startled by the first shot, wheeled around and found the second man standing between him and the bank's door, with his revolver drawn. His eyes were dark; his face, sun- and wind-burned. He had the smell of horses and wood smoke about him as he snarled, "I'll shoot you." McDowell instinctively lunged for the pistol, forcing the weapon up as it roared and blasted a ball through the ceiling. He dived for the heavy wooden door and quickly slammed it behind him. Having gotten the door between him and the gunman, McDowell stumbled as a heavy slug ripped through the frame, showering him with splinters. "Cap'n Sheets has been killed!" he shouted several times, as he dashed from the bank. The gunman sprang after McDowell, and his gun boomed and flamed as he fired two more shots at the clerk as he ran across the road and into Gallatin's dance hall. Miraculously, neither bullet hit home.[4]

Captain Sheets's sixteen-year-old brother-in-law, Edward Clingan, had been passing the dance hall across the street when he heard shots coming from the bank. Clingan saw McDowell stumble out of the bank's doorway and run toward him. He watched as a man appeared in the bank's doorway and fired twice at McDowell. Clingan quickly ducked into the dance hall with McDowell. He could hear the gunmen's bootheels pound the boardwalk and their spurs ching as they ran to their horses along Grand Street.

The first gunman had grabbed a metal box off of Sheets's desk and flew out of the bank with his accomplice. As the gunmen dashed from the bank with their guns blazing, Gallatin's citizens, aroused by the shots, quickly mustered and returned fire. As the first gunman leaped into the saddle and kicked his feet into the stirrups, his horse spooked and threw him, but one of his boots was caught in a stirrup, and the frightened horse began dragging him down the rutted road toward the bank. He freed himself and his horse raced away, stirrups flopping at the gait. He ducked into the alley between the bank and the local hotel. Several of the more daring men in the crowd followed. One of them shouted, "Let's catch him!" The killer pointed his smoking revolver menacingly at the men, who dropped for cover.[5]

The hotel had a door that opened into the alley, and a former Union captain and now silversmith, Ely Barnum, cracked it open just in time to see the thrown outlaw leap onto the back of the horse of his accomplice, who had turned back to retrieve him. Barnum jerked a quick shot at the outlaws. One of the gunmen turned and fired a bullet that smacked viciously into the wall next to the hotel's door. The two outlaws then held back the Gallatin men with a barrage of revolver shots. They galloped away in a wild run, hanging their bodies over the neck and flanks of the horse with one hand and foot, using the animal for cover like Comanche warriors.[6]

Clingan ran across the street to the bank to check on his brother-in-law, the acrid smell of gunpowder in his nostrils. Clingan found Sheets on the floor, his eyes wide and empty. His vest was dark with blood, with a pool under him, staining the floor. Clingan bent over and anxiously asked, "Are you all right, Captain Sheets?" He could smell the faint, sickish-sweet smell of blood. Sheets did not answer.[7]

On the first hill outside of Gallatin, the gunmen came across a single rider, farmer Daniel Smoote, mounted on a bay mare. The man who had been riding behind pointed his revolver at Smoote's face and ordered him to dismount. Looking into the hollow eye of death, Smoote did as he was told. The gunman pushed down off the panting horse, grabbed Smoote's saddle horn, swung up, and slammed his spurs into the animal's ribs, causing the startled mare to leap. The two men's horses' hooves beat upon the hard ground, leaving Smoote standing behind in the road.[8]

Nearly all of the men in Gallatin closed their shops and gathered their horses, shotguns, rifles, and revolvers and galloped after the outlaws. Cox led the posse. The killers rode southwest in the direction of the Hannibal & St. Joseph Railroad tracks. They found only worthless county warrants in the box they had taken from the bank and so threw the box down along the side of the road, where the posse found it.

Soon the murderers came across another rider, Methodist preacher John F. Helm, who was on the road near Kidder. Apparently fearing that the citizens of Kidder may have been alerted by telegraph of Sheets's murder, the gunmen forced Reverend Helm at gunpoint to guide them around Kidder to the railroad tracks. They told him they had just come from Gallatin where they had killed a man. The outlaws headed in the direction of Clay County and lost the posse in thick fog and forest.[9]

Someone brought Sheets's wife, Mary, to the bank. As she knelt on the floor beside her husband, cradling his head in her arms, her anguished cries could be heard throughout the town square. Shocked and disbelieving friends and relatives carried his body from the bank to his home. A hole could be seen in the building's ceiling caused by the bullet fired when McDowell had knocked the taller bandit's revolver. A furrow plowed by the other bullet fired at him scarred the door jamb.

Within hours the telegraph wires were humming with the news of the sensational murder. The St. Joseph newspaper was one of the first to break the story and described the murder as one of the boldest that had ever occurred in northwest Missouri: "It is not probable, if the murderers are caught, that any court or jury will ever be troubled with trying them."[10]

The next day, Gallatin residents Alexander M. Irving and Jessie Donohue were riding through Centerville (now Kearney), Missouri, on their way home. They rode past two men, one of whom was on a horse that looked remarkably like that owned by their friend, Daniel Smoote. Meanwhile, the drumbeat of the press continued: Captain Sheets was respected by the entire community, and "swift justice may be visited on the heads of his murderers." Sheets's funeral drew the largest crowd ever assembled in Gallatin, and emotions ran high. Local newspapers warned that the murderers, if found, "will be shot down in their tracks."[11]

The Daviess County sheriff found the horse that had escaped from one of the outlaws munching hay in the town livery barn. Among horsemen, a horse's physical features are as distinguishable and individual as any human's. The magnificent animal was identified within days as belonging to "Jesse W. James, whose mother and stepfather live about four miles from Centerville, Missouri, in Clay County, Missouri, near the Cameron branch of the Hannibal & St. Joseph Railroad." The mare's name was Kate. For the first time, Jesse James and his brother were identified in newspapers as dangerous men, "with much experience in horse and revolver work."[12]

Jesse James knew horseflesh. He had learned during his Civil War days the importance of riding horses of the finest bloodlines with the greatest speed and staying quality, which meant the difference between survival and an ugly death. After the war he was flush with cash from his earlier bank robberies, and he purchased the swiftest Kentucky thoroughbreds money could buy. Kate was one of the fastest horses in Missouri, and she had already won statewide races at the annual St. Louis Fair.[13]

One week after Sheets's murder, on Tuesday, December 14, 1869, two heavily armed Gallatin men—Alexander Irving and Ely Barnum, who had taken a shot at the murderers—rode fifty miles south from Gallatin to Liberty to meet with Clay County sheriff O. P. Moss about arresting Jesse James. Encountering criminals was nothing new to Irving. Twenty-seven, a former Union army veteran, and now Gallatin constable, Irving had helped Daviess County sheriff John Ballinger capture the notorious outlaw John Reno two years earlier.[14]

Sheriff Moss asked his deputy, John S. Thomason, to ride with Barnum and Irving and guide them to the James farm. Thomason had served as captain of Company I, 82nd Enrolled Missouri Militia during the war, when he had largely assumed the duties of law enforcement in Clay County and became a well-known and successful hunter of bushwhackers. Thomason and his twenty-year-old son, Oscar, rode with Irving and Barnum eight miles to Centerville, and then four more miles past orchards and fields of tobacco to the James farm. Twice the road dipped steeply down and crossed shallow streams between high banks thick with willows and scrubby thorn trees. These ravines led to steep hillsides, wooded with tall trees. Surrounding the James cabin and farm were dense, claustrophobic woods. Narrow trails that were a devil's nightmare were the only ways in and out. The James brothers were raised on the family farm and knew every trail and hog path, and moved along them as silently as a panther.[15]

Thomason sent Irving and Barnum to the woods north of and behind the three-room cabin, slave quarters, and barn, to prevent an escape from the rear of the cabin. Thomason and his son dismounted at the front gate and began walking up to the house, their revolvers heavy on their hips. As they approached the front door, the barn door flew open and Jesse James and another man galloped out, giving their horses a spur-whipping and shooting, crouching low in their saddles to escape the hail of bullets fired by the posse. Irving recognized one of the horses as belonging to Smoote.

The outlaws' horses leaped over the low split-rail fence surrounding the cabin and barn, but only the elder Thomason's former war horse could follow. His son and the Gallatin men had to dismount and remove the top fence rail in order to follow. John Thomason galloped after Jesse and the other rider across a meadow and over a hill toward the Centerville road. A short distance down the road, John Thomason swung off his horse, took aim and fired, but missed.[16]

◆◇◆◇◆

Back in Gallatin, Daniel Smoote was planning to get even. Although stealing horses was nothing new for Jesse James, farmer Smoote's reaction was. He hired a tall, slender, mustached Gallatin lawyer named Henry Clay McDougal, who had been practicing law for only a year, to sue Frank and Jesse James for the value of the horse Jesse had stolen. McDougal also sued for possession of the thoroughbred horse Jesse left behind. McDougal, recently married, was a Union army veteran from Virginia who had moved to Gallatin three years earlier. He was also a close friend of the murdered cashier.[17]

In Gallatin, McDougal had already proved his courage in connection with another notorious outlaw. After the Civil War, certain parts of the country suffered a period of unemployment and lawlessness, spawning a number of notorious outlaw gangs. The Reno Gang from Indiana began to terrorize the Midwest during this time. Allan Pinkerton and his Pinkerton Detective Agency, whose symbol was the all-seeing eye and motto "We Never Sleep," were soon on the gang's trail. About a year after McDougal arrived in

Gallatin, on November 17, 1867, outlaws broke open the safe in the Gallatin treasurer's office and stole $23,618 in cash and bonds. John Reno was identified as one of the robbers.[18]

Daviess County sheriff John Ballinger tracked Reno to a hotel in Indianapolis, where he found the outlaw gambling and enjoying the company of a paid "companion." Ballinger and Pinkerton detectives captured Reno without a shot being fired. Ballinger brought Reno back to Gallatin and locked him in the stone-walled jail. Worried that Reno's remaining gang members would attempt to break him out of jail, or that the infuriated citizens of Gallatin would mob the jail and lynch Reno, Ballinger asked 23-year-old Henry McDougal to sleep in the jail and help guard the prisoners. So McDougal, armed with his army revolver and a shotgun, spent Christmas Day 1867 in the Gallatin jail, guarding a dangerous outlaw.[19]

Two years later, after the latest robbery attempt and the murder of Captain Sheets, McDougal discovered that he was not Smoote's first choice for counsel: every one of the other eight lawyers in town had turned down the farmer's request for legal representation. Young, inexperienced McDougal was the only attorney in town apparently foolish enough to take the case, as to prove it would effectively hang Sheets's murder on Jesse James and possibly his brother.[20]

On Christmas Eve 1869, eight days after Smoote hired McDougal to prosecute the James boys, the Daviess County Court in Gallatin authorized a $500 reward for "the apprehension or killing of the murderers of Captain John W. Sheets of Gallatin and the delivery of their bodies to the sheriff of Daviess County or $250 for either of them." In total, the authorities posted $3,000 in reward money, one of the largest rewards ever offered in Missouri. The James boys now had dead-or-alive money on them. The reward notices marked the first time they were publicly branded as criminals and outlaws.[21]

The thoroughbred Kate was the first tangible evidence that led to criminal charges against Jesse. With the murder of cashier Sheets at Gallatin, twenty-two-year-old Jesse James had announced his outlaw presence to Missouri and the nation. He would remain a wanted man for the rest of his life.[22]

But why had Jesse ridden to remote Gallatin on December 7, 1869, to commit a sensational murder that would brand him a criminal and outlaw? Was Frank James the other gunman? If not Frank, who? In order to answer these questions, we must go back some years, to the beginning of the Civil War.

THREE

RIVERS OF BLOOD AND IRON

THE FRENCH WERE THE FIRST white men to explore the river that divides what is now the state of Missouri and gives the state its name. On June 26, 1804, Captain Meriwether Lewis and William Clark temporarily halted their journey up the river and camped for three days on a point above the confluence of the Missouri and Kansas rivers, at what the French called *le grand detour*, where the river, after running due south for hundreds of miles, is forced sharply east by a rock cliff at what is now Kansas City. The river then snakes across Missouri for four hundred river miles, cutting the state nearly in half. The Missouri River was the key to the American West for explorers and exploiters. It provided access to the furs of the wilderness and to Rocky Mountain gold and silver. The river's lurking dangers, however, rivaled its promise. Of all the western rivers, the Missouri was probably the most treacherous; every voyage up it was a chancy thing, an adventure, subject to sudden highs and lows along the river, unexpected sandbars, snags, and all sorts of dangerous drifting matter that could tear a hole in a hull. A riverboat pilot had to be equal parts gambler and magician.

The river writhed and twisted in its course, its banks in a constant state of change. The channel followed no regular and fixed course, but swung from one side of the river bed to the other, shifting with every change in the volume and velocity of the water. The broad current was a stream of flowing sand, sediment, silt, clay, and mud, studded with whole trees that had been uprooted when a bank caved in. William Clark wrote that "the water . . . contains a half . . . glass of ooze or mud to every pint." A hairy-faced trapper later quipped that he had "to chew that water before I could swallow it." The dark, strong current rapidly chewed the soil of its banks, undercutting shorelines and felling trees. During the spring, the height of the river's erosive power, the continuous falling of trees made a noise resembling the distant roar of artillery.[1]

Snags were the most dangerous obstacles. Tossed and battered against riverbank and riverbed, the drifting trees lost most of their limbs and branches. Through the absorption of water, the trees lost much of their buoyancy as well. When the subsiding floodwaters were unable to carry them farther, the heavy butt ends, with their dirt- and gravel-encrusted roots, sank to the bottom and became embedded in rapidly accumulating sand and gravel. With its shaft angled toward the surface downstream, the snag lay like a lance lurking in the muddy water, ready to pierce the wooden hulls of unhappy steamboats coming up the river. A snag lying with its shaft downstream was commonly known as a "sawyer," from the slow vibration or sawing motion given it by the action of the current.[2]

Mark Twain wrote: "We were six days from St. Louis to St. Jo. . . . No record is left in my mind now concerning it, but a confused jumble of savage-looking snags." The river was ruefully known as "Old Misery." Since 1843, steamboats had been plying its waters filled with immigrants to Oregon. Several boats sank each year to the Missouri's muddy bottom, often taking dozens of lives with them.

Steamboats usually tied up at night, as the pilots could not see the snags and sawyers in the dark.[3]

By the late 1850s, nearly fifty paddlewheel steamboats regularly churned the waters of the river, and "Steamboat a-comin!" was a welcome cry on the banks of the emerging Missouri frontier river towns, as the boats carried food and supplies to the budding settlements. The three-story, chugging steamboats could hold nearly four hundred passengers. Most of the settlers had traveled on boats from St. Louis, where they headed west on the "Big Muddy," fighting the relentless current for 457 miles. The trip was slow, tedious, and took a week or more. Huge cottonwood, hickory, ash, elm, sycamore, willow, and oak trees towered over the water, blocking out and filtering the light close to the banks. Day after day, the heavy, old-growth forests passed slowly by, broken only now and then by a meadow or a tiny clearing, with lone figures waving atop freshly cut tree stumps. The side-wheel steamers were forced to stop at numerous landings and wood yards for fuel. Most of the settlers finally disembarked in either of two muddy little river settlements, West Port (now Westport, Kansas City, Missouri) or Wayne City, which put them within a few miles of Independence, the largest settlement on the frontier.

At the aptly named village of West Port—the gateway to the great frontier named for the Kanza Indians to the west—settlers took on supplies. West Port was the jumping-off point to an entire second America of grasslands reaching to the Rocky Mountains. Its dirt streets were jammed with freighters' outfits, horses lined the hitching rails, and, in pens on every side, hundreds of horses, oxen, and cattle stamped in the mud, switching tails at swarms of flies. All day and night hammers tinkered in nine black-smith shops. Under long sheds could be seen glowing forges, and the smell of burning hooves filled the air. Bullwhips cracked like rifle fire as ox-driven wagons rumbled by. Uniformed soldiers stationed at Fort Leavenworth, one of the westernmost outposts of the United States' military power at the time, roamed the muddy roads and drank in four saloons, mingling with rough settlers, mountain men, and French fur traders.[4]

Wherever they disembarked, it was land that these settlers wanted. The rich soil of the Missouri River floodplain ranked among the best on the frontier for agriculture; in places along the river bottom it was twenty feet deep. Most of the families residing in the Missouri counties bordering the river had come from Tennessee, Virginia, and Kentucky—many from the latter had been part of a large migration forty years earlier, inspired by the glowing reports of Daniel Boone's son, Daniel Morgan Boone. The settlers believed in hard work and horse sense. In the fertile soil of the Missouri River valley, they grew the same crops they had grown back home: tobacco and hemp.

During the spring of 1842, a slave-owning Baptist minister, Robert James, stepped ashore at the Liberty, Missouri, landing with his tall, seventeen-year-old pregnant wife, Zerelda. They had been married the previous December. They were visiting Zerelda's mother, who was living in Clay County with her second husband, Robert Thomason. The Jameses had traveled from Woodford County, Kentucky, in the heart of the famed Bluegrass region.

Preacher James probably hired or bought a horse and wagon for the bone-jarring ride on the rutted roads through Clay County. The ride took the young newlyweds through the town of Liberty, the small county seat. They then rode north twelve miles, past Centerville, before arriving at the Thomason farm. On January 10, 1843, Alexander Franklin James, or Frank, was born. At first, the young family lived with Zerelda's mother and stepfather. Soon they moved a few miles away into a three-room cabin by a creek and a farm of their own.[5]

Robert James, like many Clay County farmers, primarily grew tobacco and hemp. He also owned at least two young slaves, which was common in Clay and Jackson counties, where one person out of four was a slave.

Missouri River valley farmers hauled their hemp to river landings, where they sold the rough fibers to local rope factories. The rope was then shipped back down the river toward St. Louis (when it was not frozen during three to four months each winter), and then down the Mississippi to the great plantations of the Old South where it was used to tie up cotton bales. Thus, Clay, Jackson, and the adjoining Missouri River counties were tied—culturally and economically—to the South, so much so that they would later be referred to as Little Dixie. Many residents, however, considered the area to be neither North nor South, but part of the frontier West.[6]

In March 1846, war fever gripped Clay County, as Mexico and the United States began fighting over the newly admitted state of Texas. One hundred recruits signed up in Liberty alone, under the command of Oliver P. "O. P." Moss, and rode to Mexico with Sterling Price. Meanwhile, on September 5, 1847, the Jameses added another member to their young family: Jesse Woodson James.

At the same time the Mexican War was ending in 1848, gold was discovered in California and the gold rush began. Caravans of wagons began leaving Clay County for the gold fields of California. On November 15, 1849, Zerelda gave birth to the couple's third child, Susan Lavenia James. Shortly thereafter, in April 1850, Robert James departed with one of the wagon trains for the California gold fields, leaving his 275 acre farm and young family behind. Frank was seven, Jesse not yet three. A few months later, in a gold camp called Hangtown (now Placerville, California), James died of fever.

Two years after the death of her husband, Zerelda married farmer Benjamin A. Simms, another transplanted Kentucky native, who was almost twice her age. But Zerelda's new husband had no patience for children and would not allow Zerelda's three youngsters to live under his roof. Within nine months, Zerelda left Simms and moved back with her children into their cabin. Six months later, Benjamin Simms died, after he allegedly fell off his horse.

The next year, Zerelda married Dr. Reuben Samuel, another Kentucky native, who operated his practice in a store owned by William James, Zerelda's first husband's brother, in nearby Greenville, Missouri. Samuel gave up the practice of medicine and moved to the James farm to work the fields. The Samuel/James farm prospered, due in part to its six slaves. In the list of Robert James's possessions in his probate records there appear six names, including "one black woman, Charlotte," who was thirty years old. Along with Charlotte are listed Nancy, eleven; Alexander, nine; Maria, eight; Mason, six, and Hannah, two. It is unknown whether any of the children were Charlotte's offspring. Charlotte and the children likely lived and slept in a one-room, dirt-floor cabin separate from the James cabin. There was no heat or running water. They probably ate separately from the James family, perhaps beans, potatoes, and cornbread. The children spent most of their lives at work.[7]

Unknown at that time to most Clay County tobacco and hemp farmers dependent on the Missouri River for transportation, railroad tracks were beginning to crisscross the eastern United States. Missouri statesman Thomas Hart Benton proposed that a railroad be laid to the Pacific Ocean in order to connect the eastern part of the country with the West. In early 1859, the iron horse was harnessed in Missouri, as the Hannibal & St. Joseph Railroad became the first railroad line to be completed crossing the state, pushing the farthest west of any train line in the country. So much track was laid so quickly that Missouri newspapers expressed concern that the iron tracks were causing an increase in violent storms and lightning strikes.[8]

The issue of slavery was the national fuse that smoldered in the years running up to the Civil War. Two thirds of the one hundred thousand slaves in Missouri in the 1850s were held in the counties of Clay, Jackson, Lafayette, Saline, Howard, Calloway, and Boone, arrayed along the Missouri River. In Clay and Jackson counties, farmers believed that only slaves could provide the back-breaking labor necessary to economically raise and harvest tobacco and hemp. In fact, Southerners in Clay County believed that slavery was the reason the county had become one of the most commercially successful ones in Missouri. Next to land, slaves were the single most valuable property Clay County residents owned. Free states bordering Missouri on the north (Iowa) and the east (Illinois), and the prospect of another free state to the west represented serious enforcement problems under the fugitive-slave laws for Missouri slave owners. In 1854, the newly created territory of Kansas gave Clay County slave owners nightmares and ignited five years of civil war, which raged along the Missouri-Kansas border before consuming the young nation.

In order to understand the Missouri-Kansas border political climate in the late 1850s, one must start with the 1820 Missouri Compromise, which was a temporary solution to the curse of slavery. At that time there were twenty-four states, equally divided between free and slave. In 1820, Missouri petitioned to become the twenty-fifth state, as a slave state, but there was no free state ready for admission. This meant that the balance between slave and free states would be disrupted, which was anathema to those members of Congress opposed to slavery. Henry Clay's Missouri Compromise temporarily solved the problem by establishing that from 1820 on, all states and territories north of Missouri's southern border would prohibit slavery (except Missouri), and all states and territories south of Missouri's southern border would allow slavery. The Union would be held together by the legislative bailing wire of the Missouri Compromise for thirty-four years.[9]

The tenuous legislative balance was upset by the 1854 Kansas-Nebraska Act, proposed by Abraham Lincoln's political antagonist of twenty years, US senator Stephen Douglas of Illinois. Douglas, a Democrat, had conceived of the law as a way to address political turmoil over slavery, promote a transcontinental railroad from Chicago to California through the Nebraska Territory, and perhaps lead to his nomination for president of the United States. The reasoning behind the bill was simple: open up the wild territories of Kansas and Nebraska to settlers from both North and South, and let the people (that is, white men) decide by voting whether to accept or reject slavery. Douglas failed to see that Kansas would become the cradle of a fire that would spread across the country, dividing Democrats, creating the Republican Party, hastening civil war, and destroying Douglas's political ambitions.[10]

For the first time, the slaveholding status of an entire territory, a huge swath of open plains stretching west over present-day Colorado, which Andrew Jackson had set aside as Indian territory, would rest in the hands of a few thousand voters. Before 1854, hundreds of people had emigrated to the West annually, jumping off at places like West Port, Missouri. In spring 1854, however, even as the Kansas-Nebraska bill was debated in Congress, the number swelled to the thousands. This new emigrant traffic, however, was going to Kansas, not California.[11]

The country had gone mad about Kansas. In April, the Massachusetts legislature enacted the Emigrant Aid Society bill, intended to seed Kansas with free-state settlers. Slave-owning Missourians sensed an invasion. On May 22, the Kansas-Nebraska bill passed the House of Representatives, with wild excitement, by only thirteen votes. The Senate passed it on May 25, and President Franklin Pierce signed it into law on May 30.

Illinois lawyer Abraham Lincoln equated revoking the Missouri Compromise with repudiating the Declaration of Independence. "I was losing interest in politics," he wrote, when "the repeal of the Missouri Compromise aroused me again." Lincoln, who had been a congressman from 1847 to 1849, left his practice of law and representation of the railroads to go back into politics. Pro-slavery Missourians did not wait for the bill to pass. They crossed the Missouri River in spring, staked claims on land owned by Indians, organized self-defense associations, and then went back home for the summer.[12]

The first party of emigrant aid settlers from Boston arrived by steamboat in the Kansas Territory in August 1854. The twenty-nine members in the group disembarked at the town of Kansas (now Kansas City), landing to a hostile reception from slave-owning Missourians. The little group loaded their tents, cooking utensils, and household possessions into wagons and rumbled along the wagon ruts of the twenty-two-year-old Santa Fe Trail, sometimes between ten-foot walls of big bluestem, switchgrass, and cordgrass, taller than a rider's head, interspersed with sunflowers and goldenrod.

For thirty-five miles they rode along the twin ruts of the trail, which led to the inland sea of green tall grass with no interruption save great rolling rivers and the trees that grew along the river courses, inhabited by Kanza Indians—the People of the South Wind—and buffalo. Occasionally, flocks of prairie chickens flew up, then glided away across the grass to disappear like smoke. As the lead riders stood in their stirrups and looked far off to the west, they saw black humps. Buffalo.[13]

The group rode up a hill on the southern bank of the Kaw River, from which they could look out in all directions and watch the wind walk through the tall grass. They looked into a land untouched by the plow, of infinite distance, of prairie and sky. Far, far away stretched the horizon, where the edge of the rolling plains met the sky. They stopped, pitched their tents, and built campfires. They lay awake and gazed up at a vast heaven of great white stars— it was like watching them from the deck of a ship at sea.[14]

They decided to stay and named the small village they began to build Lawrence, after their chief financial backer, the erstwhile conservative Amos Adams Lawrence. Lawrence, a Harvard-educated owner of Ipswich Mills, a large producer of knit goods, was the son of wealthy philanthropist Amos Lawrence. The son had become an abolitionist after witnessing that spring the arrest and trial in Boston of Anthony Burns, who had escaped from slavery in Virginia and stowed away on a ship to Boston. Burns, who was literate, made the mistake of writing to his brother, still a slave. Intercepting the letter, their owner learned Burns's whereabouts and headed north to reclaim his property. A federal marshal arrested Burns on May 24, 1854, and he was prosecuted and convicted under the Fugitive Slave Act. In response to an effort to rescue Burns, President Pierce ordered several companies of federal troops to Boston, who marched Burns, now in chains, from the federal courthouse through the streets "before sullen Yankees standing in front of buildings draped in black with the American flag hung upside down and church bells tolling a dirge to liberty in the cradle of the American Revolution." Burns was taken to a federal ship in the harbor and returned to slavery in Virginia.[15]

On October 16, 1854, Abraham Lincoln warned: "The Missourians . . . are within a stone's throw of the contested ground. They hold meetings . . . in which not the slightest allusion to voting is made. They resolve that slavery already exists in the territory; that more shall go there; that they, remaining in Missouri will protect it; and that abolitionists shall be hung, or driven away. Through all this, bowie knives and six-shooters are seen plainly enough. . . . [W]hat is to be the result of this? . . . [I]s it not probable that the contest will come to blows, and bloodshed?" Lincoln's prose proved prophetic. Over the next four years, nearly two hundred men would die in Kansas, and the fighting would not stop for ten years.[16]

Steamboats began to deposit thousands of settlers from New England and squatters from Missouri into the newly minted towns of Lawrence and Leavenworth. The Kansas-Nebraska Act provided for the creation of a Territorial Supreme Court, which consisted of a chief justice and two associate justices. President Pierce, a proslavery Democrat, appointed proslavery Samuel Lecompte as chief justice and other proslavery men as associate justices and to territorial government posts. Court sessions were sporadic. The earliest courtrooms were makeshift affairs in whatever space a judge could commandeer in the newly opened territory. Saloons, churches, hotels, and even the outdoors served on occasion. The stakes being high and law enforcement low, vigilantism ruled the territory. The new residents, with their extremist views, battled each other, and Kansas soon received the nickname of "Bleeding Kansas" in eastern newspapers.[17]

"We are playing for a mighty stake," said US senator David Atchison, a Missouri country lawyer given to hard liquor and plain speaking. "The game must be played boldly. If we win we carry slavery to the Pacific Ocean, if we fail we lose Missouri, Arkansas, Texas and all the territories." Fifteen years earlier, Atchison and other Missourians had burned the Mormons out of the state; Atchison was confident of their ability to give Free Soilers the same treatment in Kansas. "We are organizing," he told Secretary of War Jefferson Davis. "We will be compelled to shoot, burn and hang, but the game will soon be over. We intend to 'Mormonize' the Abolitionists."[18]

The election for the territorial legislature occurred March 30, 1855. Atchison's lieutenant in Missouri exhorted a crowd at St. Joseph: "Mark every scoundrel around you that is the least tainted with free-soilerism or abolitionism and exterminate him. Enter every election in Kansas . . . and vote at the point of the bowie knife and revolver." All but one of the territorial legislators elected were proslavery. More than six thousand votes were cast in the territory; over four thousand nine hundred were estimated to be fraudulent. The North was incensed by the fixed voting results, and newspaper reporters hurried to the territory.

The citizens of Lawrence, the Free State fortress thirty-five miles outside of the organized United States, began to build permanent fortifications. Meanwhile, the Free Soil men, led by Mexican War hero and lawyer Colonel James Henry Lane, began organizing the Free State Party and making plans for a Free State convention and constitution. Towering over six feet, Lane had a commanding presence, a powerful voice, and a mesmerizing speaking ability. The hawk-faced Lane may have done more than any other man to bring freedom to Kansas. He organized Free Soil forces to protect Kansas ballot boxes from fraudulent voting and helped defend towns from proslavery forces. He oversaw the construction of a circular, stone fort on Mount Oread that had irregular walls three to four feet high and commanded the southern and eastern approaches to Lawrence (the Kaw River protected Lawrence on the north). He also directed construction of three circular earthworks, or rifle pits, about seventy-five to one hundred feet in diameter, which guarded the main roads into town. These defenses saved Lawrence from destruction on at least one occasion, when a force of over two thousand Missourians arrived on the outskirts of the town but then retreated, apparently because they feared that Lane's fort contained cannon (which may have merely been logs tarred black). The Free State men were now in armed defiance of the federal government and its appointed authorities in the Kansas Territory.[19]

The territorial judges flouted the law almost as often as they determined it. President Pierce had to remove two justices for illegal acquisition of Indian land. The judges also furthered the cause of slavery at the expense of justice. Lecompte ordered a grand jury to indict Lane and the other Free State leaders for treason. Lane left the Kansas Territory to raise support for the Free State cause in Chicago. Since many of the Free State men lived in Lawrence, the proslavery men's efforts to arrest them provided a perfect (and probably planned) opportunity for Missourians, some of whom were now deputized as a posse, to attack this bastion of Yankee abolitionists. The first shot rang out on April 23, 1856, when Sam Jones, a Kansas Territory sheriff from Lecompton, took a bullet in the back. A year earlier, he had led a group of proslavery Missourians into the territory to stuff ballot boxes. The gunman who fired at Jones was not identified, but the shooting gave Missourians the excuse they were looking for to attack Lawrence.

On May 21, 1856, approximately eight hundred Missourians invaded the tiny town. Senator Atchison led the Platte County Rifle Company. The Missourians wore red flannel shirts for uniforms and marched in carrying rifles, revolvers, and cutlasses, with bowie knives tucked into the boots worn on the outside of their trousers, stopping every three hundred yards or so to allow five cannon to catch up. Without Lane's leadership, the Free State men surrendered the town. The Missourians stopped before the Free State Hotel and fired their cannon at the three-story structure, but they were unable to bring it down. Finally, they rolled powder kegs into a doorway, ignited them, and burned the building to the ground. Other buildings and homes were also burned and pillaged. A battle flag with a crimson star and the motto "Southern Rights" fluttered in the smoke-filled breeze. The Missourians looted the town and rode away, reeking with the smoke of Lawrence, many with pillaged satin vests and dress coats draped over their rough flannel shirts.[20]

The sack of Lawrence, the arrests and incarceration of Free State leaders by federal authorities, and news that on May 22, US representative Preston Brooks of South Carolina had severely beaten US senator Charles Sumner of Massachusetts on the Senate floor after his "Crime against Kansas" speech, unhinged the territory. On May 24, followers of a wild-looking old man named John Brown, a new Kansas settler, dragged five proslavery settlers from their cabins along little Pottawattomie Creek near Osawatomie, Kansas, and hacked them to death. Those targeted by Brown had been involved in local court proceedings to enforce the proslavery laws of the bogus legislature, such as the law declaring it to be a crime publishable by death to advocate freeing slaves. James Doyle, a grand juror in local court proceedings, and his twenty- and twenty-two-year-old sons (the latter having served as the court bailiff) were among those seized in their cabin, dragged into the woods, and killed. Allen Wilkinson, the acting district attorney and a member of the territorial legislature, and William Sherman, whose brother owned the tavern where the court convened, also died that night. Brown was indicted for murder but never brought to justice. Amid the anarchy of Bleeding Kansas, murders by both sides went unpunished.[21]

The twin traumas of Lawrence and Pottawattomie Creek escalated the war in the Kansas Territory. Lane decided to fight fire with fire. He led an army of six hundred Free State settlers into the territory on a trail he blazed through Iowa and Nebraska. He then attacked and destroyed proslavery forts at Franklin and Fort Sanders, which had been built in an effort to encircle and strangle Lawrence, and he led Free State forces at the Battle of Hickory Point. In December 1857, he "baptized" approximately 150 Free State fighters at Sugar Mound (later Mound City) as "Jayhawks." He explained the new name as follows: "As the Irish Jayhawk with a shrill cry announces his presence to his victims, so must you notify the proslavery hell hounds to clear out or vengeance will overtake them."[22]

Lane's Jayhawkers raided Missouri, liberating slaves and sometimes killing their owners. Missouri bushwhackers responded in kind. Assassination skulked in the tall grasses of the prairie. Gangs of sabered horsemen roamed the border settlements and farms, appearing out of nowhere, looting, burning, and killing, before vanishing into the tall grass. In the primeval blackness of night on the prairie, terrified settlers were forced to sleep with rifles, revolvers, hatchets, and knives within reach of their beds. Boston headlines screamed: "Murder Rules in Kansas. The bloody plot thickens. Blood flows. Freedom reels and staggers in a death grip with slavery." Bleeding Kansas was a grim dress rehearsal for the Civil War to follow. From 1855 to 1865, the Kansas-Missouri border would be the scene of the longest and most brutal guerrilla warfare ever seen on American soil. Thousands died. Every death was a lightning strike to some heart, and broke like thunder over some home.[23]

◆○◆○◆

Back in Clay County, nine-year-old Jesse and twelve-year-old Frank James were schooled in Indian and guerrilla tactics by six-foot tall "Wild Bill" Thomason, the brother of Zerelda's stepfather. Thomason had fought in the Mexican War before he returned to his earlier occupation as a mountain man, the most fabulous of persons to the boys. He dressed in a buckskin shirt ornamented with Indian work in beads and porcupine quills, with fringe on the sleeves and legs to drain the rain off. He taught the boys how to ride low on their horses like Comanche warriors and how to shoot a pistol and rifle. The boys used tree stumps as target practice, naming them for the more notorious Jayhawkers and abolitionists of the day, such as the fierce Jim Lane, "Old" John Brown, and Charles R. "Doc" Jennison, who raided the countryside dressed in red leather leggings. The boys practiced their horse-riding skills with a neighbor boy, Clell Miller. Jesse and Clell galloped their horses down the country roads, shooting fence posts that they imagined to be Free Soilers. The boys grew up playing and exploring the Fishing River bottoms, which emptied into the nearby Missouri River. Frank and Jesse James had to learn all of the rivers' crossing points, because no bridges existed. This knowledge would serve them well and may have saved their lives during the Civil War and after.[24]

For a while it seemed that Missouri's "Border Ruffians" would prevail, but in the end they could not match the overwhelming flood of free-soil settlers from New England and the northern states. In January 1861, Kansas was admitted to the Union as a free state and the thirty-fourth star on the flag. Slavery's western trajectory had met a dead end on the Kansas-Missouri line. Many folks just across the Missouri River, however, were looking for a chance to settle old grudges and tear open the scab that had formed over Bleeding Kansas. The roar of South Carolina cannons fired by the newly formed Confederate States army just three months after Kansas statehood gave them their chance.[25]

FOUR

RAVENOUS MONSTERS OF SOCIETY

AT THE OUTBREAK OF THE CIVIL WAR, it was vital that Missouri remain loyal to the Union. Missouri controlled traffic on the Mississippi, Missouri, and Ohio River networks, which were essential to access the Northwest part of the continent, and its manpower and natural resources, including large deposits of iron, were critical to the war effort. The metropolis of St. Louis, at the intersection of the flowing highways of the Missouri and Mississippi rivers, was a thriving center of commerce. Whoever controlled the upper Mississippi and the great highway to the West—the Missouri River—"would hold the country by the heart."

When the Civil War came in 1861, currents were pulling Missouri toward both the Union and the Confederacy. Although slavery was legal, most of Missouri's citizens did not own slaves and had no ties to the South, such as the German, French, and other immigrants who settled in St. Louis. On the other hand, in Kansas City, Abe Lincoln had mustered only one of every nineteen votes cast for president in 1860. If it had been possible, a majority of Missouri voters may have opted for neutrality.

But Missouri's recently elected secessionist governor, Claiborne F. Jackson, was dedicated to the cause of slavery. Six years earlier, Jackson had led nearly one thousand Missourians, armed with rifles, pistols, bowie knives, and two cannons, to Lawrence to fraudulently vote in the Kansas Territorial elections. Jackson now planned to assist the Confederacy in its bid for independence. In response to rebel troops' firing on Fort Sumter in Charleston harbor, South Carolina, President Lincoln had called for seventy-five thousand troops to suppress them. Governor Jackson raged, "Your requisition is illegal, unconstitutional, revolutionary, inhuman . . . [and] not one man will the State of Missouri furnish to carry on such an unholy war." Warring factions at the time referred to themselves as either "federals" or "secessionists"—and the latter was shortened to "secesh."[1]

Jackson directed secessionist state militia in looting the musty US arsenal in Liberty, Missouri, and distributing the one thousand muskets, three cannons, and ammunition seized to newly formed companies of state militia. Forty men were sworn into a company of pro-Southern Missouri State Guard at Centerville—including slender, long-faced, eighteen-year-old Frank James. Crowds of Clay County residents cheered for South Carolina and waived rebel flags as James and his fellow recruits drilled. Neighbors began to eye each other suspiciously, and Clay County Unionists began to worry. During the next four years, the Kansas-Missouri border war and the Civil War were fought simultaneously. As Missouri had attempted to make a slave state of Kansas, Kansas would now strive to make Missouri a free state.[2]

Frank James and the Clay County recruits of the Missouri State Guard traveled south and crossed the Missouri River in April to join former Missouri governor and Mexican War veteran Major General Sterling Price's army of secessionist militia. The battle at Wilson's Creek near Springfield, Missouri, on August 10, 1861, marked the beginning of the Civil War in Missouri. The fiery, forty-three-year-old Union commander, General Nathanial Lyon, a West Point graduate and veteran of the Mexican War, was one of the first commanders in the Civil War to make strategic use of railroads: his main column traveled over 260 miles, first by train from St. Louis to Rolla, which was approximately half way to Springfield, and then by horse and foot to Wilson's Creek, at the end of a precarious supply line two hundred miles from St. Louis. Lyon's small army of five thousand five hundred men faced a motley Southern force composed of Price's eight thousand Missourians and five thousand other Confederate troops.

In steaming, miserable conditions, Frank James fought a slow fight up and around a prominence on the banks of Wilson's Creek that became known as "Bloody Hill." In the thick of the fighting, Lyon was twice wounded and his horse shot out from under him before a bullet found his heart. The demoralized Union forces, almost out of ammunition, slowly pulled back, leaving the field to the enemy. Each side had suffered about one thousand three hundred casualties, a considerably higher proportion of losses than at Bull Run, fought three weeks earlier.[3]

Having gained confidence and prestige, Price marched north to the Missouri River, gathering recruits along the way. His eighteen thousand troops surrounded the three-thousand-five-hundred-man garrison at Lexington, the largest and most important river town between Jefferson City and Missouri's western border. Lexington surrendered three days later, on September 20. One week later, however, Union general John C. Frémont, a former Republican candidate for president, arrived at Sedalia from St. Louis with an army of thirty-eight thousand men to destroy Price's army, threatening to trap his troops against the Missouri River. Union states bordered Missouri on the west (Kansas and Nebraska), the north (Iowa), and the east (Illinois). Only sparsely populated Arkansas to the south provided a direct link to the Confederate states. Outnumbered and outflanked, General Price retreated to Missouri's southwest corner near Arkansas.

Frank James did not retreat with Price's forces but remained behind near Springfield. He was sick with measles, which struck down many farm boys who had never been exposed to these childhood diseases and which was often deadly in the 1860s. Union forces took Frank James prisoner but then paroled him. He returned home to the James farm.

Claiborne Jackson called the pro-Southern legislators into session at Neosho near the Arkansas border, and on November 3, 1861, this body enacted an ordinance of secession. The Congress of the Confederate States of America in Richmond admitted Missouri as the twelfth Confederate state on November 29, adding its star to the stars and bars. Meanwhile, the pro-Union government remained in Jefferson City. Missouri had two governments, and the strains of a house divided would rip the state in two.

The state was divided by more than just its government. Missouri was in the midst of a rapid social transition from a premodern and preindustrial agricultural society to a more market-oriented one. Missouri in the 1860s witnessed a rapid Northern-style economic development, fueled by extension of the railroads and accelerated industrialization in cities such as St. Louis. The Confederate guerrillas who rose up to fight the federals came to represent to many the best of the fading, seemingly pastoral society. The guerrillas adopted heroic and comforting legends of simpler times, masking the brutality and savagery of guerrilla warfare.[4]

As Lincoln said in the Gettysburg Address, the Civil War was a time of "testing." The rule of law practically disappeared in certain parts of Missouri. General Fremont declared martial law in the state and warned that civilians who aided the rebellion would be shot. The Union army had gained control of the Missouri railroads, the Missouri River, and the northern counties in the state by the winter of 1861–62, but the unsettled condition of the western border with Kansas and that part of the state below the Missouri River was a devil's nightmare. Small bands of mounted secessionist guerrillas sprang up, fighting without official

Confederate sanction or direction, and were referred to as "bushwhackers." Initially, they consisted of small, mounted, local bands. Soon, however, they grew in strength, skill, and effectiveness, until they began to attack federal troops, terrorize pro-Union civilians, and make raids into Kansas. Because they took no prisoners, to engage them meant two choices: fight to the death or escape. No quarter was given to those who surrendered. Missouri descended into a war of thousands of bloody incidents. The cycle of violence, with its escalating savagery by the guerrillas and ever-more-harsh reprisals by federal authorities, resulted in atrocities committed by all. Both sides prayed to the same benevolent God; both sides engaged in unholy brutality.[5]

In the first months of 1862 rebel guerrillas swarmed across Missouri like the proverbial locusts of ancient Egypt. Abraham Lincoln understood the toll guerrilla warfare was inflicting. Lincoln had traveled across Missouri just three years earlier on the Hannibal & St. Joseph Railroad on his way to speaking engagements in Leavenworth, Troy, and Atchison, Kansas, and had studied and spoken about the Kansas–Missouri border conflict since 1854. He lamented, "Each man feels an impulse to kill his neighbors, lest he first be killed by him. Revenge and retaliation follow. And all this among honest men. But this is not all. Every foul bird comes along, and every dirty reptile rises up."[6]

By March 1862, federal armies controlled St. Louis and its railroads and the towns along the railroad lines, and garrisoned troops—many of whom were non-Missourians—throughout the region. The Confederacy would never establish a permanent base in Missouri. Tens of thousands of pro-Southern families remained hundreds of miles behind Union lines, living next door to Unionists, enraged by the Union occupation and its excesses on their doorsteps. And many families had young men of military age who had not gone south to join the regular Confederate army. Local men were taken by Union soldiers and their supporters from their homes and shot to death without law or authority. Horses, corn, grain, food, and even fence rails were taken without compensation. Over time, even those loyal to the Union became resentful of the federal forces and their often-rough tactics with the local population.[7]

The state militia acted as judge and jury in court-marshaling and executing captured guerrillas by hanging or firing squad. US military commissions also did a brisk business in convicting and hanging guerrillas, although some civil courts continued to claim jurisdiction in guerrilla cases. The US military did not favor civilian courts handling guerrilla trials, however, as juries sometimes rendered verdicts of acquittal.[8]

As rebel guerrillas emerged from winter hibernation in the spring of 1863, the internal threat to Missouri became unprecedented. A Union soldier lamented that Missouri "was never so overrun with guerrillas. No one knows how to slow the flood." In May 1863, Frank James met Bill Gregg, one of Confederate guerrilla William Clarke Quantrill's lieutenants, in Clay County and joined Quantrill's bushwhacker band. Quantrill, a blue-eyed, twenty-four-year-old former Ohio schoolteacher, had become one of the most notorious bushwhackers in northwest Missouri, ambushing federal patrols and murdering Unionist civilians. He had developed a number of sophisticated tactics for conducting successful raids, such as preselecting escape routes with built-in redundancies and setting up fresh relay horses to aid in escapes. These skills were not lost on the James boys, who would use them to great success after the war.[9]

On May 25, Frank James led a band of guerrillas to a clearing in the woods near the James cabin. The Clay County Union militia soon arrived and demanded that Frank and Jesse's stepfather, Dr. Samuel, tell them where the guerrillas were hiding. When he refused, the soldiers put a noose around his neck, tossed the other end over a tree limb, and began pulling, as fifteen-year-old Jesse watched. Almost choking to death, Samuel apparently gave away the guerrillas' hideout. The soldiers charged the trees, but the band escaped.[10]

Female relatives of the guerrillas provided them with shelter and horses, and gathered supplies and information on federal troops. In July 1863, Union general Jones G. Blunt ordered the arrest and imprisonment of many of the female relatives of the guerrillas on charges of spying and aiding the rebels. The women and girls were arrested and placed in a three-story brick building at 1425 Grand Avenue in Kansas City, Missouri. The building collapsed on August 14, killing four female relatives of Quantrill's gang members. The rumor quickly spread that the collapse had been caused deliberately by Union guards weakening the building's foundation.

Five days after the collapse of the jail and the deaths of their female relatives, Quantrill's guerrillas began gathering for a strike at the heart of the Unionists and jayhawkers—Lawrence, Kansas, of which Quantrill said, "we can get more revenge and more money there than anywhere else." Lawrence was also the home of the archenemy of the rebel guerrillas, James Lane, whom President Lincoln had appointed as a general in the Union army. Lawrence also had rich banks, well-stocked stores, and fine homes with silver and jewelry.[11]

At 5 a.m. on August 21, Quantrill and about four hundred bushwhackers rode as a mob into sleeping Lawrence and began killing and robbing. For the next few hours, fierce and sweaty bearded, long-haired men, wearing no uniforms, rumbled up and down the streets and into homes and parlors, killing with guns, clubs, and knives, stealing cash and valuables, and burning homes and businesses. Smoke from the fires, rising in colossal black columns, could be seen from miles away. They killed over two hundred men and young boys before the eyes of hysterical wives, mothers, and children in a three-hour orgy of death. So many men were killed that nobody was left to build coffins. Many of the dead were buried in a mass grave. The attack left 85 widows and 250 fatherless children, and two million dollars of destroyed property, including 182 buildings.

The city lay in smoldering ashes; more than one hundred homes were burned to the ground, and mutilated bodies littered the roadside. Later that day, a resident described the aftermath: "The fires were still glowing in the cellars, which looked like great caverns with furnaces glowing in the depths. The dead lay along the street, some of them so charred that they could not be recognized, and could scarcely be taken up. At one corner, there were 17 bodies." Upon entering Lawrence, federal troops found the dead everywhere: on front porches, in bedrooms, and in the charred ruins of homes. Frank James was one of the bushwhackers.[12]

The Lawrence massacre shocked the country and captured the attention of the world. Thousands of federal troops and Kansas militia quickly pursued the bushwhackers, but by the next day they had fled back to the Missouri woods and ravines. Once the largest mass murder of unarmed American civilians on US soil (it was surpassed on September 11, 2001), the massacre prompted attorney and Union general Thomas Ewing Jr. to issue General Order No. 11, the harshest order of the war by either side against noncombatants. Ewing estimated that about two-thirds of the farmers in the Missouri counties south of the Missouri River along the Kansas border supported the guerrillas and were feeding, clothing, and providing shelter and horses to them. The farmers' lands were the swamp in which the guerrillas took refuge, and so Ewing decided to drain it.

General Order No. 11 evicted everyone living in four Missouri border counties who could not prove their loyalty to the Union cause. Ewing, whose foster brother was General William Tecumseh Sherman, wrote that he intended to "exterminate every band of guerrilla now haunting that region. I will keep a thousand men in the saddle daily in pursuit of them and will redden with their blood every road and bridle path of the border." As Missourians packed up and moved out, Kansans seeking to avenge the killings at Lawrence torched abandoned homes. Flames leapt from farm to farm, house to house, until both earth and sky seemed ablaze, transforming this once-lovely country into a silent wasteland, dotted by blackened chimneys arising out of the charred debris of burned farm homes.

Thus escalated the vicious cycle of revenge and retaliation. Quantrill's bushwhackers broke up into smaller bands. Charles Fletcher Taylor led a splinter group that crossed the Missouri River into Clay County. Perhaps the most vicious of Taylor's group was eighteen-year-old "Little Archie" Clement, so-called because of his diminutive stature—barely five feet and 130 pounds. But what he lacked in size he made up for in ferocity. Little Archie apparently liked to kill, and he was particularly fond of the bowie knife.[13]

Perhaps as a result of witnessing the near hanging of his stepfather by Union militia, in May 1864, sixteen-year-old Jesse James went to the bush. He followed hog trails and creeks to join Taylor's band, which shortly after joined Bill Anderson's guerrilla gang operating in the dark Missouri woods along the Fishing and Missouri river bottoms. These areas were a favorite of the bushwhackers, as they were rough, broken into hills and hollows by the rivers and their numerous little branches, and heavily wooded and timbered. Young Jesse knew the area well.[14]

Jesse was not alone in his youth. Most of the twenty or so members of the band were seventeen to twenty years old. They did not own uniforms but typically wore collarless, loose-fitting, large-pocketed hunting shirts. Each guerrilla also typically carried a leather pistol belt with two holstered revolvers and often a couple of more tucked into their belts. Because of its rapid fire, the six-shot revolver was the guerrillas' favorite weapon. Colt seemed to be the favorite brand, with the lighter, two-and-one-half pound "Navy" .36 caliber model favored over the heavier .44 caliber "Army" model. Loading the revolvers was time-consuming and risky on horseback in the midst of a fight, so each guerrilla carried several revolvers, drawing a new pistol when one was emptied. The fighting was at close range.[15]

Jesse started his bushwhacking days by joining in death-squad attacks on Clay County residents. During the first

few weeks of June 1864, Taylor and/or Archie Clement led
the Clay County bushwhacking crew on visits to the farms
of at least eight Unionist civilians, where they murdered
the men of the house, sometimes before the eyes of their
wives and children. Using assassination, the guerrillas
politically cleansed the countryside. The guerrillas' war on
the Clay County civilians succeeded in that general terror
prevailed—there was not one "loyal Union man who dares
to go into the harvest field."[16]

The citizens of Liberty condemned the guerrillas as "ravenous monsters of society" and said that their "speedy and
utter extermination should be sought by all brave and honorable men." By the middle of July, nearly five hundred
federal troops were in Clay County searching for the guerrillas. Many of the local citizens, however, kept the bushwhackers informed of the troops' movements and provided
little assistance to them. By attacking pro-Union civilians,
the guerrillas found their most effective weapon: terror.
Towns would first be occupied by one side and then the
other, with its citizens caught in the middle. Trade was suspended, businesses collapsed, and civil law could not be
enforced. A combination of hopelessness, uncertainty, and
terror defined peoples' lives. The statement that one man's
traitor is another man's patriot was never more true than in
Missouri during the Civil War.[17]

Bloody Bill Anderson was perhaps one of the most
vicious and feared men in Missouri. Slender and five feet
ten, he had a tangled mass of shoulder-length dark brown
hair that surrounded a tanned face framed by a full beard.
He had sharp features and vicious, blue-gray eyes that
reminded one observer of a "cross between an eagle and a
snake." His guerrilla "uniform" was all black: hat, velvet
shirt, and pants tucked into his boots. Riding on a dark
horse he looked like what he was: a killer. The scalps, ears,
and noses dangling from his bridle and horse's mane
emphasized the point.[18]

Anderson was born in 1839 in Hopkins County,
Kentucky. His family moved to Missouri in the 1840s.

They traveled down the Santa Fe Trail in 1857 to Council Grove, Kansas, where they built a log cabin on the fringe of the western frontier. Anderson and his father worked on a ranch and then began trading horses to the wagon trains heading down the Santa Fe Trail. In 1860, Anderson's mother was killed by lightning. As the hostilities along the Kansas-Missouri border escalated, twenty-year-old Anderson's horse "trading" became flat-out horse stealing. Soon Anderson's father was shot dead. Anderson and his brother Jim fled Kansas to Missouri in 1862 in order to escape horse-theft and murder charges.[19]

Anderson joined Quantrill's band of guerrillas in 1863. He was made a lieutenant under Captain George Todd in the unofficial structure of Quantrill's group. After one of Anderson's sisters was killed in the collapse of the Kansas City jail, Anderson became a homicidal maniac who showed no mercy to anyone who served or supported the Union. Eight days later, Anderson rode with Quantrill into Lawrence, where he claimed to have personally murdered fourteen civilians. "I'm here for revenge and I have got it," Anderson allegedly told one woman before riding out of Lawrence.[20]

In August 1864, Bloody Bill rode in full fury through the Missouri River counties and towns. Archie Clement was with him, and so was Jesse James. In spite of his youth, it was said that Jesse soon gained respect for his horsemanship, his ability with a revolver, and his fearlessness as he charged into the enemy. Anderson's goal was to terrorize and discourage support for the federals, and the young teenage fighters in his crew were literally soaked in blood. After Anderson's band ambushed a Union patrol near Huntersville, killing and scalping two, Anderson pinned a note on one of the dead men's bodies: "You come to hunt bush whackers, now you are skelpt." By August, the woods of Clay County were crawling with Union troops hunting for the "devil incarnate."[21]

Anderson moved his gang out of Clay County east into Ray County in August 1864. On the evening of August 30, from a bluff above the Missouri River at Rocheport, Anderson's fifty to seventy-five guerrillas fired into the steam tug *Buffington*, killing the captain of the boat. When the boat came to shore, the guerrillas climbed on board and piloted it up and down the river, ecstatic at having their own "navy." On September 5, Anderson's guerrillas fired into the steamboat *Yellowstone*, and then at another boat, bringing traffic on the Missouri River to a standstill. To run the gantlet on the Missouri, pilots demanded—and received—$1,000 for a single trip to Kansas. The carnage continued; every two or three days a new corpse was found floating in the river.[22]

On the morning of September 27, mayhem visited the railside hamlet of Centralia in the form of Bloody Bill Anderson. His men were drinking and robbing when the whistle of a locomotive was heard from the east. They stopped the train and captured the cars, which carried two dozen unarmed Union soldiers on furlough. The bushwhackers stripped them, put pistols to their heads, and murdered them. Later, companies of mounted Union infantry, largely green recruits with single-shot muskets and mounted on farm horses, rode in, viewed the bodies, and went looking for revenge. They rode into a trap. Confronted by only a small number of their foe, many more of whom were hidden in the brush on both flanks, the bluecoats dismounted for a long-range exchange of fire. They got off only one volley before being overrun; 124 were killed, many after surrendering. As Frank and Jesse James watched, Dave Pool, one of Bloody Bill's lieutenants, decided to walk on the bodies to count them. Many of the dead were decapitated and their heads rearranged on different bodies. Some heads were tied to saddles as sadistic souvenirs, a few wound up on fence posts with obscene phrases cut into their foreheads. It "had been Bloody Bill's greatest day."[23]

On the night of October 26, 1864, Anderson's guerrillas camped in the woods near the Fishing River in Ray County, just west of Albany, Missouri. Among them were Jesse

James, Archie Clement, and Clell Miller. About a mile away, Union officer Samuel P. Cox was waiting for Bloody Bill.

Tough, thirty-six-year-old Cox was another Kentucky native whose parents had settled on a farm near Gallatin. Cox had fought as a teenager in the Mexican War, and then became an Army scout who learned Indian ambush and guerrilla tactics. Wise from his twenty years west of the Missouri, he had fought in the Civil War for the Union before he came down with typhoid fever in 1862. He regained his health, and Brigadier General James Craig ordered the Indian fighter to take command of nearly three hundred federal cavalry in Ray County in order to hunt and kill Anderson. Cox's men were poorly armed, with single-shot muzzleloaders and a few pistols. But Cox had a significant advantage over previous Union officers who had faced Anderson: he was familiar with forest fighting and the art of guerrilla tactics and knew that the best way to counter them was to use them.[24]

A pro-Union woman who lived near Knoxville, Missouri, told Cox the location of Anderson's camp. Cox tried to put himself in Anderson's place and reason how to get Anderson to come to him. He hit upon the idea of tricking Anderson into thinking a federal scouting party had stumbled across his camp. Demonstrating his mastery of the use of terrain for tactical advantage, Cox concealed his men in the woods near a bridge that led to Anderson's hideout. In the faint gray of early morning light, Cox ordered one of his best riders to go to Anderson's camp. The scout glimpsed a campfire in the dark woods, a single red eye, blinking, the smoke pointing a ghostly finger up through the trees into the sky. He shot at the camp, then wheeled his horse around, galloping away.

Anderson and his men leaped into their saddles and gave chase, thinking the man was part of a federal scouting party. They galloped across the bridge after Cox's decoy, and Cox's hidden troops opened fire, emptying several saddles. Anderson and two of his men galloped through Cox's forces, shooting and yelling. As Anderson and one of his men turned and came back toward the Union picket line, Anderson was shot off his horse with a bullet to the head. After seeing their leader fall, Anderson's men fled. Cox found two human scalps swinging from Anderson's horse's bridle and a note in the dead man's pocket from General Price ordering Anderson to destroy the North Missouri Railroad bridges. He took several pistols from Anderson's body, two of which were afterward given to Cox by General Craig.

The federal soldiers loaded Anderson's corpse into a wagon and hauled it to the courthouse in Richmond, Missouri. There they allowed a photographer to capture the wild-haired guerrilla in his embroidered shirt in two photographs, in which Anderson is slumped in a chair, legs outstretched. In the first photograph, Anderson has his Colt revolver in his right hand, the barrel of which lies on top of his left wrist. In the second photo, Anderson's plumed hat is on his lap, and the lifeless fingers of his right hand are draped across the grip of his revolver, as his teeth gleam in a macabre grin.

The photos were widely published and were seen by Frank and Jesse James. Cox was a hero for doing what no other Union soldier in northern Missouri had been able to accomplish. General Craig commended Cox for "ridding the country of such a blood-thirsty villain as Anderson, who has been . . . a terror to the loyal people of Missouri."[25]

Fourteen-year-old Clell Miller, who had been wounded and taken prisoner in the skirmish, was taken to the Gratiot Street prison in St. Louis and jailed. In the spring of 1865, Clell's father met with Major Cox and begged him to help him get his son released. Cox agreed, and Clell was released in April. (Miller would repay the favor six years later in 1871, when Jesse James traveled to Gallatin to kill Cox. Miller warned Cox in time.)[26]

◆◇◆◇◆

On April 9, 1865, General Robert E. Lee surrendered to Ulysses S. Grant at Appomattox Courthouse, Virginia. The Civil War was officially over, at least in the East. Within six days, Abraham Lincoln was dead in the first assassination of an American president. Later that month, Confederate general Joseph E. Johnston surrendered the Army of Tennessee to General William Tecumseh Sherman near Durham, North Carolina. The guerrillas in the backwoods of Missouri waited, and pondered their next steps.

Missouri, like the rest of the United States, faced a significant challenge of how to reunite two separate political, social, and cultural entities that had been bitter enemies. General Grenville Dodge offered amnesty under military law for the bushwhackers if they would lay down their arms. The offer was accepted by many of the guerrillas. One of Bloody Bill's lieutenants, Dave Pool, whom even Confederate apologist John Newman Edwards described as "pitiless as a famished Bengal tiger," surrendered with a group of forty guerrillas under his command at Lexington, Missouri. But many of the former guerrillas, including Archie Clement, Jesse James, and Jim Anderson (brother of Bloody Bill), refused to lay down their arms and continued to attack and murder unarmed civilians.[27]

On May 15, 1865, seventeen-year-old Jesse James, Archie Clement, and other guerrillas were riding on the Salt Pond Road after scouting the Missouri River for a safe crossing place to escape Union patrols, when they ran into a squad of cavalrymen from the 3rd Wisconsin Cavalry. The Union soldiers yanked their pistols and fired, sending a .36 caliber bullet through the right side of Jesse's chest and into his lung. Jesse escaped into the woods, where he was first cared for by a local farmer before being driven in a wagon to Lexington, Missouri, by guerrilla Jim Cummins for medical care. There, on May 21, Jesse surrendered to Union authorities and took the Oath of Allegiance while lying on his sickbed. His wound was thought to be mortal, but he survived.

Jesse's gunshot wound brought his thirteen months in the Civil War to a painful end. The kind of education he received, like his wound, left scars that likely never went away. He made his way to his uncle's boardinghouse just across the Missouri River, north of Kansas City.

In July, his brother Frank James and several other men in Quantrill's band surrendered to Union forces in Kentucky and were then paroled.[28]

At the close of the Civil War, neither Jesse nor Frank James was a leader of their bushwhacker bands. Neither was notorious. Gallatin would change all that. The skills they had learned as guerrillas would soon lead them to become among of the most successful outlaws in American history. Meanwhile, a Union private in Virginia narrowly escaped death on a path propelling him toward a showdown with Jesse James.

FIVE

A PRIVATE IN VIRGINIA

AT THE BEGINNING OF THE CIVIL WAR, Virginia was as divided as Missouri. But Henry McDougal's Civil War experience in Virginia was vastly different from what the James brothers experienced in Missouri.

McDougal's father, John, was a farmer in Marion County, Virginia (now West Virginia). John McDougal was active in the old Whig Party and rode seventy-five miles on horseback to hear Henry Clay's speeches during the presidential campaign of 1836. McDougal believed that Clay was the greatest American statesman, so he named his second son, born December 9, 1844, in honor of him. Henry Clay McDougal worked on the family farm as a boy and received a limited education. His plans to enter college ended with the outbreak of the Civil War.[1]

On March 14, 1861, Abraham Lincoln became the sixteenth president of the United States. Shortly thereafter, the Virginia State Convention in Richmond passed an order of secession from the Union. Within twenty-four hours of the vote, Virginia rebels seized the coveted federal armory at Harpers Ferry. Delegates from the part of the state west of the Allegheny Mountains then passed a resolution in favor of the Union at the Wheeling Convention and elected attorney Francis H. Pierpont as governor of the Restored Government of Virginia—a Union government to oppose the Confederate one in Richmond.

Ten days later, Virginia citizens in the eastern part of the state voted to secede. That vote eventually led to the formation of West Virginia, which remained loyal to the Union. President Lincoln recognized West Virginia as the legitimate Virginia government, with Wheeling as its capital, and it was officially admitted into the Union in 1863 as the thirty-fifth state.[2]

After resigning his command in the US Army, Major General Robert E. Lee took command of Virginia's military forces. He had to defend an area stretching from the Atlantic Ocean to the Ohio River, but Lee quickly focused significant attention on protecting the crucial Baltimore & Ohio Railroad that ran across Virginia from Harpers Ferry to Wheeling. The railroad was the lifeline on which the federal government in Washington relied for troops, food, and supplies. From the outset of the war, both the Union and Confederate governments strove to hold western Virginia for psychological, as well as strategic, reasons. For the Union, it represented a serious inroad in the most prestigious state of the Confederacy, and for the Confederacy its retention would demonstrate strength and help preserve the South's morale.

General Lee sent Colonel Thomas Jackson—not yet known as "Stonewall"—to take command at Harpers Ferry. Lee ordered militia commanders to muster in volunteers to secure the railroads. In July 1861, Henry McDougal was living on his parents' farm in Barracksville, Virginia, when his older brother John, who believed his first allegiance was to his home state of Virginia, responded to Lee's request and enlisted in the Confederate army.

On July 21, the South won its first military victory at Manassas Junction, Virginia, an important railroad hub located near a sluggish, tree-choked stream called Bull Run. Flamboyant Confederate general Pierre G. T. Beauregard, hero of Fort Sumter, was guarding the important rail nexus at Manassas Junction, about twenty-five miles southwest of Washington, DC. Union general Irvin McDowell, a classmate of Beauregard's at West Point in 1838, devised a plan for defeating Beauregard and the Confederates and opening the way to Richmond. Beauregard received intelligence of McDowell's plan and telegraphed Jefferson Davis, who sent by railroad almost eleven thousand troops under Joe Johnston as reinforcements in the nick of time. Colonel Thomas Jackson stood like a "stone wall" during the fierce fighting and urged his men to "yell like furies." The Union's exhausted and ill-trained citizen soldiers fled back to Washington.[3]

The dramatic Confederate victory shocked the nation. The North, alarmed by the defeat at Bull Run, began to raise armies and prepare for war in earnest. President Lincoln issued a call for five hundred thousand three-year volunteers, and the country responded enthusiastically, determined to see the rebellion suppressed and the Union saved. Sixteen-year-old Henry Clay McDougal heeded Lincoln's call and enlisted in the Union army in Company A, Sixth West Virginia infantry, at Wheeling, Virginia. Governor Pierpont came to Wheeling Island as McDougal and the other raw recruits were drilling and delivered a ringing speech, reminding the recruits that he knew the father and mother of every boy from Marion County and that he expected each boy to do his duty to country and flag. Pierpont was a close friend of McDougal's father, and he had known young Henry since he was a boy. Henry never forgot Pierpont's exhortation to the fresh recruits: "Trust in God and keep your powder dry!"[4]

In early September, near Worthington, Virginia, McDougal's company was ordered on a scouting expedition. Just after midnight, they came across a Confederate blockhouse guarding a gap in the hills. McDougal's officers decided to capture the house and the sleeping rebels inside. McDougal's commanding officer whispered his order to McDougal to go in first, with fixed bayonet and gun ready to fire. McDougal felt certain that to obey meant death. He wanted to run, but obedience to orders won out, and he entered. McDougal stabbed his bayonet around in the darkness. The enemy had fled. As he enjoyed the congratulations of his company, he was thankful for the darkness, as it hid his pale face and quaking knees.[5]

McDougal's company then traveled in cattle cars on the Baltimore & Ohio Railroad from Grafton to New Creek over the Allegheny Mountains. The company marched through sleet and snow to Greenland Gap, where they camped in an old church. The chinking between the logs had fallen away, but the big wood fires were warming and cheerful. The next day, McDougal's comrades had to carry him on a cot down from the gap. Like Frank James one thousand miles to the west, he had the measles, which nearly killed him.

Twice McDougal's fellow soldiers saved his life. One morning he heard a courier gallop by the house in which he lay on his sick bed, yelling that Stonewall Jackson and seventeen thousand Confederate troops had come into the South Branch at Romney and were threatening to cut off and capture McDougal's company. His fellow soldiers carried Henry out of the house, loaded him into a farm wagon, and hauled him to safety. He thought he was going to die, but somehow he recovered. By March he was back again with his company. Soon after, McDougal was shot in a skirmish and lost so much blood that he was too weak to get up from the battlefield. A fellow soldier picked him up and carried him on his back several miles to safety.

From March to August 1862, McDougal's company was camped at Roane Court House, Virginia. On May 30, McDougal was one of a scouting party of 115 troops sent out against a Confederate force known as the Moccasin Rangers who were camped near the big bend of the Little Kanawha River. The rangers were an irregular company who were considered to be bushwhackers by many. McDougal's force surprised the rebels and killed many. Here McDougal killed his first Confederate soldier: "it was his life or mine, and I shot first."[6]

After the battle, one of the wounded rebels captured by McDougal's company came limping straight toward McDougal. A minié ball had struck him in the chin, fracturing his jaw, tearing an ugly furrow along the right side of his neck, and exposing his carotid artery, so that the pulsing of his blood could be seen with every heartbeat. His black, curling hair hung upon his shoulders, and the boy's whiskers had not felt a razor for a year. Disfigured as he was, McDougal did not recognize the soldier in gray until, with outstretched hands and tears in his eyes he exclaimed, "My God, Henry, I hoped I would never meet you like this!" It was Lys Morgan, McDougal's childhood friend and companion, who was now a sergeant in a company of Confederate rangers. McDougal bound up his friend's wounds as best he could, and Morgan, pale and haggard, limped along with McDougal's company as a prisoner.[7]

McDougal's company's supply base was sixty miles away in Ravenswood, on the Ohio River. Every wagon train and courier who had attempted to make the trip between the camp and Ravenswood had been attacked by the rebels. On July 4, another supply train was to leave Roane Court House for Ravenswood, and McDougal's commanding officer ordered that a squad of prisoners would travel with the supply train to the military prison at Camp Chase, Ohio. Among the prisoners was McDougal's friend Morgan. McDougal was ordered to be a guard on the expedition. To put a stop to the rebel attacks, the commanding officer ordered that, at the first shot from the enemy, the guards were to shoot and kill their prisoners. Each guard was quietly assigned to his particular prisoner, and by a strange fatality, Lys Morgan was McDougal's prisoner.

The order was given and the assignments made just before the men left camp at daylight. Since no convoy had failed to draw enemy fire on the road, McDougal expected an attack at any minute. When the attack came, McDougal would be forced to violate his sworn duty or kill his friend. He thought back to his boyhood, and how even the boys' fathers had been friends from childhood, and their mothers had cared for each boy as their own.

It was the longest day of McDougal's life. They marched thirty-six miles in intense heat to Jackson Court House and, unexpectedly, were not fired upon. The next day they reached Ravenswood, again without attack, and McDougal accompanied his friend to the steamboat that carried him to prison, where he said good-bye for the last time. It seemed a miracle at the time that they had not been attacked, but McDougal later learned that his commanding officer had advised the Confederates of his order two days before the troops left camp. A short time after he was imprisoned, Morgan was exchanged for a Union prisoner and rejoined his regiment. During the first battle after his release, at Droop Mountain, Morgan was killed when he was struck in the head by a Union shell.[8]

In December 1863, McDougal was in Wheeling with General Benjamin F. Kelley, the hero of the early Union victory at Philippi, West Virginia. Kelley's men had rebuilt two Marion County railroad bridges burned by the Confederates. Kelly was planning a daring raid on the Virginia & Tennessee Railroad at Salem, Virginia, with General W. W. Averill from Grafton through the Virginia mountains. Kelley ordered McDougal to carry a secret dispatch and marching orders to Averill that night. At the Baltimore & Ohio depot, MacDougal found a special train waiting for him, consisting of single car and an engine, with "steam up."[9]

The railroad tracks were cleared, and the conductor was ordered to run the engine at its top speed. From Wheeling to Grafton was ninety-nine miles—and remarkably, McDougal's train covered the distance in ninety-six minutes. The speed was so rapid and the track so uneven that as the train went over the rough track and rounded sharp turns, many of the seats in coach broke loose, and the water cooler was thrown to the floor. It was a terrifying ride, and McDougal was so concerned about his safety that had the grim conductor jumped off, McDougal was sure he would have followed. When McDougal delivered the order to General Averill, he breathed a sigh of relief that it was all over. But he had sensed the birth of the new age of the machines for both peace and war. The speed, power, and possibility of the railroad were things that he would never forget—and that would soon be the key to his fortune.[10]

As McDougal experienced firsthand, railroads played a leading role in the American Civil War. Railroads provided lines of communication and supply, and distributed troops, arms, ammunition, food, and equipment. Like rivers, they also provided avenues of invasion into hostile territory. The railroads' role in transporting supplies and troops to the Union generals substantially affected the character of the war and provided the North with a necessary element for victory.[11]

McDougal spent the last year of the war in New Creek (now Keyser), West Virginia, as his brigade's chief clerk, drafting daily, detailed reports. One day in spring 1864, the commanding officer, Colonel Nathan Wilkerson, was called away on official business to Harpers Ferry. Wilkerson ordered McDougal to run things at headquarters. A scout rode up with the news that an enemy force was going to cross the Allegheny Mountains at May's Gap, thirty miles away, after midnight the next morning to capture McDougal's outpost.

McDougal told the courier to select a fresh horse from the corral, saddle up, and report back to him. He hastily prepared an order to the commander at Greenland Gap, telling him of the situation and directing him to reach May's Gap, hide his men among the rocks and trees, and not fire on the enemy until the Confederate rearguard was well past, so that they might capture the Confederates. Knowing that a command from him might not be obeyed, McDougal signed the order "N. Wilkerson, Colonel, Commanding Brigade."

McDougal could not sleep that night, he was so worried that his plan might fail. Luckily for him, the Confederate command appeared and was captured with no bloodshed. When Colonel Wilkerson returned to headquarters, McDougal told him what he'd done. Wilkerson ordered him to never again forge an order, even with the best intentions. Wilkerson knew, as did McDougal, that had the plan failed, McDougal might have been court-martialed and shot.[12]

In August 1864, McDougal mustered out of the army. Ten days later, he accepted a position as clerk in the US quartermaster department at the old French town of Gallipolis, Ohio. Over the next two years at Gallipolis, McDougal met the young French aristocrats of the town at various parties and balls, including Emma Chapdu, the seventeen-year-old daughter of a well-to-do Frenchmen. She made a lasting impression on McDougal. Her eyes were large and dark; McDougal had never looked into eyes that were quite like hers. She caught him staring at her at a party and smiled at him, amused. He flashed a deep red. "I reckon you must think I never saw a girl before. Well, I never did see one like you before." "Thank you, Mr. Henry McDougal." Returning to his quarters that night, he kept thinking how nice his name sounded from her lips. In March 1866, he returned to his family's farm, plotting how he would make his fortune so that Emma's father would allow him to marry her.[13]

After visiting his family, McDougal spent a couple of weeks at the home of his Aunt Virlinda Boggess Atkinson in Alexandria, Virginia. Former Confederate general Fitzhugh Lee stayed in the same room with McDougal for about ten days. The two men enjoyed the high society of Old Alexandria and watched now-senator James Lane of Kansas debate in the Senate chambers. McDougal met General Robert E. Lee, Fitzhugh Lee's uncle, wizened and white-headed, who visited his nephew during McDougal's visit.[14]

McDougal also visited his father's cousin, US senator James A. McDougall, of California, who had known and been a friend of the recently assassinated President Lincoln.

(It is not known why there is a difference in spelling in their surnames, despite being close relatives.) Both McDougall and Lincoln had been frontier lawyers in and around Springfield, Illinois, in the early 1840s. Senator McDougall was the legislator most responsible for passage of the Transatlantic Railroad Act, as he was chairman of the Senate Pacific Railroad Committee and drafted the Pacific Railroad bill. Senator McDougall regaled young Henry with stories of Abe Lincoln and his frontier lawyer days, and introduced him to important railroad executives.[15]

In June 1866, Henry McDougal accompanied Senator McDougall to the White House to call upon President Andrew Johnson. McDougall encouraged Henry to become a career soldier, and at his request, the broad-shouldered, unsmiling president offered Henry an appointment as a major in the army. Henry respectfully declined, explaining that he was tired of taking orders. Privately, he was considering becoming a lawyer like his father's cousin and using his recently acquired railroad connections to begin his civilian career. Later that evening, Johnson gave a speech attended by Henry, at which the president gave thanks that he and members of Congress were becoming closer day by day. Unfortunately, Johnson was wrong, as the same Congress soon impeached and nearly convicted him.[16]

Within a few short months after bidding President Johnson goodbye, Henry left Virginia to visit his parents and family, who had decided to move to northwest Missouri for a fresh start as farmers and to take advantage of cheap farmland. McDougal wanted to explore the possibilities of becoming a frontier lawyer, much like his hero, Abraham Lincoln. He had no way of knowing that he, too, would soon become targeted for assassination.[17]

SIX

SHOWDOWN WITH FRANK AND JESSE JAMES

IN 1869, AS A NEW LAWYER and relative newcomer to Gallatin, twenty-four-year-old Henry McDougal had to search for business and take cases that no other lawyer would accept. As city clerk he had a small office on the town square east of the courthouse, and he kept busy preparing abstracts of land titles. His office was sparsely furnished with a couple of chairs, a table that he used as a desk, a simple bookcase with a few lawbooks, a wood-burning stove, and a spit box filled with sawdust. Here McDougal received clients, heard their problems, and advised what, if any, action he could take on their behalf.[1]

At that time, Missouri lawyers were not required to hold a law school degree. They trained for their law license by apprenticing themselves to another lawyer for a year or so. On November 6, 1868, McDougal received his license. That very afternoon, a farmer called on him and asked his advice on a question about road law. McDougal knew the correct answer and solved the farmer's problem. The farmer asked the amount of McDougal's fee, and he replied, "Three dollars." The farmer handed over three silver dollars, and went away just as happy as the newly minted lawyer.[2]

Shortly after receiving his license, McDougal became a law partner with Colonel James McFerran, the owner of the Daviess County Savings Association. McFerran had recently moved his family from Gallatin to nearby Chillicothe, Missouri, to open another bank and left John W. Sheets in charge of the savings association and McDougal with the legal responsibilities. Operating without a legal clerk or associate, McDougal had to master the forms and procedures of banking and other litigation, as even a minor or technical error in a filing could cause his clients to lose a case.

In filing a case with the Daviess County Circuit Court, a lawyer first had to decide whether to plead the case "in law" or "in chancery." The first referred to a formal set of proceedings and precedents handed down from the British common law, while the second, sometimes referred to as "equity proceedings," followed somewhat more flexible rules. The plaintiff's lawyer was required to draft a petition setting forth the names of the parties, the form of action under which the suit was brought, and the facts of the case.[3]

In common law, there were eleven major claims, or causes of action, including trespass, ejectment, and attachment. An action for trespass, for example, arose when a plaintiff alleged that his land or property had been interfered with or damaged. The lawyer who mistakenly identified his case might have the case dismissed by the judge. Form books suggested the proper language for various pleadings, all of which had to be written out in longhand by the lawyer. McDougal's law practice consisted of three main areas: actions to resolve questions as to the title to land, actions involving creditors and debtors, and actions involving damage to and loss of livestock and other property.

McDougal's law practice was not limited to Daviess County. No lawyer could make a living based on the one- or two-week terms during which the local circuit courts were in session. McDougal, like most country lawyers of the day, traveled several months twice a year on the large circuit that the judges were obliged to make, going from one remote county seat to the next, attending court sessions that lasted from a few days to the full two weeks.

The arrival of the lawyers and judge created a stir in each town on the circuit. People rode or drove into town on spring wagons from miles around to see the show. Trials ranged from boundary disputes to murder and robbery. In the smaller towns, trial lawyers were like stars in the theater. Lawyers often played as much to the gallery as to the jury, and some of the more flamboyant lawyers had followings who bragged about them and told story after story about what they said or who they quoted. Wagons, buckboards, surreys, and horses would be tied around the courthouse while owners were inside listening to the trials. Some lawyers drew packed houses.

Cases often were decided on common sense rather than any point of law. Trials were loose and based more on custom than statutes. Some judges admitted certain types of evidence; others did not, and so attorneys had to learn each judge's tendencies. For most cases, the country lawyers charged three dollars to twenty dollars. Lawyers typically kept records of their income in a fee book, which listed cases, the disposition, the fees charged, and expenses, such as wood for the stove that heated McDougal's office.[4]

An excellent horseman, McDougal rode the circuit over prairie trails through dense forests with a few lawbooks in his saddlebags, stopping overnight in the sparse cabins of settlers. In order to be present at the opening of court in the next county, he was sometimes forced to ford rivers and creeks on his horse. He made his trips to and from the state Supreme Court at Jefferson City on horseback or steamboat because those were the only means of travel. As he rode the circuit from county to county with the judge, he wrote out in longhand pleadings, contracts, bonds, deeds, and mortgages. McDougal believed in what he was doing and accomplishing: standing for the enforcement of law and order on the Missouri frontier. At that time, Missouri lawyers were some of the most influential leaders in the rural communities, molding and guiding public opinion and thought in politics, morals, and the law. His law practice thrived and made him a good living. By April 1869, he had acquired an interest in five hundred acres of land outside of town and was planning to build a home in town in order to persuade Emma Chapdu's father to allow him to marry her. McDougal's plan worked, and on November 2, 1869, the young couple married.[5]

A little over one month later, Henry McDougal's good friend John Sheets was shot and killed at the Daviess County Savings Association. The perpetrators were forced to leave one of their horses behind, but they encountered Daniel Smoote during their getaway and stole his horse at gunpoint. McDougal spent the Christmas holidays writing out Smoote's legal pleadings to obtain legal title to the horse left behind after the murder. The first day the Gallatin courthouse opened after the Christmas recess, on Monday, January 10, 1870, he filed the lawsuit with the clerk of the Common Pleas Court. The petition alleged that on December 7, 1869, "Jesse and Frank James [stole Smoote's] horse" and put Smoote "in fear of some immediate injury to his person."[6]

Since no photographs of the brothers were known by authorities to exist before 1876, and they were not known by any of the witnesses to Sheets's murder, the identification of Frank and Jesse James as defendants was apparently made on the basis of the thoroughbred left behind in Gallatin. McDougal, like almost everyone else in Gallatin, visited Jesse's magnificent mare in the livery barn. She was almost fifteen hands high and had wide-spaced, intelligent eyes. McDougal's petition valued Smoote's horse at $150, his saddle at $20, the bridle at $2, and the halter at $1.50.[7]

McDougal also filed a Writ of Attachment with the petition, supported by a handwritten affidavit by Smoote that tracked the allegations in the petition. Smoote says in his affidavit, "Jesse James and Frank James did, on the 7th day of December, 1869, feloniously steal, take, and carry away from affiant, and in his presence, and against his will by putting him in fear of immediate injury to his person: one bay horse. . . ." Smoote apparently did not dictate the affidavit in his own words, since it is full of legal terminology. The practice of attorney ghostwriting was common at the time.[8]

McDougal also filed an Attachment Bond in the amount of $450 as security for any damages to Jesse James as a result of the attachment of Jesse's property (the thoroughbred horse, saddle, and bridle left in Gallatin after Sheets's murder), should the court rule in the James brothers' favor. The Writ of Attachment sought possession of the horse, saddle, and bridle to compensate Smoote for the judgment that he might receive against Jesse James for the value of his stolen horse.[9]

In February, the sheriff of Daviess County filed an affidavit of service of the Writ of Attachment (which probably meant he left a copy of the writ with the owner of the Gallatin livery stable in which the horse was kept). Smoote now held a lien on Jesse's prized racehorse. McDougal then faced the tough task of trying to serve, or formally give, a copy of the petition to Jesse and Frank James so they would be required to respond to Smoote's charges. McDougal first contacted the Clay County sheriff to see if he would be willing to serve a copy of the complaint on Jesse and Frank. Meanwhile, authorities in Gallatin were apparently confident that they would capture Frank and Jesse James alive. On February 12, 1870, the court authorized money to rebuild Gallatin's one-cell jail into two cells.[10]

On March 12, 1870, Deputy Sheriff John S. Thomason, who had had a shoot-out with Jesse James just three months earlier when he attempted to arrest him, filed with the court a sheriff's return regarding service of the petition. Thomason said in the papers that he had left a copy of Smoote's petition and the Writ of Attachment with a "white person and member of the family over the age of 15 years" at the James family farm in Clay County where "Jesse James and Frank James usually reside." In other words, Thomason had not actually given the petition to Jesse or Frank, but to a person at their cabin (which was not an uncommon means of service at the time). The only people meeting Thomason's description who were living on the James farm at the time were the boys' mother, Zerelda Samuel, their stepfather, Dr. Samuel, and their sister, Susan. The James brothers would now be forced to respond to the petition or lose the case.[11]

At about the same time, fellow attorney and close friend Samuel Hardwicke of Liberty, Missouri, took McDougal around the corner of the old Gallatin courthouse for a confidential conversation. Hardwicke had been born in Clay County in 1833 and was admitted to the bar in the spring of 1857. He had a reputation as one of the most able lawyers in the county, and he and McDougal were on opposite sides of several cases in 1869 and thereafter. Hardwicke told McDougal that Jesse James had sworn to kill McDougal for seeking possession of the outlaw's favorite racing mare. "As Jesse knew me and I did not know him," McDougal later wrote, "there was nothing for me to do but to take my medicine in silence, and I did." But Jesse had picked the wrong lawyer to threaten. The threats prompted McDougal to begin working with Hardwicke and the Pinkerton Detective Agency to track down Jesse.[12]

After the Civil War, the fast and furious development of the United States took place against a background of sometimes mounting lawlessness. The forces of law and order operated at a county or local level and were often inept, untrained, or even corrupt. Into this vacuum stepped the Pinkerton National Detective Agency. Although a private enterprise, Pinkerton was virtually a national police force. Its founder, Allan Pinkerton, was quick to exploit new technology, such as the railroads, telegraph, and extensive files on known and suspected criminals, including photographs when available, in mobilizing the forces of the law against interstate crime.

Hardwicke and the Pinkerton detectives in Chicago sent telegrams back and forth coded in a word-substitute cipher, keeping each other informed on the James brothers' movements and on strategy as to their capture. Hardwicke gave McDougal the key to the cipher, so McDougal was able to stay informed in real time. McDougal also conferred with Hardwicke as to the strategy in capturing the brothers.[13]

McDougal's prosecution of Frank and Jesse James didn't hurt the young lawyer's popularity in Gallatin. In fact, it made him something of a celebrity. On the first Tuesday in April 1870, McDougal was elected mayor of the town without opposition, a position he would hold unopposed for two terms before declining a third.[14]

McDougal was also instrumental in bringing the railroad to Gallatin. As a lawyer who rode the circuit on horseback, McDougal knew how great the demand was for passenger trains. Using railroad contacts provided by his father's cousin, Senator James McDougall, McDougal arranged to bring a spur of the Chicago, Rock Island & Pacific Railroad to Missouri. With the last spike of the Transcontinental Railroad being driven at Promontory Point, Utah, the previous May, Gallatin residents were abuzz that their little town would soon be connected to that famous railroad.[15] A train depot brought prosperity and economic growth to any town fortunate enough to land one. The railroad would soon transform Gallatin from a sleepy backwater town to a growing hub of commerce for the county and the surrounding area. Buoyed by his success with the railroad, in 1872, McDougal was elected as the youngest probate judge in Missouri state history. He would thereafter be called "Judge McDougal."[16]

In response to the service of the petition, Frank and Jesse James hired the formidable forty-three-year-old Samuel Arbuckle Richardson as their lawyer. Richardson was born on July 6, 1826, in Anderson County, Kentucky. In 1845, he enrolled at the University of Missouri, where he completed his studies in two years. Afterward he took up the study of law under the Honorable Edward A. Lewis, who later became a member of the Missouri Supreme Court. He became a lawyer in 1852, and in 1859 moved to Gallatin. He apparently owned slaves before the Civil War. Richardson did not fight during the war but served as the Daviess County attorney, and was appointed Daviess County commissioner in 1864.[17]

At the time the Jameses hired him in 1870, Richardson owned more than four city blocks, and a street would later be named after him. He was the most experienced and successful lawyer in the county, and his extensive knowledge of the law made him one of the most formidable legal opponents in the state. Men loved or feared him. He served as the Daviess County attorney almost continuously from the time he came to Gallatin until his election as the first judge of the newly created Twenty-Eighth Judicial Circuit in 1872.[18]

Richardson's first move was to ask the judge to quash the service of the petition, which the Clay County deputy sheriff had left at the James family cabin outside Kearney, Missouri. Richardson knew that the case could be won or lost on whether legal service of the petition was effected on Frank and Jesse. Without legal service of the complaint, the lawsuit could not proceed. Richardson argued that the sheriff had not established whether a James family member received the lawsuit, or that the service was made at the "usual place of abode of the defendants." Of course, Frank and Jesse James were now wanted outlaws as a result of Sheets's murder and on the run from the law, so no one knew their current "usual place of abode." The court granted Richardson's requested relief, giving the James brothers a stunning, albeit temporary, victory. McDougal refused to give up. He again requested that the sheriff attempt personal service of the petition on Frank and Jesse.[19]

About this time, in May 1870, a Daviess County grand jury issued a murder indictment against the James brothers for the killing of John Sheets. No written record of the testimony before the grand jury exists, but the May 1870 handwritten indictment states that the witnesses who testified before it were "W.A. McDowal" [McDowell], "Daniel Smoot" [Smoote], John F. Helm, "A.M. Erwin" [Irving], and "Jessie Danaho" [Donohue]. McDowell, the bank clerk, no doubt testified about the appearance of the two gunmen and the December 7, 1869, murder of Sheets in the Daviess County Savings Association building. Smoote described the two men who stole his horse at gunpoint. John F. Helm was the minister who had guided the fleeing gunmen, at gunpoint, around the town of Kidder, Missouri, to the Hannibal & St. Joseph Railroad. Alexander M. Irving, a veteran of the Union army, was the Gallatin constable. He and Donohue had seen two men in Kearney with Smoote's horse the day after Sheets's murder. One week after the murder, on December 14, 1869, Irving rode to the James farm with Deputy Sheriff Thomason in a failed effort to arrest the James brothers, which resulted in a shoot-out. Irving identified the horse ridden by one of the fleeing riders as belonging to Smoote.

Based on the testimony of the witnesses, the murder indictment issued by the grand jury states in the baroque legalese typical of the late 19th century:

> Frank James and Jesse James on the 7th Day of December 1869 . . . did fire Revolving Pistols charged with gunpowder and leaden bullets which did strike, penetrate, and wound John W. Sheets upon the left breast of the body . . . and one other mortal wound . . . in and upon the left check near the left eye of . . . John W. Sheets [and] John W. Sheets . . . did instantly die.[20]

◆◇◆◇◆

Meanwhile, in the media storm surrounding Sheets's murder, Jesse James came to the attention of John Newman Edwards, an aide to Confederate general Joseph O. Shelby during the Civil War and the author of the book *Shelby and His Men*. During the war, Major Edwards had written

Shelby's official reports and was famous for his overblown and poetic rhetoric, turning a run-of-the-mill cavalry skirmish into another "Charge of the Light Brigade." His well-known alcoholism may have contributed to his excesses in writing. Historians today almost universally criticize Edwards for his exaggerations and defense of all things Confederate, no matter the facts. Edwards was then the editor of the *Kansas City Times*, railing against injustices (perceived and real) being inflicted on former Confederates and encouraging them to jump back into politics. The overt political bias of newspapers at the time was even reflected in some of their names—for example, the *Lexington Caucasian*.

The fiery and flamboyant Edwards had read about the Gallatin robbery and heard the rumor that Jesse James had killed the cashier not for money but because he believed the man to be Major Samuel P. Cox. Edwards was intrigued that Jesse had apparently committed murder in the name of the Confederate cause. The publisher arranged for a meeting with the outlaw, after which he decided Jesse's story could be useful in furthering the postwar Southern cause.

In June 1870, Edwards assisted the outlaw in writing the first of his many letters to newspapers. Newspapers were very influential in the 1870s. No other form of mass media existed at the time. People of the era had little chance of understanding the unfolding events around them except through the eyes of a newspaper. It was the newspapers that would end up setting Jesse James apart from hundreds of other outlaws. Every thief and murderer realized an immediate disadvantage whenever a newspaper branded him an outlaw. But Jesse James was one of the first criminals who benefited from the newspapers. His alleged letters to the editor after the murder of Sheets and later robberies denied guilt and played to the sympathies of many by waving the Stars and Bars of the Old South. What followed Sheets's murder was one of the most unusual public relations collaborations in American history. In fact, Edwards is more responsible than anyone for the creation of Jesse

James's "noble robber" image. One reason for the success of Edwards's myth is that it fit into the larger contested narrative of the Civil War.[21]

After the war, some white Southerners began to spin grand, romantic fables of the Lost Cause that had been fought for states' rights or constitutional principles, or any other reason they could conjure as long as it was not slavery. Jefferson Davis, who before the war had declared "the labor of African slaves" as the cause of the rebellion, wrote after the war that slavery had nothing to do with it. An early use of the term occurred in 1867, when Edward A. Pollard, the influential wartime editor of the *Richmond Examiner*, published *The Lost Cause: A New Southern History of the War of the Confederates.* It is a full-blown, argumentative statement of the Confederate point of view with respect to the Civil War.[22] Proponents of the Lost Cause created and glorified tales of Confederate martyrdom in the face of Yankee depravity. Edwards embraced the legend, and he decided he could cast Jesse James as the postwar embodiment of the Lost Cause, a figure for whom he could create a narrative in which James was a noble soldier turned political criminal, a defender of a Southern tradition of honor, family, and friendship. On the other hand, his persecutors were faceless, corporate cowards who cared nothing for family and friendship.

The pattern of Jesse James's letters in the *Kansas City Times* was set in the first one addressed to Missouri's governor, appearing June 24, 1870. It reflected themes that would become his trademark for over a decade. He claimed that he was innocent, but, as a Southern bushwhacker, he could not surrender without fear of being lynched. He would turn himself in as soon as he could be assured he could get a fair trial. A controversy exists as to whether Jesse James or John Edwards wrote this letter to Governor Joseph W. McClurg:

> Governor McClurg:
> Dear Sir: I and my brother Frank are charged with the crime of killing the cashier and robbing the

bank at Gallatin, Missouri, December 7, 1869. I deny the charge. There is not a word of truth in it. I can prove, by some of the best men in Missouri, where I was the day of the robbery, and the day previous to it, but I well know if I was to submit to an arrest, that I would be mobbed and hanged without a trial. The past is sufficient to show that bushwhackers do not have any show in law in Missouri. Several bushwhackers have been arrested in Missouri since the war, charged with bank robbery, and they most all have been mobbed without trials. I will cite you to the case of Thomas Little of Lafayette County. A few days after the bank was robbed at Richmond, in 1867, Mr. Little was arrested in St. Louis, charged with being one of the parties who perpetrated the deed. He was sent from St. Louis to Warrensburg under a heavy guard. As soon as the parties arrived there, they found out that he (Mr. Little) could prove, by the citizens of Dover, that he was innocent of the charge. As soon as these scoundrels found out that he was innocent a mob was raised, broke into the jail, took him out and hanged him.

Governor, when I think I can get a fair trial, I will surrender myself to the civil authorities of Missouri. But I never will surrender to be mobbed by a set of blood-thirsty poltroons. It is true that during the war I was a Confederate soldier, and fought under the black flag, but since then I have lived as a peaceable citizen and obeyed the laws of the United States to the best of my knowledge. The authorities of Gallatin say the reason that led them to suspect me, was that the mare left at Gallatin by the robbers was identified as belonging to me; that is false. I can prove that I sold the mare previous to the robbery. It is true that I fought Deputy Sheriff Thomason, of Clay County, but was not my brother with me when we had the fight. I do not think that I violated the law when I fought Thomason, as his posse refused to tell me who they were.

Three different statements have been published in reference to the fight that I had with Thomason, but they are all a pack of falsehoods. Deputy Sheriff Thomason has never yet given any report of the fight that I have seen. I am personally acquainted with Oscar Thomason, the deputy's son, but when the shooting began, his face was so muffled up with furs that I did not recognize him. But if I did violate the law when I fought Thomason I am perfectly willing to abide by it. But as to them mobbing me for a crime that I am innocent of, that is played out. As soon as I think that I can get a fair trial I will surrender myself to the civil authorities of Missouri, and prove to the world that I am innocent of the crime charged against me.
Respectfully,
Jesse W. James[23]

Jesse was smart, but relatively unschooled. It is doubtful he would ever have used phrases such as "parties who perpetrated." The letter contains hyperbole, for which Edwards was famous: "prove, by some of the best men in Missouri," "blood-thirsty poltroons," and "prove to the world." Significantly, the metaphor "under the black flag"—equating the guerrillas to pirates sailing under the skull and crossbones and taking no prisoners—was a term Edwards used in his book, *Shelby and His Men*. In light of the sophisticated, literary style of this letter, particularly when compared with later correspondence known to have been written by James, Edwards likely wrote or heavily edited it. By way of comparison, a letter Jesse wrote a few years later to George Shepherd asking Shepherd to meet with him after the Glendale train robbery states:

Friend Georg. I cant wate for you hear, . . . I would wate for you but the boys want to leave hear, don't fale to come and if we don't by them cattle I will come back with you. Come to the plase where we meet going south that time and stay in that naborhood until I find you. Your Friend, J.J.

Edwards may have attempted to make the letter sound as if it were written by an unsophisticated hand, but his literary talent and tendencies give him away.[24]

In addition to the style of the letter, its substance also suggests that it was not written by Jesse James. The letter refers four times to "robbing the bank," the "robbery," and "robbers." But as the two men who went inside the Daviess County Savings Association knew, there was no robbery. The men took only a box of worthless county warrants, which they threw away alongside the road. No cash was taken. If James had written the letter, why would he have referred to "robbing the bank" and the "robbery"? It is almost as if the person writing the letter knew about the crime only from reading the newspaper accounts (which mistakenly reported the crime as a bank robbery). This would suggest that Jesse never saw the letter before it was published in the newspaper.

It is possible, perhaps likely, that Edwards spoke to Jesse about the crime before Edwards wrote the letter. The letter contains certain details—such as the explanation that Jesse did not recognize Thomason because his face "was so muffled up with furs" and "was not my brother with me when we had the fight"—that ring of an eyewitness account. If Edwards did interview Jesse, the outlaw likely denied being at Gallatin, argued that he had an alibi, and claimed that his pursuers had the wrong man, as most criminals tend to do. But it is doubtful that James actually put an ink pen to paper to write the letter. If Jesse did write the letter, why did Edwards not keep it?

The newspaper's readers knew that it was true, however, that there was a possibility that Jesse James may be lynched if he turned himself in. In fact, at least three newspaper articles after Sheets's murder so much as said so. The recent lynchings of suspects in the Richmond, Missouri, bank robbery provided evidence for the point. The failure of the legal system and Radical Republican rule of law in Missouri gave Jesse an excuse to continue his criminal activities—and Edwards a platform to further his political agenda.

On June 16, 1870, Clay County Sheriff O. P. Moss filed yet another sheriff's return with the court clerk, which said that "Jesse James and Frank James cannot be found in my county." Given the Clay County sheriff's repeated trips to the James farm in 1870 in an effort to arrest Frank and Jesse for Sheets's murder and the theft of Smoote's horse, and to serve them with Smoote's lawsuit, Jesse's later claim that he left for Texas during at least part of the summer of 1870 may be true. A fugitive who was comfortable in the saddle could easily disappear in Texas. Jesse was familiar with the area, as he had traveled there during the winter of 1864–65 with Arch Clement, and Thomas Coleman "Cole" Younger had a ranch in Dallas County, Texas. Younger was a Confederate guerrilla with William Quantrill during the Civil War and the oldest brother of Jim, John, and Bob Younger. Colonel Henry Younger, the boys' father, had owned a three-thousand-five-hundred-acre farm before his death at the hands of Union soldiers during the war. Cole participated in bank robberies after the war as early as the 1868 robbery of the Nimrod Long & Co. bank in Russellville, Kentucky. Cole's brothers then joined the newly formed James-Younger Gang.[25]

On July 15, 1870, a second letter purporting to be from Jesse James to Governor McClurg was printed in the *Times* of Kansas City. It promised to provide an alibi "to let those men know who accused me of the Gallatin murder and robbery that they have tried to swear away the life of an innocent man." One week later, the *Times* published affidavits of five Clay County residents in an effort to provide Jesse an alibi. Mexican War veteran and former Confederate captain John S. Groom, the Kearney merchant who had been accosted by Jesse on December 14, 1869, and who would later become sheriff of Clay County, said that he had known Jesse since 1866, that he had "never known a more honest person," and that Jesse had been in his store at Kearney, Missouri, on December 6, the day before the robbery.[26]

Another businessman and justice of the peace, James M. Gow, swore that he, too, had seen Jesse in his store on

December 6, 1869, the day before the murder. Alfred A. McGinnis swore that he saw Jesse in Clay County the day after the murder at Mrs. Fox's in Clay County. Reuben and Zerelda Samuel stated that the mare that had been left behind in Gallatin had been sold by Jesse on Sunday, December 5, for five one-hundred-dollar bills to a man who said he was from Topeka, Kansas. Finally, Susan James, Jesse's sister, swore that her brother and she attended preaching in Greenville (three miles east of their home), and after their return, Jesse sold her bay mare Kate to a stranger who said he was from Topeka, Kansas. Her story that Jesse had been riding and racing her horse the last few years was obviously far-fetched, and probably designed to distance Jesse from the murder. She further testified that her brother was at home the day after the murder.[27]

Gallatin was only forty-nine miles away, however, and a skilled rider could have made the trip and returned in the time not accounted for by the witnesses (the evening of December 6 until the afternoon of December 8). Only members of Jesse's immediate family swore to his where-abouts on the day of the murder, and the claim that the horse was sold to a stranger who happened to be a Kansan was either a transparent attempt to blame the crime on Jesse's Jayhawker enemies, or upon Bloody Bill's brother, Jim Anderson, who was from Kansas. The $500 alleged to have been the sale price of the horse was an incredible sum for a mare in 1869. By contrast, Smoote valued his horse at $150, which was a good price for an excellent saddle horse. Newspaper accounts did not express surprise at the $500 sum, however, which was perhaps a testimonial to the magnificent thoroughbred that Jesse had left behind in Gallatin.[28]

On July 12, 1870, the clerk of the court filed an affidavit stating that "Frank and Jesse James . . . have absconded or absented themselves from their usual place of abode," such that Smoote's petition could not be served on them. The brothers were still in the Clay County area, however. On August 1, they rode into Kearney and up to Judge Gow's store. Gow had a general mercantile business at the time and was also justice of the peace, so he could legally notarize deeds conveying real estate.

Two warranty deeds are recorded in Book 35 in the deeds for Clay County, Missouri, one signed by Jesse W. James at page 26 and one signed by Frank James at page 27, each dated August 1, 1870. The deeds convey the brothers' legal interests in their family farm, which they, as minors, had inherited from their father at his death, to their mother, Zerelda Samuel. Judge Gow filled in the names of Frank James and Jesse W. James on the respective deeds in the acknowledgment portion. It was said that things were so hot for the outlaws that the brothers stayed mounted in front of Gow's store and each signed the deed while in the saddle. On August 5, 1870, the Kearney correspondent to the *Liberty Tribune* reported, "The James brothers were in town this week. They were heavily armed and well mounted. They soon left."[29]

Back in Gallatin, Jesse's letters in the newspaper gave McDougal a creative idea. If Jesse James was going to defend himself in a public forum, McDougal would fight fire with fire and inform the Jameses of the complaint by publishing notice of it in the same medium. McDougal filed a motion with the court, and on August 9, 1870, he received an order allowing the Smoote complaint to be served upon the James brothers by publication in the *Gallatin Weekly Democrat*.[30]

In August and again in September, the Gallatin newspaper published the order notifying Jesse and Frank James that a lawsuit had been filed against them. The notice told them that Smoote sought to recover a money judgment from them in the amount of $223.50, and that, unless they appeared in court on October 10, their property—Kate and the saddle, halter, and bridle—would be "sold to satisfy the same."

On October 10, McDougal obtained an Affidavit of Publication from D. Harfield Davis, the publisher of the *Gallatin Weekly Democrat*, confirming publication of the order in the newspaper, which McDougal filed into the court record. McDougal then asked the judge to find that the James brothers now had notice of the lawsuit, such that the lawsuit could proceed and they should be required to answer the charges in court.[31]

The next day, the court approved the service of the complaint on the Jameses by publication in the newspaper, and gave the brothers forty-five days in which to file their answer to the complaint.

Meanwhile the criminal charges against them arising out of Sheets's murder were moving forward. On November 21, 1870, Sheriff Moss filed papers with the court saying he had again attempted to arrest Frank and Jesse James pursuant to the separate murder and grand larceny charges, but they were "not found in Clay County." The James brothers were probably either still in Kentucky, where their sister had married former Quantrill guerrilla Allen Parmer on November 4, or were on their way to Texas, often their winter quarters.[32]

On Valentine's Day 1871, the hearing on Smoote's case was continued by agreement. Almost eight weeks later, on April 11, Samuel Richardson finally filed a handwritten answer on behalf of Frank and Jesse James. Their response to Smoote's accusations foreshadows what was to fuel their emerging legend. Richardson wrote that Frank and Jesse James denied being at Gallatin on December 7, 1869. Thus, they denied stealing Smoote's horse. Unknown to McDougal, spring 1871 was about the same time that Jesse James traveled to Gallatin with two of his gang members, Clell Miller and Dick Liddil, in an effort to kill McDougal. Jesse also is believed to have participated in a bank robbery just north of Gallatin in Corydon, Iowa, on June 3, 1871, while he was in the area, perhaps in part to raise money to pay his lawyer's fees.[33]

◆◇◆◇◆

In the spring of 1871, lumbermen invaded the woods around Gallatin, which rang with the strokes of axmen.

Lumbermen's camps sprang up along the banks of the
Grand River and its tributary streams, and floating logs
filled the water. The buzzing of sawmills also filled the air.
On April 5, 1871, the first railroad tie was laid in Daviess
County on the railroad line running from Chillicothe,
which was completed to Pattonsburg by the end of 1871. It
was the Council Bluffs-Omaha division of the Wabash, St.
Louis & Pacific Railroad. Lumber, iron, and material of
every description lined the railroad tracks, and the wake of
the advancing workmen was marked by the debris and
deserted camps along the tracks. The Chicago &
Southwestern Railroad line was also constructed through
Daviess County in 1871, and the first telegraph in the
county was operational by at least August 17, 1871. On
that day, a message was sent to Chicago and an answer
received that afternoon.[34]

On September 26, the southwest spur of the Chicago,
Rock Island & Pacific Railroad was completed to Gallatin.
Henry McDougal, as mayor, presided over a huge celebra-
tion. As part of the festivities, he hosted President Ulysses
S. Grant and many other distinguished guests on the first
westbound train from Gallatin to Leavenworth, Kansas.
McDougal met Grant's train at the new Gallatin depot,
along with most of the town's residents, who crowded
around the depot and tracks. McDougal gave a short wel-
coming speech as Grant appeared at the rear of the train
with the stub of a cigar clamped in his teeth, his coat
unbuttoned, and his tie somewhat askew. He bowed as the
crowd cheered.[35]

◆◇◆◇◆

After nearly two years of legal gun-slinging, on October 30,
1871, Smoote's case against Frank and Jesse James was set
for trial. But the Jameses knew that they couldn't fight
their way out of the Gallatin courtroom. They failed to
appear for the trial to deny Smoote's allegations. Of course,
they would have been arrested for Sheets's murder if they

had shown up. Richardson was forced to withdraw the answer he had filed on the Jameses' behalf, in which they had denied Smoote's allegations. The judge therefore found, based on Smoote's sworn testimony, that he was entitled to recover damages for the value of his horse, saddle, and bridle. The judge also ordered that Jesse's property—Kate and the saddle, bridle, and halter—be given to Smoote to satisfy the judgment in Smoote's favor. Smoote now owned Jesse's racehorse. Kate remained the object of considerable interest to visitors over the years. Smoote raised several fine colts from her, and, as it turned out, he ended up getting the better end of the bargain.[36]

Jesse James apparently had romance on his mind as Smoote was taking possession of his horse in Gallatin. In 1871, twenty-three-year-old Jesse began to court Zerelda Mimms, his first cousin who had cared for him when he was bedridden after being shot through the lung in 1865. "Zee" had been named for Jesse's mother, Zerelda. Frank James would begin to court Annie Ralston, whom he may have met at a racetrack near Kansas City.[37]

Jesse elected not to appeal the judgment against him, but, true to his outlaw nature, he sought revenge against McDougal. McDougal continued collaborating with the Pinkertons in an effort to track down Frank and Jesse James. This effort would soon result in the capture and first trial of a member of the James-Younger Gang—Clell Miller.

SEVEN

THE TRIAL OF CLELL MILLER

THE FIRST SUCCESS OF THE Pinkerton-Hardwicke-McDougal collaboration may have been the arrest of Clell Miller for the June 3, 1871, robbery of the Ocobock Brothers' Bank in Corydon, Iowa. Cleland D. Miller grew up on a farm about five miles from the James farm and was the oldest of five brothers. His father, Moses Miller, was a farmer and blacksmith. Fourteen-year-old Clell was with Jesse James and Bloody Bill Anderson when they were ambushed by Major Cox's troops near Knoxville, Missouri, in October 1864.[1]

Clell was a stock driver for Charles Robb, perhaps with Jesse James at times. Clell had a keen interest in horses and won awards for the best gelding at the fall 1870 Clay and Jackson county fairs. Clell's horse was named Kato, which was curiously similar to the name of Jesse's mare, Kate. It was about this time that Clell was also rumored to be a horse thief.[2]

Miller family stories recount that Clell looked up to Jesse James, who was two years older. Clell and Jesse practiced racing their horses around trees, shooting their pistols at the trees until they toppled. They also raced their horses down the road, shooting their pistols at fence posts. Clell's brother Ed was also a good horseman, an excellent shot, and a member of the gang during some of its robberies.[3]

At about 1:00 p.m. on Saturday, June 3, 1871, five months before McDougal obtained a judgment against Frank and Jesse, four men, thought to be the James brothers, Cole Younger, and Clell Miller, rode into the public square of Corydon, Iowa, a few miles north of the Missouri state line. Corydon was the seat of Wayne County, in the heart of the hog and corn belt. The four strangers dismounted in front of the Ocobock Brothers' Bank, located on a corner of the public square. One man held the horses and guarded the front door while another guarded the back door. Two others entered the bank and pointed their large Colt revolvers at the cashier. They forced the cashier to unlock the bank's vault, from which they took $5,242 in currency and stamps. A posse was quickly organized by W. M. Litell, a Union army veteran who had been the sheriff of Wayne County from 1865 to 1869. But the posse's horses were no match for the robbers' thoroughbreds.[4]

The outlaws lost the posse in woods southwest of town, and crossed the Missouri state line as darkness fell. The bank's owners established a $1,000 reward for the capture of the robbers and sent a telegram to Pinkerton's National Detective Agency in Chicago, seeking its assistance. Robert Pinkerton, the son of Allan Pinkerton, travelled by train and then horseback to join the posse the next day, which continued to pursue the bandits for over one hundred miles.[5]

At about noon on Monday, June 5, two days after the robbery, a posse of approximately ninety men, including Pinkerton, spied four men sitting and resting with their backs against a school building in a part of Daviess County called Civil Bend, just northwest of Gallatin. The men jumped up and ran into a nearby stable, where they had left their horses. Money wrappers were left at the spot, so the gang may have been dividing the bank loot. As the robbers galloped out of the barn, about twenty shots were quickly fired in a wild shoot-out, killing one of the posse's horses. One member of the posse fired a shotgun blast, at least part of which struck one of the robbers (possibly Frank James) in the back, nearly knocking him off his horse, causing him to drop his coat. A member of the posse picked up the coat and found it stained with blood.[6]

Pinkerton followed the robbers' trail to Clay County and the Missouri River. He crossed the river at the Blue Mills Ferry but wisely gave up the chase at the crossing of the Independence and Lexington wagon roads. Another Pinkerton detective from Chicago, R. W. Westfall, either accompanied Pinkerton to Clay County in June or went there shortly thereafter. Frank James may have made his way to former Confederate general Joseph Shelby's farm in Lafayette County, where he convalesced for two or three months. Because he was wanted for the murder of Sheets, Jesse James did not remain in Clay County after the robbery.

Another letter allegedly from Jesse James but clearly ghostwritten by John Edwards appeared in the *Kansas City Times*:

> As to Frank and I robbing a bank in Iowa or elsewhere it is as base a falsehood as ever was uttered from human lips. . . . I don't care what the Radical [Republican] Party thinks about me. . . . But I am satisfied that if I was disarmed at present, those brave Radical heroes in Missouri would try to mob [hang] me.

It is unlikely that such prose came from a little-educated farm boy like Jesse James. An example of an actual letter from Jesse James to a newspaper reads:

> Dear Sir I have lately bin reading so much about me and my friendt in your Paper som is tru and some is fals I do denie writing . . . it is fals I was in urope for two years I have bin back one year . . . I defie eny man to arrest me or eney of my companum.[7]

Because Clell Miller was neither wanted nor notorious, the twenty-one-year-old went back to live at his parents' farmhouse in Clay County after the robbery. Detective Westfall, who was working undercover, obtained information suggesting that Miller was involved in the robbery. The month following the robbery, Westfall, pretending to be in the horse business, met with Miller in Liberty. Westfall testified later that the two men discussed the Corydon bank robbery during their meeting, and that Miller claimed that he had an alibi.[8]

Westfall met with Miller again in Kearney in January 1872, along with some of Miller's acquaintances, in a cabin. After some drinks and discussion of recent events, they left the cabin, and Miller drew his revolver as he came up behind another man and placed the revolver across the man's neck. He snarled at Westfall, "We are rattlers in this part of the country." He also bragged that there were "not enough men in the state of Iowa to take me out of Clay County" to answer for the robbery.[9]

Westfall visited Miller a third time, in February at the Miller farm home near Holt. Westfall said he asked the Liberty sheriff to help him arrest Miller, but the sheriff said he would not arrest Miller or the James boys for all the money in Clay County, as he was afraid of being murdered. Westfall decided to lure Miller out of Clay County so he could get help from the local sheriff in arresting Miller. Westfall told Miller at their meeting that he had run into financial trouble and that a bank was going to take two horses he owned outside of Cameron, Missouri. He asked Miller to come and help him steal the horses.[10]

Miller agreed, and the two men boarded the Rock Island train at Kearney for the twenty-mile ride north to Cameron, located in Clinton County. By this time, McDougal was the primary lawyer in northwest Missouri for the Rock Island Railroad. Cameron was at the junction of the east-west Hannibal & St. Joseph and the north-south Chicago, Rock Island & Pacific Railroad lines, and therefore easily accessible to the Pinkerton detectives from

Chicago. Allan Pinkerton and Hardwicke would routinely meet in Cameron rather than in Clay County, where Pinkerton feared reports of their meetings would reach the James boys.[11]

After the train reached Cameron, Westfall and Miller checked into the Combs House hotel. The two men went into the bar, where they sat down at a table for a drink. Westfall had arranged the arrest with the town sheriff, who was waiting to help the agent. Westfall drew his revolver on Miller while the sheriff grabbed Miller from behind, took his revolvers, and handcuffed him. The sheriff took the angry Miller to the Corydon jail to await trial. Miller was not "mobbed."[12]

On March 20, 1872, a grand jury in Wayne County, Iowa, issued an indictment for bank robbery against Clell Miller. The Wayne County District Court then set bail for Miller at $5,000. According to the bail note, Clell's father mortgaged 240 acres of his farmland to raise Clell's bail so he could be released from jail until his trial. But first-rate improved land in Missouri could be bought for five to ten dollars per acre, and a bank would not have given a mortgage for the full value. It is therefore unlikely that 240 acres could have generated even half the amount needed. In addition, Frank and Jesse James and Cole Younger would not have wanted Miller sitting in jail, subject to potential daily visits from the prosecutor encouraging him to enter into a plea agreement to assist the prosecutors in capturing Frank and Jesse and agreeing to testify against them, in exchange for a reduced prison sentence. Accordingly, the Jameses and Younger may have contributed funds for Miller's bail.[13]

Miller's lawyer, John W. McClanahan, a former Union army captain, moved for a continuance of the case until the October 1872 court term in order to allow him and two other lawyers defending Miller to question the prosecutor's witnesses and prepare the defense. McClanahan had been admitted to the bar in 1861 and practiced in Corydon until he entered the Union army as a captain of the 34th Iowa Infantry. He returned to Corydon and by 1872 was one of its leading attorneys. Whoever had hired McClanahan had made a wise move in choosing a former Union soldier to represent the former Confederate guerrilla Miller, an attempt to offset any prejudice against Miller that the Iowa jury may have felt.

The fact that Miller had three lawyers defending him was highly unusual and lavish for a mere "farmer." Obviously, Miller's defense was well-funded. Frank and Jesse are thought to have committed at least two robberies in the five months before Miller's trial (the April 29, 1872, Columbia, Kentucky, bank robbery and the September 26, 1872, Kansas City Industrial Exposition robbery in Missouri). A portion of the proceeds of these robberies may have gone to help pay Miller's bond to get him out of jail and to his lawyers for their gold-plated trial defense.

Just over one month after Miller's indictment and arrest, on Monday morning, April 29, 1872, five men—thought to include Frank and Jesse James and Cole Younger—rode into Columbia, Kentucky. The men took different roads and wore long overcoats that concealed their revolvers. They gathered in the town square, where they were noticed because of their magnificent horses and expensive saddles. One of the bandits had been seen scouting the bank the day before, and another (possibly Frank) allegedly had been seen studying a map of the area, perhaps planning an escape route. Three men, one thought to be Jesse, tied up their horses in an alley next to the Bank of Columbia, pulled off their saddlebags, and went inside. Another man, thought to be Cole Younger, and the fifth robber kept a lookout on the town square.[14]

Inside, cashier R. A. C. Martin was at the bank's counter talking with a state representative, James Garnett; Court Clerk James T. Page; and a local merchant, William H. Hudson. The first robber (Jesse?) said, "Good morning," as he pulled out his revolver and, in a careless move, fired at the cashier, whom the robbers were counting on to open the safe. The muzzle of the revolver was so close that the exploding gunpowder singed the cashier's shirt as the bul-

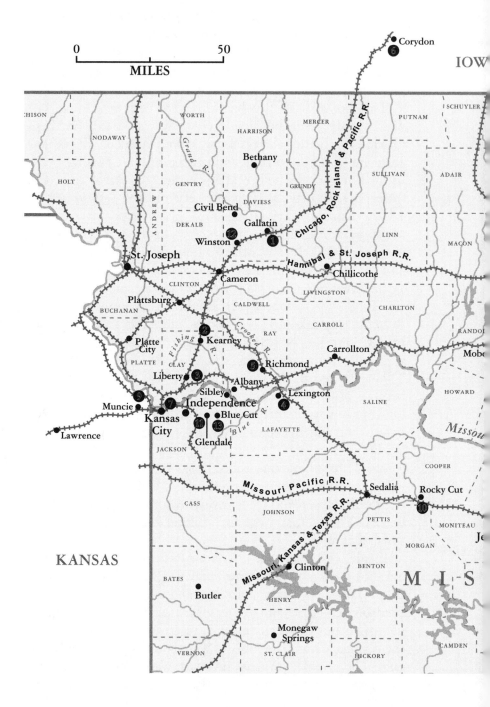

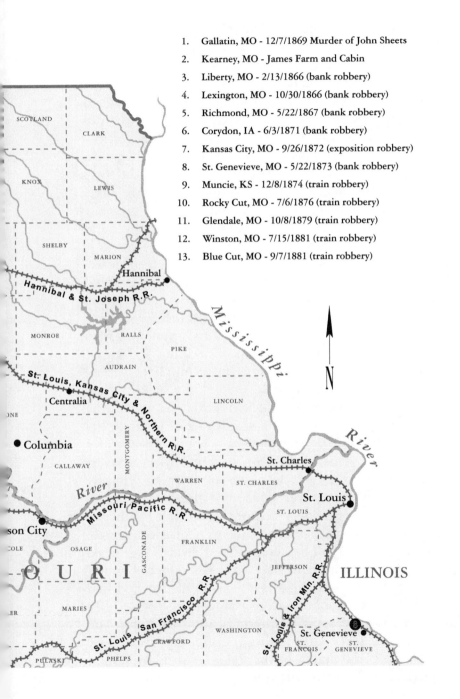

1. Gallatin, MO - 12/7/1869 Murder of John Sheets
2. Kearney, MO - James Farm and Cabin
3. Liberty, MO - 2/13/1866 (bank robbery)
4. Lexington, MO - 10/30/1866 (bank robbery)
5. Richmond, MO - 5/22/1867 (bank robbery)
6. Corydon, IA - 6/3/1871 (bank robbery)
7. Kansas City, MO - 9/26/1872 (exposition robbery)
8. St. Genevieve, MO - 5/22/1873 (bank robbery)
9. Muncie, KS - 12/8/1874 (train robbery)
10. Rocky Cut, MO - 7/6/1876 (train robbery)
11. Glendale, MO - 10/8/1879 (train robbery)
12. Winston, MO - 7/15/1881 (train robbery)
13. Blue Cut, MO - 9/7/1881 (train robbery)

let burned through the side of his body. The bank's three patrons bolted for the door as the robber fired at Hudson, who knocked the pistol's barrel to one side, burning his hand as the shot went wide. Outside the bank, Younger and his accomplice started firing wildly into the air, yelling for everyone to get off the street. Inside, the robbers dragged the mortally wounded cashier into the vault, leaned him against the safe, and ordered him to open it. Not surprisingly, and perhaps realizing the lethal nature of his wounds, he refused. A sandy-haired robber (Jesse?), hearing the shots outside, ran out to his horse, yelling, "For God's sake, hurry," to the other bandits in the bank. Unable to open the safe, the robbers grabbed $1,500 from the cash drawer and galloped away.[15]

Fewer than thirty days before Miller's trial, on the afternoon of September 26, 1872, three men wearing checkered bandannas pulled over their faces guided their horses through the crowds and rode up to the Twelfth Street ticket booth of the Kansas City Industrial Exposition. One man dismounted and grabbed a tin box containing $978 that was lying just inside the window, as his accomplices warned the startled crowd to stay back. One of the bandits then fired at the ticket taker, who ducked out of the way, as the robbers galloped off toward the woods east of town. A little girl was shot during the robbery.[16] The motivation for this risky robbery may have been to pay Miller's lawyers their pretrial retainer fee, as criminal lawyers typically demand a retainer to cover their anticipated fees during trial, since they are generally skeptical about their ability to get paid after trial, particularly if their client is convicted.

Shortly thereafter, on September 29, Edwards published one of his most famous editorials, "The Chivalry of Crime," in which he began knitting a new legend: he declared that the Kansas City robbers were "chivalric, poetic." To Confederate Democrats still suffering from their defeat and losses in the war, with gross public corruption by Republicans at the state and national level in the Grant administration, Edwards provided a literary analogy: the robbers, who most suspected were some combination of Frank and Jesse James and the Younger brothers, were American Robin Hoods with bands of merry men. He argued that such noble robbers would "never go upon a highway in lonesome places to plunder the pilgrim" but would only rob in daylight, and that they belonged to the "times of King Arthur and legend."

To modern readers, this may make little sense, but to the Democrats and former Confederate readers of Edwards's editorial, the erstwhile guerrillas were seen as striking back against the Republican authorities, who appeared helpless to stop them, much like the sheriff of Nottingham's lack of success against Robin Hood. One aspect of Edwards's analogy was accurate, however: the robbers and their supporters lived in and sought refuge in the thick forests of Clay and Jackson counties. In the latter, they favored the "Cracker's Neck" area, a rough and heavily timbered area near Independence, along Cracker's Neck Road, which was said to be so narrow and crooked that if you rode too fast you could crack your neck. The local outlaws liked to travel the road and stay in the area because the residents were their friends and supporters. Over the decades, the former Confederates' battling the Republicans' context of Edwards's arguments was forgotten, leaving only the Robin Hood myth. There was no mention in Edwards's editorial about the child shot by the bandits during the robbery.[17]

A couple of weeks later, Edwards published a purported letter from one of the alleged robbers (supposedly Jesse) denying that those who took the money were thieves. Rather, the letter asserted that the men were "bold robbers, and I am proud of the name, for Alexander the Great was a bold robber, as was Julius Caesar, Napoleon Bonaparte, and Sir William Wallace." The letter went on to denounce the Republican Party, and the writer argued that it was an insult for him to be compared to President Grant, as "Grant's party has no respect for anyone. They rob the poor and rich, and we rob the rich and give to the poor." By this time, Edwards was an influential leader of the Missouri

Democratic Party, and the letter reads as if it were written by a college-educated political operative rather than an unschooled farm boy. There is no evidence that Jesse James wrote the letter. Significantly, once again, Edwards apparently failed to show the letter to anyone or even retain a copy. Nor is there any evidence that Frank and Jesse James robbed in order to give to the poor. In fact, as discussed later, it appears that they spent much of their stolen money buying and racing thoroughbred horses, gambling, and drinking.[18]

Back in Iowa, the prosecutor offered a deal to Miller's lawyers: if Miller would identify the other robbers and testify against them, the charges against him would be dropped. Miller refused.[19]

Clell Miller's trial started on Monday, October 22, 1872, and lasted five days. Most murder trials of the time lasted only a day or two. The prosecutor called a couple of witnesses, the defense attorney did the same, they made their arguments, the judge instructed the jury, and the verdict came back. Miller's trial was quite different: over thirty witnesses testified.

The prosecution's case was handled by District Attorney Milt Jones. Twelve Wayne County men were sworn as jurors. On Monday afternoon, after the jury was selected, prosecutor Jones began the trial testimony by calling Ted Wock, the cashier of the bank. Jones wanted to begin with a dramatic yet credible witness. Wock fit the bill. He told the jury that he was sitting at his desk inside the bank facing the front door at about one o'clock on June 3, 1871, when two men walked in, pulled long-barreled revolvers, and "told me to keep still, or they would shoot me. I concluded the best thing to do was to mind them." One man went behind the bank's counter with saddlebags and began to fill them with money from the cash drawer. The other man stayed with Wock, "holding his revolvers pointing at me." The man with the saddlebags told Wock to unlock the vault. Wock hesitated, and the man pointing the revolver at his face said he would shoot him if he didn't unlock the vault. Wock did as he was told, and the robber grabbed the contents.[20]

The men warned Wock that if he stepped out of the bank they would shoot him. They left and mounted their horses, which were hitched outside of the bank door, guarded by a third man on horseback to whom they handed the saddle-bags. The man on the horse also held a revolver in his hand, and as he rode off, said, "Good day." The robbers had stolen $5,242.

Wock described the man who held his revolvers on him as "thick set, not very high, well-built, a little sunburned." The other man in the bank was about the same height, but not so heavily built, with a thinner face. Wock could not identify Miller as any of the three men. This is, perhaps, not surprising. As the youngest and least experienced man in the gang, Miller likely would have been assigned one of the simpler tasks necessary for the robbery, such as acting as the lookout on the public square. The Jameses and Cole Younger likely would have either gone inside the bank and/or guarded the outside of the bank and the all-important horses for their getaway. Without a photograph of Frank or Jesse James, the bank cashier was not able to say whether they were involved in the robbery.

The prosecutor called the second witness, Iowa farmer John A. Corbet, to identify Miller as one of the robbers. Corbet told the jury that four or five men had been involved in the robbery and that one of them was of the same general physical appearance and walked very much like the defendant Miller. Corbet was with the posse when, two days after the robbery, it came upon four men sitting against the Civil Bend, Missouri, schoolhouse, about seventeen miles northwest of Gallatin. It was cloudy and raining. The four men ran into a nearby stable and began shooting. Corbet went to the west of the stable in a wheat field, about sixty yards from the men. A member of the posse yelled at them to surrender. One of the men called out in a loud voice, "We cannot see it." The men then bolted from the stable, riding low on their horses, firing their revolvers and galloping south. Their horses were too fast for the posse, which lost their trail. On the floor of the stable, the posse found a pair of gloves, four large revolver holsters, and a large revolver.[21]

Having begun his case with good witnesses and testimony to establish the facts of the robbery and that one of the robbers looked like Miller, prosecutor Jones next called Pinkerton detective Westfall, whom he anticipated would be subjected to a scathing cross-examination. Westfall testified that he first met Miller in July 1871, in Liberty, Missouri. Westfall met with him again on January 16, 1872, in Kearney. Miller told Westfall that he had been accused of bank robbery but that he had an alibi. Westfall asked Miller why he carried two revolvers; Miller drawled that he had carried them during his bushwhacking days with Bill Anderson. As they drank in a saloon, Miller also almost confessed to the crime by bragging to Westfall that if any members of the posse "had any sand in their craws, they could have captured the whole of us while we were in the barn."[22]

Westfall testified that he met with Miller again in February 1872, at Miller's father's farmhouse. He lied to Miller and told him that he had fallen into debt and was afraid that the bank would take two horses he owned to satisfy his debts. Westfall asked Miller to help him steal the horses; Miller agreed. The two men took the train from Kearney to Cameron, Missouri. While on the train, Westfall tried to persuade Miller to take off his holsters and pistols and put the pistols in a valise to keep people from becoming suspicious. Miller finally shoved the pistols inside the waistband of his trousers.[23]

When they got to Cameron, they checked into the Combs House hotel. Westfall drew his pistol on Miller as the two were dining, and the sheriff arrested him. Westfall said he then consulted a lawyer, John W. McClanahan, to obtain a requisition, or warrant, for the arrest of the robbers of the bank in Corydon. In other words, in order to arrest Miller, Westfall had spoken with and enlisted the assistance of McClanahan, the very lawyer who now represented

Miller. McClanahan would likely have been disqualified to represent Miller under today's standards, as he was a witness with material facts in the case. Such ethical standards had not yet been established in Iowa in 1872.

Under a long, fierce cross-examination, McClanahan attempted to impeach Westfall's credibility by accusing him of making statements to McClanahan while obtaining the arrest requisition. In a question that echoed the purported James letters that had appeared in the *Kansas City Times*, McClanahan accused Westfall of saying that he intended to "have a mob hang Miller." Westfall denied making the statement. McClanahan also accused Westfall of telling him that "he did not care a damn for Miller" and that the reward was all he wanted. Westfall protested, "I never made such a statement." The unfairness and impropriety of suggesting that Westfall was not truthful through McClanahan's unsworn assertions, as an attorney representing Miller, should have been apparent to anyone in the courtroom. Moreover, the jurors in a small town such as Corydon would have been well acquainted with McClanahan, whereas Westfall was a stranger in town. Whoever had hired McClanahan as Miller's lawyer had been clever indeed.[24]

Prosecutor Jones next called fifteen-year-old Edward Fennell to the stand in an effort to bolster Westfall's testimony and confirm Miller's guilt. Fennell had been standing in a churchyard on the edge of town listening to the famous orator Henry Clay Dean speak when four men rode by at "a pretty keen gallop." One man took off his hat and waved it at the crowd as he rode by, shouting that they had just taken a "lot of money from your bank." Fennell identified Miller as the man who had taken off his hat and waved it at the crowd. But Fennell's youth and his quick look at the robbers made his testimony tenuous.

Every prosecutor wants to end his case with a strong witness. Jones finished his case however by calling a couple of witnesses who were members of the posse and who were inconsistent in their testimony as to whether Miller was one of the men they had seen at the Civil Bend schoolhouse. The testimony revealed a lack of preparation by Jones.[25]

It was now the defense's turn. McClanahan called eight witnesses, the first four of whom were relatives of Miller's, who provided an alibi as to Miller's whereabouts the day of the robbery. This was reminiscent of the affiants Jesse James and or Edwards had lined up to provide Jesse with an alibi after Sheets's murder. First was William Miller, a thirty-one-year-old veteran of the Confederate army and Clell Miller's cousin. Miller testified that he saw and spoke to Clell on June 3, 1871, the day of the robbery, at a store in Gentryville, Missouri, and that he had borrowed Clell's horse that evening. He admitted during cross-examination that Clell carried two Colt revolvers at all times.[26]

Next to testify was Isaac Miller, Clell's fifty-nine-year-old uncle, who was a farmer. He told the jury that he saw Clell outside of the store in Gentryville on June 3. He also testified that Clell went to church with him the day after the robbery, as well as the following Sunday. After Clell was accused of robbing the bank, Isaac Miller went with him into Gentryville to locate witnesses who provided affidavits and testimony as to Clell's whereabouts in Gentryville the day of the robbery. During cross-examination, Isaac Miller gave conflicting testimony as to which church he and Clell had supposedly attended on which date. He admitted that Clell was generally armed.[27]

The next witness in the defense's parade of family members was the grandly named Napoleon Bonaparte Robertson, a son-in-law of Isaac Miller's. He testified that he had seen Clell in a store in Gentryville on June 3. F. M. Setzer, who owned the drugstore in Gentryville, then testified that in his store on June 3, he saw Clell and all of the family members who had just testified.[28]

Like the prosecution, the defense wanted to begin and end its case with a strong witness. McClanahan planned to have his final defense witness call into question the character of the prosecution's chief witness, R. W. Westfall.

Presley Anderson lived four miles from Clell Miller's family farm and said that Clell was a "peaceable man." He admitted during Jones's cross-examination that Miller carried two revolvers at all times. But Anderson then dropped the bomb that McClanahan had probably planned: he gratuitously volunteered that Westfall shared a room in a hotel that Anderson managed in Holt, Missouri, with a woman whom Anderson said he had seen "in a whorehouse in Kansas City."[29]

Prosecutor Jones now faced the daunting task of rebutting the alibi testimony of the defense's Missouri witnesses. He did the best he could by calling witnesses who placed Clell Miller in Corydon the night before the robbery. Jones first called Harriet Gallop, who was a waitress at the Coddington Hotel in the town. She told the jury that she waited on Miller during evening supper at the hotel the night before the robbery. Next to testify was the owner of the hotel, James D. Coddington, who also identified Miller as one of two men who stayed at his hotel the night before the robbery, both of whom rode horses with saddlebags.[30]

Coddington said that Miller and the other man left the hotel the morning of the robbery. They walked into the barn to saddle their horses, leaving their saddlebags outside the barn door. As they were leading their horses away from the barn, the other man said, "We forgot our saddlebags." Coddington told the man that he "would fetch them to you," but the man whirled around, hurried past Coddington, and grabbed the bags. Coddington was so suspicious of the man's behavior that he asked, "Have you got money in them saddlebags?" Before Miller's lawyer could object, Coddington testified that the man replied, "No, but we have got something that will make it damned fast." The man's statement to Coddington was inadmissible as hearsay evidence. The prosecutor knew it but elicited the testimony anyway.[31]

In an unusual and unexplained decision (perhaps because the prosecution had intentionally introduced hearsay evidence from Coddington), the trial judge allowed the

defense to then call the final witnesses at the trial (typically, the prosecution's rebuttal case ends the testimony and
evidence in the trial). The judge allowed the defense to call
a dozen witnesses, all of whom testified as to detective
Westfall's allegedly bad character: he drank and was a gambler, and he had a reputation for not telling the truth. Many
prosecutors believe it is essential to call at least one witness
on rebuttal, if only to take advantage of the crucial last
word. Jones did not do so. It should be noted that the testimony contains no suggestion that the motive behind the
robbery was political or somehow related to the Civil War.[32]

After closing arguments, the jury retired Friday afternoon to consider its verdict. The jurors returned by the
close of business with a verdict of "not guilty."

Clell Miller's trial displayed a combination of prosecutorial lack of preparation and misjudgment, and defense
savvy. The prosecutor was overwhelmed and out-lawyered.
Miller's lawyers had succeeded in their strategy of creating
reasonable doubt as to Miller's guilt by arguing that he was
a mere farmer and the detective was an immoral liar.
Corydon's citizens, however, believed that justice had been
defeated by the Missouri witnesses.[33]

◆◇◆◇◆

In Kansas City, John Newman Edwards continued his public relations campaign for the James brothers. On
November 23, 1873, he caused a sensation when he published "A Terrible Quintet," a special newspaper supplement of twenty pages for a national audience. Eleven of the
pages were devoted to a breathless biography of Frank and
Jesse James, calling them the "two most wonderful men in
Missouri" and providing a lengthy excuse for their actions,
while at the same time denying that they had committed
any crimes. In his introduction, Edwards wrote "much that
has been said and written concerning these men was purely
sensational, fictitious and romantic." Edwards then added
to the "sensational, fictitious and romantic" with a gener-

ous mix of facts and fiction. He crafted a glorified image of persecuted former Confederate guerrillas, replete with the overblown rhetoric for which he was famous: Frank James had a "tiger in his heart." Even undisputed geographical facts were misstated and exaggerated for dramatic effect. Edwards claimed that "Kearney to Gallatin was 80 miles" (rather than forty-nine), as supposed evidence as to why Jesse James could not have traveled to and from Gallatin and murdered Sheets in the time unaccounted for in the affidavits of his family and friends. Edwards even botched the date of the murder, claiming it occurred on December 16, rather than December 7, 1869.[34]

Meanwhile, the Pinkertons, Hardwicke, and McDougal continued in their efforts to capture or kill the James brothers. On March 4, 1874, Pinkerton sent agent Joseph Whicher to Clay County with a scheme to bring in the two outlaws. He posed as a farmhand but made the mistake of depositing fifty dollars in the Commercial Bank in Liberty, a far larger sum than a typical farmhand would carry. He also revealed his identity to the bank's president and Sheriff Moss, who told Whicher to stay away from the James farm, as "the old woman [Zerelda Samuel] would kill him as quick as the boys would." Whicher ignored the advice and took the train to Kearney dressed as a laborer. He arrived about sundown and started walking to the James farm three miles away.

About three the next morning, four men on horseback crossed the Missouri River on the Liberty Ferry. One of the men was bound and gagged. The three other riders told the ferryman that they were a posse and that the bound man was a horse thief they were taking to the Independence jail. Three of the men were later identified, based upon the ferryman's descriptions, as Jesse James, Jim Anderson, and Arthur McCoy (another former bushwhacker). Whicher's corpse, shot at close range in the temple, neck, and shoulder, was found on the road four miles east of Independence. Wild pigs had eaten some of the corpse's face. On the body's clothing was pinned a handwritten note that read, "This to all detectives." Allan Pinkerton had never suffered a defeat like this, and he began to fund the investigation at his own expense.[35]

Hardwicke was communicating by telegram with Pinkerton at least by 1874, keeping him (and McDougal) informed of efforts to capture or kill the James brothers. In December 1874, Hardwicke met with L. W. Towne, the general superintendent of the Hannibal & St. Joseph Railroad, to arrange for a special train to carry Pinkerton's men in an attempt to arrest Frank and Jesse James. The train was unusual in that it consisted of only an engine, a tender, and a caboose.[36]

On Christmas Day 1874, Hardwicke sent Pinkerton a telegram outlining his ideas on how to capture the James brothers. The plan called for Robert Pinkerton and six other detectives to take the train arranged for by Hardwicke from Illinois to a wooded area two miles north of Kearney. There the Pinkerton men were led by a guide arranged for by Hardwicke to the James-Samuel farm. Hardwicke was to hold the train at that location after the raid until all of Pinkerton's men had returned safely. Hardwicke also arranged with one of the Jameses' neighbors, Daniel Askew, to use his farm as a staging area before the attempt to capture or kill the brothers.

On the evening of January 25, 1875, Frank and Jesse James and Clell Miller had dinner at the James-Samuel farmhouse. Unknown to Hardwicke and the Pinkerton men, however, they apparently rode away after dark. Shortly after midnight, the Pinkertons surrounded the farmhouse and threw an incendiary device through one of the windows to illuminate the interior and/or start a fire to force the occupants outside. Dr. Samuel kicked the device into the fireplace, where it exploded. Portions of the exploding device shattered Zerelda Samuel's right wrist and hit thirteen-year-old Archie Peyton Samuel, Jesse's thirteen-year-old half brother (named in honor of bushwhackers Archie Clement and Peyton Long), in the midsection.

Archie later died of his injuries, and Mrs. Samuel's right arm had to be amputated below the elbow.

Word of the attack spread quickly across western Missouri, and within days the entire state and most of the nation were reporting on the event. The attack provoked rage across the state. The media were outraged at the death of a child, and the atrocity reawakened memories of the war. John Edwards wrote the most ferocious editorial of his career, calling on Missouri citizens to "rise up and hunt the midnight cowards and assassins to their death. . . . [Y]ou who fought under Anderson, Quantrill . . . recall your woodcraft and give up these scoundrels to the Henry rifle and Colt's revolver." He added, "It is not for the robberies that Pinkerton hates the James Brothers. It is because like you they were at Lawrence, . . . when the Black Flag floated and men neither knew nor wanted quarter." In a follow-up editorial, "Pinkerton's Vendetta," Edwards claimed to have a letter from the attackers or their sympathizers that said, "If the d——d Rebel Gov. of Mo . . . wants to know who committed the murder at Dr. Samuel's I can tell them who it was, it was the friends of Capt. Sheets," potentially implicating McDougal and Hardwicke.[37]

John Edwards apparently urged the Missouri General Assembly to condemn the raid. The assembly quickly passed a resolution demanding an investigation. Thereafter, it almost passed a bill to grant amnesty to the Jameses. In legislation offered March 17, 1875, which was apparently written by Edwards, the bill declared that the James brothers had "gallantly periled their lives . . . in the defense of their principles" and were driven to become outlaws by necessity. Declaring the brothers to be "brave . . . generous . . . gallant and honorable" men, it urged that amnesty be extended for acts committed during the war. The amnesty bill received a majority vote but failed to achieve the two thirds needed for passage.[38]

The amnesty bill is compelling evidence of the success of Edwards's efforts to create a mythology for the Jameses.

Through his pen, the robbers and murderers had become noble bandits. The Civil War in Missouri, in which many young men had fought with the North, became a war where the virtuous Southerners had fought against Northern occupiers. The invasion of the James farm by Pinkerton detectives only served to prove the extent of Northern treachery against Missouri's Confederates during the Civil War and its aftermath.[39]

A grand jury interrogated Hardwicke and Askew, and Hardwicke's work for the detectives soon came to light. Hardwicke and Askew were not charged, but they now faced the wrath of the James brothers. During the night of April 12, 1875, Askew was shot three times in the face outside his cabin as he fetched a pail of water. A few minutes after the shooting, a neighbor of Askew's heard a mounted stranger shout, "We have killed Dan Askew tonight, and if anyone wishes to know who did it, say the detectives did it." Jesse James was reported to have crossed the Blue Mills Ferry after the shooting of Askew, being recognized by his horse. Samuel Hardwicke fled Liberty for St. Paul, Minnesota, in fear for his life.[40]

◆◇◆◇◆

Nearly nine years of fighting had scourged Missouri and it remained an open wound after the Civil War. Roughly one out of every three of its citizens had been killed, driven out by guerrillas, banished by Union authorities, or simply fled. The peace imposed by the Jameses' Unionist neighbors was punitive. In June 1865, the Radical Republicans in Missouri enacted a requirement that each officeholder, juror, educator, voter, and even minister swear an oath, as a condition of employment and voting, that he had not supported the rebellion. This effectively precluded all former Confederates and their supporters from voting and returning to their prewar professions. Without an income, many farms owned by former Confederates fell behind in their bank payments and were foreclosed on and sold to

Unionists and/or new settlers who flocked to Missouri, mostly from the north.

In 1870, the infamous oath law was repealed, and in 1872, approximately seventy-five thousand formerly disenfranchised ex-Confederates were again allowed to vote. The Democrats swept the state elections and by the end of 1875 controlled state politics. That year they created a new Missouri Constitution that segregated schools, banned interracial marriages, and included an amnesty provision for all wartime activity. The former insurgents had created their own social order and rejected the laws imposed by what some viewed to be Northern occupiers. Edwards's glorification of Frank and Jesse James coincided with the resurrection of pro-Southern political activity in Missouri.[41]

Perhaps now believing Edwards's fawning accounts of their invincibility, Frank and Jesse James decided to take their criminal show to Minnesota. At least eight men were involved in the 1876 bank robbery in Northfield: Frank and Jesse James; Cole, Bob, and Jim Younger; Clell Miller; Charlie Pitts; and Bob Stiles and/or Bill Chadwell. The Jameses and Youngers were apparently lured to Minnesota by promises of rich pickings by Minnesota native Bob Stiles, who may have gone by the alias of Bill Chadwell (some authors believe that Stiles and Chadwell were different men). It has been suggested that the bank in Northfield was targeted in part because it was owned by Adelbert Ames, a former Union general and governor of Mississippi during Reconstruction. But the gang members arrived in Minnesota the last week of August 1876 and scouted possible targets in Mankato, where they met on September 2. It was only after they determined that a grasshopper plague had wiped out the farmers in the area, and thus their deposits at the Mankato banks, that the gang settled on the First National Bank of Northfield.

On Thursday, September 7, at 2:00 p.m., the Jameses and Pitts dismounted in front of the bank, hitched their horses, and went inside. One of them carried a grain sack. Clell Miller and Cole Younger had ridden up to the bank from a different direction. Miller dismounted and stood outside the bank's door, guarding the entrance and the horses. Younger also dismounted and watched the street outside of the bank. Things did not go well for the robbers inside the bank. Despite being pistol-whipped, the assistant cashier refused to open the vault. Incredibly, Frank and Jesse James did not realize the safe was not even locked. Two citizens were also in the bank, and the James brothers found themselves short-handed in covering all three men and scooping up the loot from the cash drawer. The bank teller bolted for the back door and, despite being shot in the back as he fled, escaped.[42]

Northfield's citizens began arming themselves and running toward the bank. Miller and Cole Younger fired into the air, trying to clear the street. Jim and Bob Younger came galloping toward the bank, shooting and screaming. Shotguns and revolvers began to appear from windows and storefronts. Miller was shot from his horse and killed with a blast of birdshot to the head and a bullet through his chest. Jesse James shot and killed the assistant cashier, and then he and the other bandits in the bank came flying out and leaped onto their horses. They clung to their horses' necks, using the animals for cover as they galloped away. Bob Stiles was shot dead off his horse. As the Younger brothers continued to fire their revolvers in an effort to clear the street, Bob Younger's right elbow and shooting arm was shattered by a bullet. Another bullet lodged in Jim Younger's shoulder. All three Younger brothers were captured. Only Frank and Jesse James escaped.

The gang had run into a bunch of farmers and small-town businessman and had been shot to doll rags. Rather than focusing on the gang's near annihilation, however, John Edwards and the Southern press emphasized the James brothers' "daring" escape from a relentless posse of hundreds across five hundred miles. The two brothers good fortune to survive unscathed and escape could only add to their legend in the eyes of their supporters.[43]

◆◇◆◇◆

After the Northfield debacle, there was a three-year hiatus in robberies by the James brothers. Frank, perhaps cured for the moment of a desire for further robbery and tired of living in the saddle, now married and with a son, moved to Nashville, Tennessee, where he succeeded as a farmer. Jesse also apparently wanted out of the robbery business and attempted to make his living as a gambler and horseman in Humphreys County, not far from the Tennessee River, about seventy-five miles west of Nashville, but he was not as successful as Frank. Jesse and Frank James were expert horsemen. Accordingly, they always rode in style, mounted on the finest Kentucky thoroughbreds money could buy.[44]

In 1877, John Newman Edwards published his book *Noted Guerrillas, or Warfare of the Border*, which cemented the legend of Missouri's noble guerrilla fighters. The book glorified the wartime exploits of Jesse James and many of his guerrilla compatriots. Albert Castel, in his foreword to the 1976 reprint of Edwards's book, wrote, "It did more than any other book to establish and perpetuate the fame of the James Boys." It was, however, Edwards's earlier editorials and the letters he wrote for Jesse James that had the greatest effect on establishing and perpetuating the myth of Jesse as a noble robber.

In September 1879, three years after the botched Northfield robbery and needing money, Jesse James recruited a new gang consisting of James A. "Dick" Liddil, a dapper young man from Vernon County, Missouri; Bill Ryan, a hard-drinking Irishman who lived in the Cracker's Neck (now referred to as the Crackerneck) region near Independence, and an unsophisticated country boy, Tucker Bassham, also from the Independence area. These new recruits had not been trained in the war like the three Younger brothers, who were lost to the gang at Northfield; in fact, they were little more than petty thieves. These men, with James's cousin Wood Hite and Ed Miller, the brother of the dead Clell, would conduct the final crimes of the gang.

In spring 1880, Ed Miller introduced Jesse to two young brothers who lived in Ray County, Charlie and Robert "Bob" Ford. James befriended them, particularly the older brother, Charlie. The gang's social life centered on the farm home, one mile east of Richmond, of the Fords' sister, a young, attractive widow named Martha "Mattie" Bolton. During that summer, while out away from the farm, Miller and James had a heated argument. It could have been over Clell's death or money. Jesse shot Ed dead off his horse, but he wanted to keep the killing quiet, for fear that some of his gang members or supporters might turn against him. He asked Charlie Ford to keep Miller's horse and told him that Miller was ill and had gone to Hot Springs, Arkansas, for his health.

Miller's disappearance and the later discovery of his body caused concern among Miller's friends, including Jim Cummins. Cummins was a former guerrilla who had helped Jesse James get to Lexington in May 1865 so he could get medical care for the gunshot wound to his lung. Cummins had either given or sold Miller the horse he was riding at the time James killed him. James later picked up the horse from Charlie Ford and rode it back to the Nashville area, with Dick Liddil and Bill Ryan in tow to his brother's farm.

Frank James did not like Ryan and allegedly told Jesse not to bring that "damned Irishman to my house." Frank was afraid that Ryan's drinking would lead to trouble, and he turned out to be right. On Friday March 25, 1881, Bill Ryan, alias "Tom Hill," rode north from Nashville toward Adairville, Kentucky. Ryan stopped that night in a saloon and got very drunk, which would soon lead to more trouble than Frank James imagined.[45]

The Daviess County Savings Association building photographed around 1900 before it was demolished. Employee John W. Sheets was murdered here in December 1869 by Jesse James and an accomplice. (*Daviess County Historical Society*)

A contemporary but inaccurate illustration of the attack on John W. Sheets to avenge the Civil War death of Confederate paramilitary leader William T. "Bloody Bill" Anderson. There were only two men involved in the crime. (*Daviess County Historical Society*)

John W. Sheets, left, a Union veteran, was mistaken for Samuel P. Cox, right (in a later photograph), who led the ambush of "Bloody Bill" Anderson. Anderson's former soldiers, including Jesse James, vowed revenge against Cox. (*Daviess County Historical Society*)

> Daniel Smoote   Plaintiff
>   against
> Jesse James + Frank James   Defendants
>   In the Common Pleas
>   Court of Davies Co Mo
>   Jany Term 1870
> Plaintiff state that on the 1st day of
> December 1869 at or near the city of
> Gallatin in the County of Davies and
> State of Missouri, the defendants Jesse
> and Frank James did feloniously
> steal take and carry away from
> this plaintiff and in his presence and
> against his will, by putting him the
> said plaintiff in fear of some immediate
> injury to his person the following per-
> sonal property to wit: One bay horse with
> four white feet and a white snip in the
> nose of the value of One Hundred and
> fifty Dollars. One Saddle of the value of
> Twenty Dollars One Bridle of the value of
> Two Dollars and One Halter of the value
> of One and 00/100 Dollars. the property of this
> plaintiff by which the plaintiff says he is
> damaged in the sum of Two Hundred
> and Twenty three and 00/100 Dollars for
> which he asks judgment
>   H. C. McDougal
>   atty for Plaintiff

The 1870 petition filed on behalf of Daniel Smoote against Jesse and Frank James by Henry McDougal, the first legal complaint against the James brothers. Following the murder of John Sheets, Jesse James lost his horse and stole Smoote's bay at gunpoint during his getaway. (*Author*)

Jesse Woodson James, left, became the target of young lawyer, Henry Clay McDougal, right, following Sheets's murder. McDougal would pursue the conviction of the James brothers over the course of more than a decade. (*Library of Congress/Author*)

The Daviess County Courthouse, cater-corner from the Daviess County Savings Association and site of McDougal's complaint against Frank and Jesse James. (*Daviess County Historical Society*)

The James-Samuels Farm near Centerville, Clay County, Missouri. It was here that a Pinkerton detective threw a device that exploded and killed Jesse and Frank's younger brother and disfigured their mother. Note the fence and woods that played a role in the December 14, 1869, attempt to capture the brothers. (*Library of Congress*)

William T. "Bloody Bill" Anderson in a posed photograph after he was dead. Two of Anderson's pistols were presented to Samuel P. Cox at the time, and when Anderson's brother demanded their return after the Civil War, Cox refused, which set in motion the events that led to the death of John Sheets and the identification of Jesse and Frank James as criminals. (*Original photograph by Robert B. Kice*)

Henry C. McDougal as a twenty-four-year-old private in the Union army. He served mostly in West Virginia. (*McDougal family*)

Henry's father's cousin United States senator from California James A. McDougall. Senator McDougall introduced his nephew to key persons in the railroad industry. (*Author*)

Jesse James photographed toward the end of the Civil War at about age seventeen. (*Library of Congress*)

Frank James, center, just after the Civil War, wearing his Confederate uniform. Jesse is standing at right. Frank would have been twenty-two years old at the time. (*State Historical Society of Missouri*)

Former Confederate officer and editor of the *Kansas City Times*, John Newman Edwards promoted Jesse James and his crimes as upholding Southern honor. (*State Historical Society of Missouri*)

Samuel A. Richardson was one of the most experienced lawyers in Missouri when he became counsel for Frank and Jesse James following the Sheets murder. (*Daviess County Historical Society*)

Thomas T. Crittenden, governor of Missouri, recognized that the James Gang would have to be stopped in order for the state to continue to attract railroads and other modern industries rather than be bypassed due to uncontrolled crime. (*Library of Congress*)

Allan Pinkerton and his agency also sought to capture the gang members on behalf of their railroad clients. (*Library of Congress*)

Newspaper illustrations of the James Gang's December 8, 1874, robbery of the Kansas Pacific Railroad train near Muncie, Kansas. At top, one of the bandits forces a general store owner to signal the train to stop. Bottom, gang members swarm aboard the train and take control at gunpoint. They then forced a Wells Fargo employee to open a safe containing thousands of dollars in currency and gold which they stole. Note the sacks with eye holes cut out of them that the gang often used as a disguise, and their use of multiple firearms. (*Leslie's Illustrated News*)

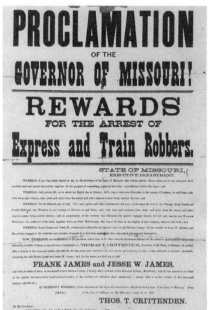

Gang member Richard "Dick" Liddil surrendered to authorities in January 1882 and offered to provide information leading to the arrest of Frank and Jesse James in exchange for a pardon. (*State Historical Society of Missouri*)

Governor Crittenden authorized a reward for the capture of Frank and Jesse James. (*State Historical Society of Missouri*)

The First National Bank of Northfield, Minnesota, was the scene of the September 7, 1876, failed bank robbery where the James-Younger Gang suffered its worst defeat. Two gang members were killed and the Younger brothers were eventually captured. Only Frank and Jesse James remained at large. (*Northfield Historical Society*)

Jesse James photographed in his coffin. James was shot and killed by Robert Ford on April 3, 1882, in James's St. Joseph, Missouri, home. (*Library of Congress*)

Former Confederate general Joseph Shelby testified in defense of Frank James during his murder trial in 1883. (*Library of Congress*)

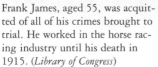

Frank James, aged 55, was acquitted of all of his crimes brought to trial. He worked in the horse racing industry until his death in 1915. (*Library of Congress*)

The author holding the *Daniel Smoote v. Frank and Jesse James* lawsuit that he discovered in 2007. This was the only successful legal action against Jesse James. (*Author*)

EIGHT

THE ARREST AND TRIAL OF BILL RYAN

ON MARCH 25, 1881, an elegantly dressed man on an expensive horse rode up to a saloon in a town a few miles north of Nashville, Tennessee. Nobody knew him. He began to drink whiskey and became very drunk. He got into an argument with another man and tried to pull his pistols, shouting in an Irish accent, "Stand back, I'm Tom Hill, outlaw against state, county and the United States Government!" The saloon owner, William L. Earthman, who also happened to be the justice of the peace, threw his arms around the man, pinning his arms so that he couldn't shoot. "Tom Hill" was searched and found to be wearing a buckskin vest containing about $400 in twenty-dollar gold coin "eagles" and $980 in other currency. Tied up in a chair, he was hauled outside, hoisted into the back of a wagon, and driven to Nashville, where he was locked up in the jail.[1]

The Nashville chief of police believed that the prisoner might be a member of the James Gang and telegraphed a description of him to Kansas City police chief Thomas Spears. Spears asked newly elected Jackson County prosecutor William H. Wallace to look at the description, since Wallace had been investigating and studying the gang members. Wallace recognized the Tennessee prisoner as Bill Ryan. Wallace knew Ryan from Independence, where he had grown up, before Ryan became an outlaw. He was about twenty-nine and had a reputation as a drunk who was often seen in the Independence saloons. This was a great stroke of good luck. Purely by accident, the law had arrested a key member of the James Gang. Wallace ordered Ryan to be transported to Independence and placed in the stone jail.[2]

The last phase of the James Gang's robberies had begun sixteen months before Ryan's arrest with the armed robbery at 8:30 p.m. on October 8, 1879, of a Chicago & Alton train running from Denver, Colorado, to Chicago. The robbery took place just outside of Independence, in Glendale, a lonely and isolated stop consisting of a two-story depot, where telegraph operator John Andrews lived with his elderly mother. That night, Jesse James and five others—Bill Ryan, Dick Liddil, Tucker Bassham, Jesse's cousin Wood Hite, and Ed Miller—rode their horses at a fast trot over a bridge across the Little Blue River, along the road that led to the depot. The robbers entered the telegraph office and took operator Andrews prisoner. James shoved a cocked revolver into Andrews's mouth to force him to stop the train. Mrs. Andrews became hysterical, crying, "Don't kill my son!" The robbers frightened her so badly that she almost died of a heart attack, but she survived and had to be committed to an asylum. Upstairs in the living quarters the gang captured W. E. Bridges, a traveling railroad auditor who had the misfortune of stopping there for the night, and robbed him.[3]

The robbers walked down the track and piled stones between the tracks to stop the train. They boarded it and pistol-whipped the express company guard. The gang stole about $6,000 from the U.S. Express Co. safe on the train, far less than the $60,000 or so in gold they thought the train might be carrying from Colorado's mines. Jesse left a note with the telegraph operator that said, "We are the boys who are hard to handle, and will make it hard for the party that tries to take us. James brothers." Of course, this was false bravado—the farmers and merchants at Northfield had found the more experienced James-Younger Gang relatively easy to handle three years earlier.

The robbery caused public outrage and calls for the apprehension of the criminals. In the years between 1876 and 1879, public sentiment toward the gang had changed. Whatever sympathy the public might have had prior to 1876 by reason of their Civil War connection, there could be no such justification for crimes after a three-year hiatus in robberies and after the Democrats and ex-Confederates had swept the Missouri elections in 1875. The gang's robbing and beating of innocent civilians now seemed senseless, cowardly, and cruel. Frank and Jesse James became an embarrassment to many in Missouri, and pressure began to build to put an end to the outlaws. Not even John Newman Edwards stood up for Jesse this time. Thomas T. Crittenden, the Democratic governor elected in 1880, promised in his inaugural address to rid the state of the robbers.[4]

The James brothers and the success of their vicious crimes had become a financial disaster for Missouri, particularly after Eastern newspapers began referring to it as the "Robber State." For fifteen years, Missouri's land had depreciated, and thousands of train, stagecoach, and other travelers going east or west passed around the state to avoid being robbed, costing it millions of dollars. Yet it was still considered political, if not actual, suicide to criticize the outlaws in their home counties, and no Missouri politician had ever denounced them by name in the Crackerneck and other country districts where their families, friends, and supporters still lived.

During the summer and fall of 1880, before Bill Ryan's arrest, tall, slender, thirty-one-year-old William H. Wallace conducted his campaign for Jackson County prosecuting attorney on horseback, usually speaking at night in the rural districts of the county, where many of the inhabitants were supportive of, if not related to, the outlaws. Wallace's dark brown eyes flashed as he boldly denounced the outlaws in the midst of some of their friends and supporters, and called them out by name, including Frank and Jesse James. This caused astonishment and threats. He promised the people that if elected, he would prosecute the gang to the full extent of the law. The Democratic Party saw this as an attack on former Confederates and refused him the nomination. He ran as an independent and, despite death threats, won.[5]

Wallace hailed from Clark County, Kentucky. His father, Rev. Joseph William Wallace, was a Presbyterian minister. Wallace's great-grandfather, John Wallace, was a captain during the Revolutionary War and had been with George Washington at Valley Forge in 1778. When Wallace was eight, he and his family moved to Missouri, traveling by steamboat and landing at Wayne City, just north of Independence.[6]

The family settled on a farm in Jackson County on the open prairie southeast of Independence between what is now Lee's Summit and Blue Springs. The settlers found wild geese, prairie chickens, and partridges in great numbers, and the nearby woods held pheasant, wild turkeys, and deer. Wallace had four brothers, all of whom worked on the family farm, plowing, planting, and harvesting. Wallace's family owned five male slaves, who worked alongside the five Wallace boys. Wallace's father owned about twenty horses, most of them brought from Kentucky. By 1860, eleven-year-old William was a skilled farmhand with the plow, behind Wiley and Rock, the family oxen.

In 1861, with the start of the Civil War, twelve-year-old William became an errand boy for the surrounding farmers. Given the fact that the state was violently divided, the men hesitated to go to the towns for fear of arrest, or worse. Wallace thought himself to be too young to be harmed, so he went with the women on "war calls" for supplies, information, or to locate missing property and slaves. As an errand boy, Wallace was frequently in the camps of both sides. He sometimes helped feed the horses of the federals at his father's farm in the morning, then helped feed the horses of the guerrillas in the afternoon.[7]

Over the course of the war, Kansas jayhawkers and Missouri bushwhackers depleted the Wallace farm's livestock, crops, and even fence rails. One day a band of soldiers under a Captain Pardee, belonging to the Kansas Regiment of Colonel Charles Jennison, rode up to the Wallace farm. They looted the home of everything of value, including the family's horses. One of the soldiers cocked his pistol and gave William's father three minutes to retrieve a gold watch he had been told his wife had in bed with her, as she was sick. William watched in fear and amazement as his father said, "You can shoot on. The watch is my wife's, and I will never ask her to give it up." The soldier stormed off without shooting the old man. Reverend Wallace had defeated an armed enemy by the strength of his conviction. This was a lesson young William would not forget.[8]

In August 1863, Union general Thomas Ewing Jr. issued the infamous General Order No. 11, requiring everyone in Jackson County and other adjacent counties to move within one mile of the Union provost marshal's post or leave in fifteen days. On the night of the last day, Wallace heard dogs left behind begin to howl from miles around. Kansans then began to torch Jackson County farmhouses, which could be seen blazing away at distances of twenty-five miles. One night Wallace counted twenty-two homes on fire. Soot rained down from the sky. The prairies and surrounding countryside also caught fire from the burning homes.[9]

The Wallaces loaded their few remaining possessions and drove their wagon to Lexington, where they crossed the Missouri River. They rode to Fulton, Missouri, where Wallace's father was given a professorship at Westminster College. Wallace had only a pair of linen trousers and a cotton shirt for clothes for that winter and their food was as scant as their clothing.[10]

William Wallace earned a college degree at Westminster. After the war, his father returned to what remained of the family farm. William and his father taught school in an old stable to support the family as they hauled wood, built fences, replanted, plowed, and rebuilt the farm. William worked for a short time as a reporter for the *Kansas City Times*, then began to study law at Fulton. He then moved to Independence, where he first apprenticed and then practiced law for the next five years.[11]

Wallace proved to be a powerful orator with a keen intellect. He earned his first public reputation when attorney James H. Slover allowed him to make the closing argument to the jury in a murder case. Slover and Wallace represented a man who was charged with killing a man whom the defendant had found in a compromising situation with his wife. Wallace argued that the "unwritten law" allowed the jurors to acquit his client for killing a man who had "ruined" his marriage. The jury found Wallace's client not guilty.[12]

Another of Wallace's cases would have implications later in his prosecutions of the James Gang. Wallace was hired to represent Mattie Collins, who was accused of murdering her brother-in-law, Jonathon Dark, on February 2, 1879. Dark had apparently objected to Mattie's being visited by a young man. Accounts vary as to whether her suitor was soon-to-be James Gang member Dick Liddil, or another man. According to Mattie, Dark had a revolver in his pocket and threatened her with it before she drew her own pistol and shot him dead. Before the killing, however, Mattie was said to have vowed, "I'll see his heart's blood before dawn."

Wallace claimed at Collins's September 1879 trial that she was temporarily insane at the time of the murder. The prosecutor's witnesses, including Mattie's mother, testified that Mattie was not insane but merely had a terrible temper. The jury took fifteen minutes to return a verdict of not guilty by reason of insanity. Collins lived with Liddil after her acquittal and later claimed that they were married.[13]

In 1880, Wallace moved from Independence to Kansas City. He had been raised in the same part of the state as the James-Younger Gang members and in the immediate neighborhood with several of them. He had studied them and knew more about their friends and their relatives than he did about his own. About twenty-two men had belonged to the gang over its fifteen-year existence. When one was killed or imprisoned, a new recruit was added.[14]

This was an area where groups of men banded together for the purpose of plunder, riding through the streets, swaggering in hotels and barrooms, and even courthouses, with three to six revolvers belted on them, taunting the officers of the law, firing their pistols into houses, and robbing men on the highway. Many Missouri citizens were terrified of the outlaws, and it was rumored to mean death to report their activities to the authorities. A Jackson County judge told Wallace a story about a bank robbery committed in the county. A man who knew the robbers was called to testify before the grand jury. He gave it the facts and names of the robbers. As he was being excused he said, "Gentlemen, I have told the truth. I will never swear a lie," and drawing a pistol, he added, "The notches on this pistol give the number of men I have killed. My life is now in danger and . . . if anybody is indicted, each man on this grand jury can dig his grave." No one was indicted.[15]

Even after the botched Northfield raid, Wallace's clients told him the Northern press was "lying on the boys again." They were astonished when Wallace pointed out that the photographs of the captured and dead robbers in the newspapers were members of the gang. Wallace harbored no personal animosity toward the outlaws. In fact, some of his closest friends were among their relatives and defenders.[16]

Wallace used facts and evidence to gradually change the minds of many who believed the myth peddled by Edwards and others that the accusations against "the boys" were false. But Wallace also defended Missouri's ex-Confederates against charges that they supported crime in the state. His actions took courage and earned him grudging respect from many Jackson County residents who had earlier sympathized with the James brothers. His election showed that the residents of Jackson County generally sympathized with his stand against crime, even though some of the same citizens had supported the Confederates during the Civil War, as had Wallace.

To convict Bill Ryan, Wallace needed an eyewitness to testify about the October 8, 1879, train robbery in Glendale, which was the indictment pending against Ryan in Jackson County. Wallace traveled to the state penitentiary to talk to Tucker Bassham, who had been captured the year before, in July 1880, and imprisoned after pleading guilty to the robbery. Wallace convinced Bassham, who had been a newcomer to the gang, to testify against Ryan in exchange for a pardon. Wallace then went to Governor Crittenden and persuaded him to grant Bassham the pardon.

With Ryan in jail, Wallace now confronted what everyone said was an impossible task: convicting a member of the James Gang in Missouri. The prevailing belief was that no jury would have the courage to convict, even if convinced of Ryan's guilt. With Bassham's testimony in his pocket, Wallace prepared to put Ryan on trial for the Glendale train robbery.[17]

Wallace forced the Ryan case to trial in Independence during the last week of September 1881, five months after Ryan's arrest. The trial caused intense excitement and discussion. Newspapers called it "the most thrilling contest ever had in any court in Missouri or in the West." Many of Wallace's friends encouraged him to dismiss the case and let Ryan go free. They argued it was not worth his life to prosecute the case, which would only result in an acquittal anyway, as no Jackson County jury would dare convict a member of the James Gang. Wallace, demonstrating the conviction and determination of his father, said he would rather be shot than dismiss the charges. Governor Crittenden attended Ryan's trial—guarded by eight marshals.[18]

Unlike the prosecutor in the Clell Miller trial, Wallace had spent months thoroughly preparing the state's case, as he correctly anticipated a well-funded and fierce defense. First, he visited the Crackerneck neighborhood near Independence, interviewing witnesses and obtaining information. Then he traveled to Nashville and interviewed Earthman and other possible Tennessee witnesses. Wallace requested that the railroad officials allow the men in charge of the train who had witnessed the robbery to come to Independence to testify at the trial. The officials refused, much to Wallace's astonishment and dismay. They said it was hopeless, that no jury would convict one of the James Gang in Missouri, and that the gang would target their trains in retaliation and kill their conductors and engineers.

As expected, Ryan had hired an impressive team of four lawyers to represent him, including R. L. Yeager, the former prosecuting attorney of Jackson County. In fact, Yeager had been the prosecutor on Bassham's case when he was arrested just a year earlier. Yeager had also presented witnesses and evidence on behalf of the state at Bassham's preliminary hearing, so he knew the state's case and the witnesses. Rounding out the defense team were Blake L. Woodson, an experienced criminal lawyer; B. J. Franklin, a former congressman; and former Independence mayor James Slover. Friends of the outlaws packed the courtroom; many of them slept in the courthouse yard in order to secure a seat when the courthouse opened. Most were rumored to be armed.[19]

Officials suspected that Jesse James was hiding a short distance from Independence. Primitive fireworks were shot into the sky from the countryside surrounding Independence at night; it was said that was done to let the defendants—and the jury—know that Ryan's friends were watching the trial and supporting him. The judge kept a firm rein on the proceedings. Sensational newspaper accounts proclaimed that the trial would be a test case between the banner of the law and the black flag of the bandit.[20]

The *Independence Sentinel* warned that there is "a desperate organization in the county banded to prevent the arrest, trial, and conviction of the train robbers or, failing this, to rescue them from the officers in case of conviction." Wallace received a letter during the trial warning him that unless he dropped the case he would be killed. The letter was signed "League of 12." Witnesses had reported that twelve gunmen had been involved in the September 7, 1881, train robbery at Blue Cut near Glendale, Missouri, which had taken place just two weeks before the trial began. A detective had also heard Ryan talking about the letter in jail before it was delivered to Wallace, so Wallace suspected that the letter may have indeed come from Jesse James and his gang.[21]

Dick Liddil told Wallace after the trial that Jesse James had organized a rescue. The plan was to shoot the prosecutor and other officials in the courtroom and, during the confusion, lead Ryan to a waiting horse. Liddil said that James had abandoned the escape attempt when he found out that Maurice Langhorne—an ex-Confederate captain said to be one of the toughest and deadliest men in General Joseph Shelby's Civil War cavalry brigade—was assigned to guard Ryan. Langhorne was a formidable foe, and his presence, along with twenty other lawmen, made a rescue attempt too risky.

On September 22, 1881, the jury was selected for Bill Ryan's trial, and Wallace made his opening statement, laying out in detail the facts the state expected to prove. For the first time, the state identified all of the alleged participants in the crime: Jesse James, Dick Liddil, Ed Miller, Bill Ryan, and Tucker Bassham. James Slover made the opening statement for Bill Ryan. He told the jury that Ryan was a farmer who had worked in his fields the day of the robbery, that he went to bed early that evening, and that he had nothing to do with the robbery. Ryan had an excellent reputation in the community, whereas the state's chief witness, Bassham, was a convicted thief who had lied about Ryan in order to free himself from prison. In other words, the defense planned to use tactics similar to those that had been successful in Clell Miller's trial: demonize the state's chief witness and beatify the defendant.

At nine the next morning, Wallace began calling witnesses. He decided to open his case with the dramatic testimony of the neutral and credible Tennessee witnesses, who told the jury about Ryan's drunken and belligerent behavior, his attempt to draw his pistols when confronted, the gold coins found in his pockets, and his use of the alias "Tom Hill."[22]

Wallace then called Missouri witnesses to testify as to the robbery and Ryan's presence in the area. An ex-Confederate and a young farmer testified that on the night of the robbery, several horsemen rode by their houses coming from the direction of Glendale and that they recognized Ryan's voice, having known him since they were boys. The train's express messenger, William R. Grimes, testified that a large man—Liddil said later it was Jesse James—struck him over the head with a revolver, which knocked him out, and that when he awoke, $9,400 had been taken from his safe.

Wallace's key witness was Tucker Bassham, a new recruit added to the gang for that one robbery who had already pleaded guilty and been sentenced to the penitentiary. Bassham had to be guarded around the clock in order to protect him from assassination. Someone burned down Bassham's home, an old log cabin in the Crackerneck region, during his testimony. Bassham's wife and children were forced to flee for their lives. She told Wallace that Jesse James had sat at her dinner table before the train robbery and threatened that he would kill a woman who informed on him just as quickly as he would a man.[23]

Just before Bassham was sworn as a witness, Wallace cleverly handed him the governor's pardon in the presence of the jury, telling them that it had been issued upon the express promise of Bassham to become a witness and tell the whole truth, and that, as was usual in such cases, he was to go free. Wallace's strategy drew the sting out of what he knew would be a scathing cross-examination by the defense. Bassham testified that Jesse James and Ed Miller were the leaders of the gang, which included Dick Liddil, Bill Ryan, and a man called "Bob." Bassham provided details that tied Ryan to the robbery. He testified that Ryan had first approached Bassham in his field, demanding, "What are you plowing for?" Bassham replied that he was supporting his family. "Dammit, why do you do that? Let's go knock off a train on the Pacific track," Ryan urged. It was obvious that politics was not a motivation for the robbery. Ryan and Ed Miller visited Bassham again two days before the robbery. They said that Jesse James was in the county and that they were going to rob the train at Glendale.[24]

On October 8, the men met at a schoolhouse at sundown. Bassham did not own a gun, so Jesse James gave him a shotgun that belonged to a man named Kit Rose. The men rode to the woods near the little Glendale depot just south of Independence, dismounted, tied up their horses, and walked to the depot. Once there, Jesse James, Ed Miller, and Bob pulled their revolvers on the telegraph operator and took control of the depot. Liddil, Miller, and Bassham had handkerchiefs tied over their faces with mouth and eye holes cut in them. Ryan had a winter cap pulled down over his face. James wore no disguise. He told Ryan and Bassham, whom he called "Arkansas," to take over a small store about seventy-five feet from the depot.

James smashed the telegraph and ordered the operator at gunpoint to bring out a red light to signal the train to stop. The operator said he had no red light. Furious, James told him to put out a green light—a signal for the train to stop for passengers. "But the train will stop if I do that," protested the operator. James cocked one of his revolvers and put it into the operator's mouth. "That is what we want," he snarled. The operator did as he was ordered. Bassham heard a lady crying and shrieking, "Don't kill my son." James and Miller also rolled a boulder onto the track, just to make sure the train stopped.

When it did, James and Miller entered the express car. They demanded the keys to the safe. The express messenger, Grimes, was a little slow to respond, so they beat him over the head with their revolvers until he was unconscious. They stuffed the contents of the safe into a grain bag. Ryan and Bassham guarded the engineer, and Bob guarded the rest of the train. There was a great deal of shooting. Ryan shot at someone who was carrying a lantern toward the train.[25]

After the robbery, the men leaped onto their horses and rode south down the Harrisonville road through the heart of the Crackerneck region to an abandoned farmhouse to divide the loot, which totaled about $6,000. Bassham's share was about $900. The men then separated. James told Bassham to go home and go to work the next day as usual and "no one will suspicion you." He also told Bassham to be careful about spending too much money, to never carry more than fifteen dollars with him at any one time, and to return the shotgun to Kit Rose. Bassham said that when he tried to give the shotgun back, Rose told him to get rid of it because it had been used in the robbery. Bassham threw the weapon into the Little Blue River. Having established all the facts necessary for a conviction, Wallace announced that the prosecution's evidence had concluded. Wallace's case had been quick, efficient, and thorough.

As in the Clell Miller trial, the defense called several witnesses to establish Ryan's alibi and good character. While most testified that Ryan had an excellent reputation for character, they were not able to withstand Wallace's well-prepared and fierce cross-examination. An experienced prosecutor is able to predict the defense's likely approach, counter it, and close the case with effective rebuttal witnesses. The Ryan trial showed Wallace was up to the challenge. He seemed to have anticipated the defense approach, and he was even able to force the witnesses to admit under his relentless questioning that Ryan had been arrested several times for carrying concealed weapons, public drunkenness, and even disturbing public worship.[26]

Ryan's sister, Mollie Ryan, then testified that her brother was gathering corn with Jack Williams on the day of the robbery and that he did not leave the house that night. Jack Williams testified next, but he appeared confused about dates and events. During Wallace's cross-examination, Williams contradicted himself several times, became flustered, and finally exclaimed, "I'm not a walking almanac!" The defense then called two other men to contradict Bassham's testimony and attack his reputation for truth and honesty, but Wallace's cross-examination again undermined their credibility. The defense then ended its case.

Wallace called three witnesses in a well-planned rebuttal to corroborate Bassham's testimony. One witness testified to meeting five armed men late on the night of the robbery going west on the Harrisonville Road, at exactly the point where Bassham had said he left the rest of the gang after dividing the loot. Another testified that he found the shotgun that Bassham said he threw into the Little Blue River after the robbery, and the weapon was introduced into evidence and shown to the jury. Finally, Wallace called Mattie Collins to the stand. The mere fact that a woman was testifying in a criminal trial was noteworthy enough, but she was also notorious as a result of her earlier murder trial. She would not admit to being gang member Dick Liddil's wife, but she acknowledged that she had brought substantial sums of money to "farmer" Ryan while he had been in jail to defray "his expenses." The implication was that the money was to buy Ryan's silence to keep him from making a deal with the prosecution in which he would testify against Jesse James and help authorities kill or capture him in exchange for a reduced sentence and/or support to his family in the case of a conviction. James no doubt knew that with a man like Ryan, loyalty was based largely on money.[27]

The situation became tense as the trial neared its finish. Governor Crittenden ordered two crates of rifles shipped to the city to provide additional firepower to the police and eight marshals who attended the trial. He told reporters that "it will be very dangerous indeed for the desperadoes to undertake the liberation of their friend." Thirty years after the trial, Wallace admitted, "With a family to care for, I would not do now what I did then."[28]

Wallace's closing argument to the jury on September 27 was a masterpiece. He knew that he had to inspire the jury to have the courage to convict, because he was afraid that some of the members, knowing the danger of such a vote, might falter. There is no reference to any alleged political motivation for the crime:

> We are now engaged in the hottest and most important trial in the history of this glorious Commonwealth. It is a test case. For fifteen years this band of men . . . has so terrorized Western Missouri that no citizen has dared give information or institute proceedings against them for fear of losing his life. Meantime they have startled the world with their deeds of daring—their bank robberies, their train robberies, their murders, their assassinations. At last one of their numbers is compelled to face a Missouri jury. . . . You are soon to say which you prefer, the mask of the bandit or the torch of civilization. . . . I defy Jesse James and the defendant himself, . . . I defy all who uphold them in their nefarious calling of death and plunder, and in the pernicious work of bringing shame and disgrace upon the fair name of our State. . . . May God fill your hearts with courage and lead you to a righteous verdict.[29]

The jury was out but fifteen minutes before coming back with a guilty verdict. Ryan, who had stood for the jury's verdict, turned pale and had to support himself with a chair to keep from falling. He was sentenced to the state penitentiary for twenty-five years. Newspapers said the conviction broke the backbone of the James Gang. A jury had done what it was supposed that no Missouri jury would ever dare do. Courage sprang up, and mouths began to be opened.

Squads of men began to scour the country in search of the James brothers. Jesse became suspicious of his own men.

Shortly after Ryan was convicted and sent to prison, a former deputy sheriff in Jackson County came to Wallace and asked for a list of men in the county who harbored and supported the Jameses. Wallace asked why he wanted such a list. The man refused to answer but said that those who sent him believed that Wallace was the only man who could provide such a list. Wallace suspected the list would be used for illegal retribution and so refused to provide it.

A few days later, a railroad official traveled from St. Louis to see Wallace. He also asked Wallace if he could provide a list of supporters of Frank and Jesse James. Wallace again asked the purpose of such a list. The official explained that the railroads had decided to put an end to train robbery in Missouri by making it impossible in the future for the Jameses to find anyone who would be willing to harbor them. He then admitted that the plan was to prepare a train of box cars in St. Louis containing nothing but men, guns, and horses. The train was to stop at Little Blue in Jackson County on the Missouri Pacific Railroad line just after dark, where the men would unload the horses, mount them, and ride in squads to kill every man whose name appeared on the list. Wallace told the official that he would have no part in such a plan and refused to cooperate. The railroad companies' plan to unleash death squads into the night was abandoned. Events would soon prove the wisdom of Wallace's decision.[30]

NINE

THE DEATH OF JESSE JAMES

WHEN ATTORNEY AND FORMER Union officer Thomas T. Crittenden became Missouri's governor in January 1881, he devoted much of his inaugural address to a declaration of war on Missouri's bands of outlaws, the most notorious of which were Frank and Jesse James. He argued that the end justified the means: "When your house is burning you stand not upon the method of extinction." His public opposition to the bandits required courage, since a large number of Missouri Democrats were more sympathetic to the outlaws than the law. State law would not permit him to offer more than three hundred dollars each for the capture of the outlaws. He realized that this paltry amount would not be enough to motivate informers to risk their lives to come forward.[1]

On July 27, 1881, Crittenden called a meeting of the lead lawyers for the railroads that had been victimized by the gang's armed robberies. Marcus A. Low, Henry McDougal's law partner, attended on behalf of the Rock Island Railroad, which had been hit twice by the James

Gang, and Low authorized a cash contribution from the railroad for Frank and Jesse's capture. In addition to Low's representation of the Rock Island Railroad, another of McDougal's clients, the Wabash Railroad, was also represented by counsel at the meeting. After the meeting, Low drafted a proclamation for a $10,000 reward for each of the James brothers, which was signed by the governor and published in newspapers across the state. Low may have been motivated to offer the reward as much to protect the life of his friend and law partner McDougal as to protect his client's property and profits.[2]

The last train robbery attributed to the James Gang occurred a little over a month after the reward offer was publicized, on September 7, 1881, just two weeks before the Bill Ryan trial. The robbery took place at a sharp curve and steep grade of the track that forced trains to sharply reduce their speed, called Blue Cut, only three miles from the Independence courthouse where Ryan was tried. The train crew consisted of conductor J. M. Hazenbaker, engineer L. "Choppy" Foote, brakeman Frank Burton, and a fireman, who were in charge of four coaches, a smoking car, a baggage car, and a sleeper car. Foote provided a detailed account of how the train was stopped and the terror and injuries inflicted upon the train's passengers by the robbers:

> We were turning a short, sharp curve, when I was flagged with a red light. I put on the brakes, and brought her to a stand. By the headlight I could see two men on the tracks, standing near a pile of stones between the rails, and the red light was on top of it. Seeing one of the men was masked, I knew we were going to be robbed. I hardly had time to say it to my fireman before we were covered by the pistols of the two men, and were invited to get down. God d—n you, and the threatening flourish of the revolvers, made me do as they asked. Getting off the engine I found myself in the company of six masked men and one unmasked man. There were others of them up

on the bank of the cut. They showed every disposition to murder me but I reasoned with them, and then altogether we went to the express car, and I was told to knock in the doors. I gave it one or two whacks, and it was opened.[3]

H. A. Fox, the U.S. Express Co. messenger, who was in the baggage car when the train came to a halt, picked up the story:

My first knowledge that anything was wrong was when the baggage master said, 'Hallo, this is a funny place to stop.' He got up and looked out of the window, and as he did so someone began pounding on the door with a heavy piece of iron, or with an axe, and it was either broken down or flew open as the robbers entered, some four or five in number. I retreated to the other end of the car, but two of the robbers followed me with pistols in both hands and demanded the keys of the safe. They threatened to kill me and I gave it to them, and one . . . quickly opened the safe and took what was in it. . . . One big, burly fellow came up to me, and with a revolver hit me a terrible blow on the head, knocking me down, and two or three of them tried to strike me with their revolvers at the same time. I don't quite remember what took place then, as they hit me hard, and I was bleeding a good deal.[4]

During the attack on the baggage car, conductor Hazenbaker realized that a freight car was bearing down on them and that a fatal crash was inevitable unless he acted quickly:

I saw the train surrounded by a number of masked men heavily armed, and at once started back, passing through all the cars, warning the passengers to hide their valuables, as a gang of robbers were aboard. . . . I passed to the rear platform when a man with two revolvers leveled at me commanded a halt.

> I told him an approaching freight train would smash into us directly, and I was going back to flag it unless someone killed me before I got there. I took a lantern and one brakeman [Burton] and stepping off started back around the curve to signal the freight train.[5]

Hazenbaker's assistant jumped off and ran with his lantern down the track. The robbers began shooting at him. "The bullets whistled all around me and struck the rails and stones," Hazenbaker said. "'For God's sake, don't shoot the boy, he is saving the lives of these people,'" he told the robbers. "Then one of them threw up his arms and cried 'Stop shooting.' I waved my lantern. The train stopped only a car length off."

Passenger John J. Price gave a graphic description of the scene in the Pullman car:

> My first warning was when the conductor came running in and said, "Gentlemen and ladies, robbers are on the train, hide your valuables." At once everyone took off their watches, rings, diamond earrings and hid them as best they could. . . . Just then a short man with a mask on rushed into the car with a pistol in each hand and said: "Everyone hold up your hands; we are robbers." He was quickly followed by four more men, all of whom had shotguns or revolvers. One of the robbers had a grain sack and into this the men threw watches, pocketbooks and whatever else they got. In some cases they took off rings from ladies hands, laughing as they did so."

The women were all screaming, and one man knelt down in the car and prayed.[6]

The public was outraged. Newspapers in other states mocked Missouri law enforcement, claiming that only Missouri would have tolerated the robbers for twelve years (it had actually been fifteen). At nine the next morning, Governor Crittenden telegraphed the sheriffs of Jackson,

Clay, and six other counties to send armed men in pursuit. By this time Sheriff Henry Timberlake of Clay County had already organized a posse to try to track down the robbers. The governor traveled to Kansas City to take charge and to meet with the man-hunters.[7]

The squads of men scouring the countryside for the James brothers soon arrested three young men. John Bugler and brothers Matt and Creed Chapman lived within two miles of the scene of the robbery and were well armed, with Bugler packing two revolvers. The sheriff's deputies also found in their possession some material used in patching rifle bullets that matched material found at the scene of the robbery. Other evidence against them was a spur, found where the train was stopped, belonging to Bugler.[8]

Two days later, on the Saturday following the robbery, John Land and Andy Ryan were arrested. Land was said to be a "bad character" and in his possession the authorities found a rifle loaded with a cartridge matching an unexploded cartridge picked up at the scene of the robbery. Andy Ryan was a brother of Bill Ryan's, convicted for the earlier Glendale train robbery. The men had also been seen peering into an express car as the train stopped at Glendale, a short distance from Blue Cut, a few nights before the train was robbed. The men were incarcerated in the Jackson County jail in Kansas City.

In March 1882, about seven months after the train robbery (and six months after the Bill Ryan trial), William Wallace was assigned as the prosecutor on Bugler's and Land's cases. He placed a detective named Gorham under cover in the Kansas City jail cell with John Land, hoping to obtain a confession and/or information on the James brothers. Unknown to Wallace, Gorham took the newspapers giving the train passengers' accounts of the robbery into the cell and shared them with Land. Land agreed to be a witness for the state in exchange for full immunity.

Land told the undercover detective that he was not approached until the morning of the robbery, when John Bugler and Creed Chapman met him while he was digging fence posts. At first he was hesitant about joining them, but after meeting them at Glendale with a man he thought to be Jesse James, he changed his mind. Land claimed that there were twelve members of the gang in the raid, five from the "old gang" and seven recruits from the neighborhood, presumably himself, Creed and Matt Chapman, John and Henry Bugler, George Matt, and one other, perhaps Andy Ryan. Land said that the members of the old gang had entered the cars and did the robbing while the new recruits guarded the train alongside the track.

On March 28, 1882, John Bugler's trial began in Independence. Sandwiched between the sensational Bill Ryan trial and the Frank James trial to come, it is perhaps understandable that this notable chapter in Missouri legal history has been overlooked by historians. But Wallace's prosecution of John Bugler for the Blue Cut train robbery is, in many ways, just as significant to Missouri's history as the Ryan and James trials. The courtroom was overflowing with spectators. Wallace first made a motion that created a sensation: he argued that the assembled group of potential jurors should be dismissed and a new one selected because twenty-two of the thirty-three men on the list came from Blue Township, a stronghold of support for the James Gang. One immediate effect of Wallace's motion was the disappearance from the case of Independence attorney James H. Slover, who had been the mayor of Independence in 1870 and who had apparently been responsible for assembling the potential jurors. Whispers of a "packed" jury quickly spread around the courtroom. The judge granted Wallace's motion and excused the potential jury members.

When the jury was seated on March 30, more sensations burst on Independence, the biggest being a rumor of the surrender and confession of gang member Dick Liddil. (Liddil had surrendered to Sheriff Timberlake on January 24, but his surrender and confession did not make it into the newspapers until after the Bugler trial had started.) In his confession, Liddil gave almost day-by-day details describing the train robbery for which Bugler was being tried and the others who were to be tried. Liddil's confession resulted in Wallace's issuing a subpoena for Jesse James to be a witness in Bugler's trial—more of a legal exercise than something that had a chance of happening. According to Liddil, the robbers divided various stolen pieces of jewelry about half a mile from the scene of the robbery. Liddil's arrest caused a dispute between Wallace and Kansas City police commissioner Henry Craig as to whether Bugler's trial should continue (Wallace's position) or charges against Bugler should be dismissed and efforts focused on catching Frank and Jesse James (Craig's position). The dispute over tactics ended with Craig being summoned to meet with Governor Crittenden, who tried to smooth over the disagreement. Craig received a $2,500 reward for the capture of Clarence Hite, on information supplied by Liddil, which may have improved Craig's disposition.[9]

Wallace had again thoroughly and methodically prepared his case. Unlike in the Ryan trial, Wallace's evidence against Bugler was more forensic and circumstantial in nature. One of Wallace's first witnesses was a gunsmith who testified that he sold .44 caliber Remington revolvers to John Bugler before the robbery. Witnesses also testified as to the rifle cartridges found in the possession of Land shortly after the robbery. In a cutting-edge nineteenth-century precursor to crime-scene forensics, Wallace introduced evidence in the form of a ballistics test on the shell casing showing that "the extension of the hammer exactly fitted the indenture in the butt of the shell."

Land then testified as to Bugler's participation in the robbery. Bugler's lawyer failed during cross-examination to make Land contradict himself, although Land admitted that the undercover detective had shown him newspaper stories describing the robbery while he was in jail. Land's testimony seemed to sway the jury and court observers as to Bugler's guilt.[10]

But Wallace, who did not know that the detective had shown the newspaper accounts to Land until hearing the cross-examination at trial, became suspicious of Land's testimony. On Saturday afternoon, April 1, 1882, Wallace asked the judge to postpone the trial during the state's case until Wallace could interview Liddil about the train robbery. The judge granted Wallace's request. Liddil gave Wallace a detailed account of the Blue Cut robbery, told Wallace that he didn't know the six young men charged with the robbery, that they had not been involved, and that Frank and Jesse James would have never taken such raw youngsters into a robbery with them. In an interview with a reporter for the *Kansas City Evening Star*, Liddil said, "John Land don't know one of the old party [gang] anymore than you do and he is just lying like hell about it." Wallace then traveled to Jefferson City to the state penitentiary to interview Clarence Hite, who also participated in the robbery and told Wallace a similar story.[11]

On April 3, sensational news swept through the state: Jesse James had been shot in St. Joseph, Missouri. He had moved from a house in Kansas City thirty miles north to St. Joseph the first week of November 1881, as law enforcement escalated its efforts to capture James in Jackson County after Bill Ryan's conviction.

On Sunday morning, December 5, 1881, a lethal gun battle occurred at Mattie Bolton's farm home, one mile east of Richmond, Missouri. Mattie was the sister of Robert and Charlie Ford, who had met James in summer 1879. Dick Liddil and Wood Hite, Jesse's cousin and Clarence Hite's brother, had arrived at the farmhouse the night before. Hite was handsome and fancied himself a ladies' man. It was said that Mattie loved both Liddil and Hite. The two men argued, which led to a shoot-out at the breakfast table. Robert Ford also happened to be staying there at the time. He heard the shooting, threw open the kitchen door, and fired at Hite. It was never established whose bullet killed Hite. Liddil took a bullet in the leg. Ford and Liddil knew their lives would be in danger as soon as James discovered they had killed his cousin, one of his closest companions.

On January 13, 1882, Robert Ford met secretly with Governor Crittenden and Sheriff Timberlake and offered to assist in capturing the James brothers. Crittenden offered $10,000 in return. Dick Liddil surrendered to Timberlake eleven days later, seeking a plea agreement in which he would testify against the Jameses in exchange for a pardon. Shortly after, Bob and Charlie Ford moved in with Jesse at his new home in St. Joseph, as he scouted banks for a possible robbery. Jesse, getting more and more suspicious, may have also wanted to keep a close eye on them.

Charlie Ford later testified that on Monday morning, April 3, Jesse had read an article in the paper stating that Dick Liddil had surrendered to authorities. The Ford brothers became nervous, worrying whether Jesse's plan to rob the Platte City, Missouri, bank was true or was an excuse for him to get Charlie and Bob out of the house in order to kill them, as he had apparently done to Ed Miller the year before. After breakfast, Jesse complained of being warm and pulled off his coat and threw it onto the bed. He then "opened the door [to the house] and said that he would pull off his [gun] belt as someone might see it." As Jesse turned his back on the brothers, Robert Ford shot him in the back of the head. He was dead at thirty-four. For almost half of his life—all of his adult life—totaling sixteen years, he was an outlaw, robbing and murdering across at least ten states. If he had not been shot, he probably would have added to his number of robberies, and perhaps murders.[12]

Ten days after Jesse James's death, John Edwards published an editorial more bizarre than anything else he had written about the outlaw, epitomizing him as the "noble robber":

THE MURDER OF JESSE JAMES. Let not Caesar's servile minions; Mock the lion thus laid low; Was no foeman's hand that slew him; Twas his own that struck the blow. Not one among all the hired cowards, hard on the hunt for blood-money, dared face this wonderful outlaw, one even against twenty, until he had disarmed himself and turned his back to his assassins, the first and only time in a career which has passed from the realms of an almost fabulous romance into that of history. . . . Tear the two bears from the flag of Missouri. Put thereon in place of them as more appropriate a thief blowing out the brains of an unarmed victim, and a brazen harlot, naked to the waist, and splashed to the brows in blood.[13]

On Tuesday, April 4, the day after Jesse James was killed, William Wallace traveled to St. Joseph with Mattie Collins so she could identify the body. Upon seeing the body, Collins became distraught and started raging against the Fords. While he was in St. Joseph, Wallace interviewed Charlie Ford, who had been jailed with Bob for James's murder and who had also participated in the Blue Cut robbery. Ford also allegedly told Wallace that Bugler and the other young men arrested had not been involved in the robbery. Wallace now had three men, each not knowing that Wallace had talked with the others, telling the same story as to the identity of the participants in the robbery. All three said Bugler and the other young men in custody were innocent.

Every attorney Wallace consulted told him to leave it to the jury to decide Bugler's guilt or innocence. After consulting with Governor Crittenden on Wednesday, April 5, 1882, however, Wallace went back into court and shocked the judge, the jury, and the spectators by asking the court to dismiss the case against Bugler, stating only that he had positive knowledge that Bugler was not guilty of the train robbery. The judge granted Wallace's request, but he delivered a lecture to Bugler about the evil of carrying concealed weapons and emulating outlaws. One of the jurors told Wallace afterward that Bugler was "beyond all question guilty" and that Wallace had made the mistake of his life. In fact, after Bugler was discharged, the jury took an informal vote and came up with a verdict of guilty. The press raised a firestorm over the dismissal of the case, which became the subject of heated conversation across the state and nation.[14]

Wallace was criticized mercilessly for the dismissal, but he steadfastly maintained that he was convinced Bugler was innocent and that he could do nothing else as a sworn officer of the court but ask that the case be dismissed. Wallace explained that sending an innocent man to jail would have haunted him the rest of his life.

A reporter then interviewed Land, who allegedly confirmed that his story was false and that neither he nor the other young men charged with a crime were involved in the robbery. Land said that he'd gotten into a fight with Matt Chapman (another of the young men falsely accused and charged), who told Land that he was going to "swear me into the penitentiary for the Blue Cut train robbery." About the same time, Land received a message from John Bugler leading Land to believe that Bugler was also going to falsely accuse him of involvement in the train robbery. Land said "this made me mad and, as I was sure we would all be sent up anyway, I saw Tucker Bassham get out of the Glendale robbery by squealing on Bill Ryan and I was determined to make a confession." Land told the reporter that he was able to testify as to so many of the actual details of the robbery because he had read the newspapers and incorporated all of those details into his confession, which he "studied every day so that I knew it all by heart and when my time came to testify I knew it all as well as I knew my name."[15]

Wallace maintained that Bugler and the other men charged with the robbery were innocent, yet he could have easily convicted them. The newspaper articles on which Wallace based his justification for seeking dismissal of the charges primarily contained the accounts of the train's employees and passengers as to what occurred inside the train. Land had consistently maintained that he and the other new recruits were stationed outside the train along the tracks. It is difficult to understand how newspaper reports as to what transpired inside the train could have shaped Land's testimony as to what occurred outside the train.

Moreover, most of the witnesses who were interviewed for the newspapers said there were at least six men outside the train along the tracks, which was consistent with Land's testimony, at least before he recanted. Finally, would a band of experienced robbers, including Jesse James, huddle together inside the train during the robbery without stationing anyone outside to warn of the arrival of law enforcement? Who were the men whom engineer Foote said he saw along the tracks and whom brakeman Burton said shot at him from along the tracks? At least one other possible explanation exists for Wallace's dismissal of the charges against Bugler and the other alleged new recruits to the gang.

Wallace, an experienced and capable prosecutor, would not have gone to trial if he did not believe he had sufficient evidence for a conviction. Indeed, the physical evidence against Bugler and Land was fairly strong: when Bugler was captured he had two revolvers and material used in patching rifle bullets that matched material found at the scene of the robbery, and he was missing a spur that was also found at the scene of the robbery. When Land was captured he had a rifle, the cartridges to which corresponded to an empty shell found at Blue Cut. Moreover, Wallace was an astute judge of witnesses such as Land, having just masterfully dealt with gang member Tucker Bassham's testimony about the Glendale robbery during Bill Ryan's trial.

Dick Liddil had surrendered on January 24, but his surrender was kept quiet to prevent arousing Jesse and Frank James's suspicions. On February 11, Liddil led Sheriff Timberlake and Police Commissioner Craig to the Hite home, where they captured Jesse's cousin, Clarence Hite. Accordingly, both Liddil and Hite would have been available for interview by Wallace before beginning the Bugler trial in late March. Indeed, based on information provided by Liddil, Wallace issued a subpoena to Jesse James. If

Liddil or Hite had claimed that Bugler and the other new recruits had not been at Blue Cut, Wallace would not have issued a subpoena to Jesse James nor proceeded to trial against Bugler.

On Sunday, April 2, 1882, news of Liddil's surrender made its way to the front pages of the Kansas City newspapers. The next day, April 3, 1882, Robert Ford, afraid that Jesse James would become suspicious of him, shot and killed James. This leads to another reason why Walllace sought to dismiss the case against Bugler.

A controversy arose almost immediately over the rumored involvement by Governor Crittenden and other state officials in James's murder, because the Fords mentioned during the coroner's inquest that Crittenden had sanctioned the killing. Once Liddil had surrendered and the news became public, the governor and law enforcement did not want to expose Liddil to an interview by Bugler's lawyers, or to an examination by Bugler's lawyer at Bugler's trial. The authorities wanted to save Liddil's testimony for any trial of Frank James. Regardless of what Liddil would say about Bugler's participation in the Blue Cut robbery, the only way to prevent interviews of Liddil by Bugler's lawyer and/or Bugler's lawyer from calling Liddil as a witness at Bugler's trial was to dismiss the charges against Bugler. If Bugler's lawyer had called Liddil as a witness and Liddil testified that Bugler was not involved in the robbery, it also would have been damaging to Wallace's reputation and credibility.

Similarly, the governor and law enforcement did not want to expose Robert and Charlie Ford to cross-examination at the trial after James's murder on April 3. In addition to the concerns already mentioned, Crittenden did not want either of the Fords to be subject to questioning that might reveal that the governor had met with Robert Ford on January 13, 1882, in Kansas City at the St. John's Hotel, where Crittenden allegedly offered reward money and a pardon in exchange for Jesse James's murder. The public revelation of these facts could have easily led to criminal charges of conspiracy to commit murder being filed against Crittenden.[16]

Under these circumstances, Crittenden may have persuaded Wallace at their meeting the day before Wallace dropped the charges against Bugler to do so in order to protect Crittenden from charges and to preserve the testimony of Liddil for any trial against Frank James. Once the decision was made to dismiss the charges, Wallace needed a justification that would pass public muster. The recently revealed fact that newspaper articles describing the crime had been shown to Land in prison provided a basis for dismissal of the charges. Wallace's explanation, however, was based on statements from known criminals; he failed to refute the forensic evidence. The dismissal therefore remains controversial.[17]

At the time of the dismissal of the Bugler trial, Jesse James, Wood Hite, and Ed Miller had been killed by their comrades; Bill Ryan and Clarence Hite were in the penitentiary; and Dick Liddil had surrendered. At about the same time, the Ford brothers were indicted for Jesse's murder, pleaded guilty, and were sentenced to death by hanging on May 19, but Governor Crittenden sent a telegram granting them a full pardon. Only Frank James now remained at large, and he had a $10,000 reward hanging over his head.[18]

◆◇◆◇◆

A few months after Wallace dropped the charges against Bugler, two women came to his office. One of them was a tall, older lady dressed in black with her right sleeve pinned up. The face of the other woman was hidden by a veil. The older lady told Wallace they wished to see him on a private matter in his office. When the door was closed, the woman with the veil lifted it and asked Wallace if he remembered her. Wallace said that it had been a good many years since he had seen her but that he certainly did—the blond, blue-eyed woman was Annie Ralston of Jackson County, whom Wallace now understood was Frank James's wife. Wallace had known her years earlier when she was growing up in Independence. She introduced the other woman as Frank's mother.[19]

Annie James had come to propose to have Frank surrender to Wallace, but she was afraid her husband would be killed for the reward in the act of giving himself up. "Frank can't even cut a stick of wood without looking around to see if whether or not someone was slipping up behind him to kill him," she said. She trusted that Wallace would protect him, given his conduct at the Ryan and Bugler trials and based on her knowledge of him in their youth. "Mrs. James, if your husband surrenders to me, if he is harmed it will be over my dead body," Wallace assured her. She asked Wallace about the terms of the surrender. Wallace said he would have to consult the governor, since Wallace only had the authority to make agreements for crimes committed in Jackson County.[20]

Wallace immediately telegraphed Crittenden, who telegraphed back that he would let Wallace name the terms of James's surrender. The response stunned Wallace until he realized that the governor was washing his hands of the matter and would let Wallace take the criticism. Wallace sent a note to Annie James that the state could not agree that her husband could go absolutely free, but that if he would surrender, the state would be satisfied with a short prison term. Two days later, Wallace received Annie James's note rejecting the offer. John Newman Edwards then began to attempt to negotiate Frank James's surrender to the governor.[21]

Edwards succeeded, and James's arrest was unlike any other in American history. Edwards and James traveled to Jefferson City on October 4 and checked themselves into the McCarty House, a local hotel. Late that afternoon, they went to Crittenden's office in the Capitol, where the governor, numerous state officials, including Missouri Supreme Court justice John Ward Henry, and the press waited. Those gathered heard the sound of footsteps entering the rotunda of the building. A moment later, Edwards appeared in the open doorway. Behind him came the erect figure of Frank James.

The governor and the outlaw were now face-to-face. Edwards introduced James to Crittenden. James deftly unbuckled his gun belt and held out his holstered revolvers. He said quietly, "Governor, I want to hand over to you that which no man has been permitted to touch since 1861 and to say that I am your prisoner."[22]

Crittenden told Edwards that he was putting James in Edwards's charge for the night. James was then allowed to return to his hotel room, where he entertained guests, including the governor and his wife, until about 11 p.m. Early the next morning, Edwards, James, the governor's secretary, and Frank O'Neill, a reporter with the *St. Louis Missouri Republican*, left by train for Independence. Along the route, James pointed out to the reporters a number of the locations he visited while fighting in the Civil War. "I know every foot of that ground; many a time I watched from these hills and seen soldiers pass up and down," he said.

James's return to Independence was more like that of a hero than a felon. By now he was a celebrity in pulp fiction. News of the train was widespread, and hundreds of people lined its route. When the train arrived in Independence, James's wife, son, and father-in-law were there to meet him, along with several hundred others. James was allowed to check into the Merchant's Hotel, where he registered under his own name for the first time in sixteen years. An immediate bidding war broke out among souvenir hunters for the page.[23]

James's surrender was media catnip. A barrage of newspaper stories designed to distance him from the sordid crimes of the James Gang coincided with his arrest. At the time of the surrender, the press released a letter allegedly written by Frank James, and a reply by the governor. In his letter, James said his decision to surrender was the culmination of a "determination which has been forming for years, and which has already stood the test of four years of sober, industrious farm life." The press also reported his claim, made at his surrender, that he had not been in Missouri for four years and that he was now an industrious farmer. The articles included comments by Justice Henry that James had won his sympathy and that, if Henry were governor, he would pardon James. Frank O'Neill, the reporter given access to James, published a long article in which he described James's efforts to reform and in which he portrayed the robber as a refined gentleman.[24]

Wallace met James at Independence on October 6, and turned him over to the Jackson County marshal, who placed him in the Independence stone jail. A great crowd gathered to see him. He entertained visitors in his small cell, which was decorated with an expensive European carpet, and photographs and pictures on the walls. The iron-barred cell door remained unlocked, and a rocking chair was placed in the corridor outside. His wife brought him books and morning papers, and a restaurant delivered steak dinners. He received scores of visitors, including the governor. His story, and the media frenzy it generated, increased his popularity.

The question of bail came up. Edwards told Wallace that James had friends in Independence worth over a million dollars ready to provide assets to cover James's bail. But the indictment against James was for first-degree murder, which was not bailable without a court hearing. Wallace was asked to consent to bail but refused, saying he could not agree without a court hearing and order. Edwards took Wallace aside at the Merchant's Hotel and told him that if he would consent to James's bail, it would make him the most popular man in Missouri; it would assure Wallace of the governorship, and Edwards would do all he could to bring it about. Wallace replied, "Major, I would like to be governor, but I am on oath, and it comes too high." Wallace had never consented to bail and freedom for any other defendant charged with murder, and if he had done so for Frank James he would be sending a message to potential jurors that James was either not a public safety risk, was innocent, or both, which would have made obtaining a conviction against him nearly impossible.[25]

Edwards set out to use the newspapers to publicize James's defense themes: "Everybody has been forgiven and forgotten except Frank James. . . . [I]t is time to draw the veil of charity over the terrible past and deal honorably and fairly with Frank James." James, however, was charged not for his Civil War actions but for postwar robberies and murders. Nevertheless, the fact that he had surrendered to authorities was a public relations bonanza. Edwards wrote to James at the end of October:

> Your stay in the jail has been worth millions to you as far as public opinion is concerned. In fact, it was the best thing that could have happened. You can have no idea of the number of friends you have, nor how rapidly public sentiment is gravitating in your favor. You have borne yourself admirably, and every man who has seen you has become your friend. Do not refuse to see anybody, and talk pleasantly to all. There is a great deal in diplomacy. A soft answer turns away a heap of wrath.[26]

Edwards also began busying himself with lining up James's "dream team" of seven lawyers: former lieutenant governor Charles P. Johnson; John F. Philips of Kansas City, a former congressman who later would become a federal judge; and five others. All apparently served without charging a fee. The roster of lawyers was not only a testament to James's fame, it was a testament to his political power. Here was a robber-murderer who personally surrendered to the governor and was then represented, free of charge, by an ex-lieutenant governor and ex-congressman.[27]

Wallace now had to decide for which crime he would try Frank James. He first considered a murder indictment against him for the 1874 killing of Joseph Whicher, the Pinkerton detective from Chicago who had gone to the James farm undercover as a farmhand to arrange for the capture of the James brothers and whose bullet-ridden body was later found outside of Independence. Wallace was then a newspaper reporter who had covered the story and had seen the body close up. Liddil told Wallace, however, that Jesse James had told him that he had killed Whicher. Wallace interviewed the ferryman, John Brickman, who remembered that two men had carried a bound and gagged man across the river on his boat, telling him that they were lawmen and the prisoner was a horse thief they were taking to the Independence jail. He could not identify Frank James as one of them. Wallace had no proof on which he could prosecute Frank James for Whicher's murder, so he turned his attention to Gallatin, Missouri.[28]

THE ATTEMPTED ASSASSINATION OF MAJOR SAMUEL P. COX

FRANK JAMES HAD THREE CRIMINAL CHARGES pending against him in Gallatin, including the 1869 murder of John Sheets. Wallace likely consulted with the Daviess County prosecutor and Henry McDougal as to the possibility of bringing James to trial for Sheets's murder. Prosecutors are trained to prepare a case for trial by focusing on three issues: did the defendant have the motive, the opportunity, and the means to commit the crime with which he is charged? In life, motive is what causes a person to act. In law, motive is an inducement that leads to a criminal act. The presence of motive gives the prosecutor a reason to consider a suspect for a particular crime. In the Sheets murder case, Wallace and the prosecutors assumed that the murder was done for a reason. The prosecutors therefore had to determine the motive for Sheets's murder: did the two men ride to Gallatin intending to murder Sheets, rob the bank, or both?

A controversy exists even today as to the nature of the crime. Some writers accept that Sheets was murdered in the course of a bank robbery during which, irritated by Sheets's alleged slowness in handing over cash, the robber shot the cashier.[1] Others think the motive for shooting Sheets was the mistaken belief that he was Major Samuel P. Cox, the Union commander who had killed Confederate bushwhacker Bloody Bill Anderson toward the end of the Civil War.[2]

What do the facts set forth in the legal filings and circumstantial evidence suggest? The evidence strongly suggests that the murder was an assassination, rather than the tragic result of a failed bank robbery. The only witness to the crime, William McDowell, reported that the killer shot Sheets after accusing him of killing Bill Anderson. One of the murderers also told Reverend Helm, whom the two gunmen forced to guide them around Kidder during their getaway, that they had killed Major Cox in revenge for the death of a brother. This implicated Jim Anderson, who was Bill's brother, in Sheets's murder.

Cox had reported to the Gallatin sheriff that a few months before Sheets's murder, he had received a letter purportedly from Jim Anderson, who had refused to surrender at the end of the Civil War. Anderson was well known and had been identified as one of the participants in the robbery of a Liberty bank in 1866. Anderson's letter demanded that Cox return the two revolvers he had taken from Bloody Bill's body. The letter threatened that if Cox failed to hand over the pistols, Anderson would come and get them.[3]

Cox's and Helm's testimony, and the killer's reference to Bill Anderson as he shot Sheets, led to the belief in Gallatin after the murder that the two strangers had come to kill Cox. It was thought that the two gunmen had inquired of someone on the street about Cox, had him pointed out as Cox and Sheets were standing in front of the bank, and, mistaking which one of the two men was meant, had entered the bank and killed the wrong man. The mistake would have been easy for a stranger to make, since Cox and Sheets strongly resembled each other—both men were of the same height and build, and both had short, dark beards. The execution style of the murder—one shot through the heart and another through the brain—also suggests an assassination.[4]

The Daviess County court records also do not reflect that a charge of bank robbery—or even attempted bank robbery—was filed against the James brothers. Rather, Frank and Jesse James were indicted by the county grand jury in May 1870 for the murder of Sheets. Both were also charged with felony grand larceny for the theft of Daniel Smoote's horse. Why would criminal charges have been filed for the theft of the horse but not for the taking of cash from the bank—unless no cash was taken? Prosecutors are trained to file all charges available against criminal defendants in order to give themselves the widest possible latitude at trial for the admission of evidence and for plea-bargaining purposes. Bank robbery and/or attempted bank robbery were serious felony charges that no prosecutor would have failed to file against Frank and Jesse James if the facts supported them.[5]

The facts surrounding Sheets's murder also differed significantly from other bank robberies in which Frank and Jesse James were implicated. In their other robberies, the gang had carried a grain sack or saddlebags into the bank in which to carry the gold and silver coins and paper currency. No evidence exists that McDowell and the other witnesses reported any sign of a grain sack or saddlebag carried by the murderers, nor did the two gunmen apparently attempt to gain access to the bank vault in the Daviess County Savings Association, unlike in other bank robberies.

Other differences between Sheets's murder and the James brothers' suspected bank robberies include the number of men involved and the tactics used in the crimes.

Only two men were involved in Sheets's killing. The gang's practice for bank robberies was to use a minimum of four men. One or two men were always stationed outside the bank, one to watch the horses, which were critical for a successful getaway, and the other to prevent anyone from entering the bank during the holdup. At least two other men always entered the bank—one or two to pull pistols on the bank employees, and another to scoop money into the grain sack that the gang typically used. Anywhere between four and a dozen men were involved in each of the ten bank robberies attributed to the James-Younger Gang. The usual number of men involved was at least four.[6]

Moreover, the other bank robberies thought to have been committed by the members of the James-Younger Gang in Missouri—Liberty, Richmond, Ste. Genevieve, and Lexington—occurred in towns on the Missouri River (or the Mississippi River in the case of Ste. Genevieve) or within six or seven miles thereof. Gallatin, however, was over seventy miles from the Missouri River. Of course, most of the larger towns in Missouri at the time had banks and were located on or near the Missouri or Mississippi rivers. So the location of the target banks may have been more than coincidence; they may have been chosen because the James brothers and other gang members had gained extensive knowledge of the river bottoms as youths. Until 1869, no bridge existed across the Missouri River. The river provided the gang with cover and a natural barrier to any pursuing posse, whose members may not have known the crossing points on the river as well as the James brothers. The gang escaped after the Liberty and Richmond bank robberies by crossing the Missouri.

Thus, analyzing the bank robberies in which it is generally accepted that Frank and Jesse James were involved distinguishes those crimes from what occurred at Gallatin and is also revealing as to whether politics provided any motivation for the robberies.

◆◇◆◇◆

In the three years before Sheets's murder, there were four bank robberies in which Frank and Jesse James were suspected of participating. The first, and most successful, took place February 13, 1866, in Liberty, Missouri, just eight miles from the James farm and several miles from a bend of the Missouri River. At 2:00 p.m. that day, twelve or thirteen men, many clad in blue Union army overcoats, rode into Liberty. Three men took positions outside of town, acting as lookouts, while the remainder rode into town. Nine or ten of the men posted themselves at strategic locations in the town, guarding the entrance to the Clay County Savings Bank and the town square. Two of the men walked into the bank and warmed themselves at the stove before one of them walked to the counter and asked for change for a bill. As the cashier stepped to the counter, one of the men pulled a revolver and told him that if he made any noise he would shoot him. The other man pulled his pistol on the other bank employee, gave a similar order, and demanded all of the bank's money.[7]

The robbers forced the cashier to fill a wheat sack with cash and bearer bonds from the safe totaling nearly $60,000. The robbers shoved the employees into the bank's vault and slammed the heavy door shut, but they failed to notice the door was not locked. The cashier pushed the door open, rushed to the bank window, hoisted it, and began to shout "robbery!"

As the robbers mounted their horses outside the bank, one of them pulled his revolver and shot and killed a nineteen-year-old college student who was across the street from the bank. The outlaws then began firing into the air and yelling in an effort to clear the street. They galloped east toward the Missouri River. A posse quickly gathered and galloped off in pursuit. It followed the bandits near Centerville and then to a spot on the Missouri River at Sibley, which had been one of the bushwhackers' favorite Missouri River crossing points during the war. A snowstorm covered the gang's tracks on the opposite bank, however, and the posse lost the trail.

In the days following the robbery, at least nine of the robbers were identified by witnesses: Jim Anderson, Archie Clement, Oliver "Ole" Shepherd (brother of George Shepherd), Bud and Donny Pence, Jim and Bill Wilkerson,

Frank Gregg, and Joab Perry. These men had all been core members of Bill Anderson's gang and had followed Clement and Jim Anderson back from Texas in 1865. The Pences were relatives of the James brothers', and the Pences' Kentucky home would later be used as hideouts by Frank and Jesse. The gang may have been led by Clement, who was killed in a saloon in Lexington, Missouri, ten months later. It is unknown whether Jesse James was one of the bank robbers. He claimed later that he did not participate in the robbery, as he was still recovering from the gunshot wound to his lung suffered nine months earlier.[8]

The next robbery took place at noon on October 30, 1866, in Lexington, Missouri. Cashier J. Thomas was alone at his desk at the banking house of Alexander Mitchell & Co. in the battle-scarred town of Lexington, the seat of Lafayette County that sits on a bluff south of and overlooking the Missouri River, east of Liberty and Kansas City. It was an easy horseback ride southeast of the James brothers' farm. Two men entered the bank and asked the cashier the "discount" on a bond. When Thomas said he wasn't buying bonds, the men pulled two big revolvers each on the banker and pointed them at his head. "Give us all the money," they ordered. The bandits stuffed $2,000 from the cash drawer into a wheat sack and left, telling the banker not to give an alarm, or "you'll get your head blown off." Two other men waited outside, having hitched their horses in an adjacent alley. The four bandits galloped out of town, heading west.[9]

The gang's bloodiest bank robbery took place in Richmond, Missouri, where Bill Anderson's corpse lay moldering in its coffin three years after it had been posed for souvenir photographs. At 3:30 on Friday afternoon, May 23, 1867, twelve men converged on Richmond, about seven miles north of the Missouri River, a few miles east of adjoining Clay County, and about forty miles from the James farm. The twelve men rode in small, separate clusters before they gathered in front of the Hughes & Wasson banking house on the town square. Four of the men got off their horses while the others rested in their saddles and

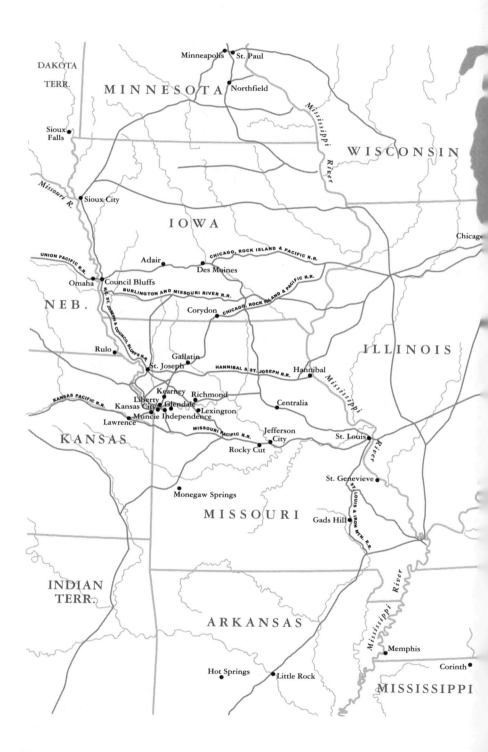

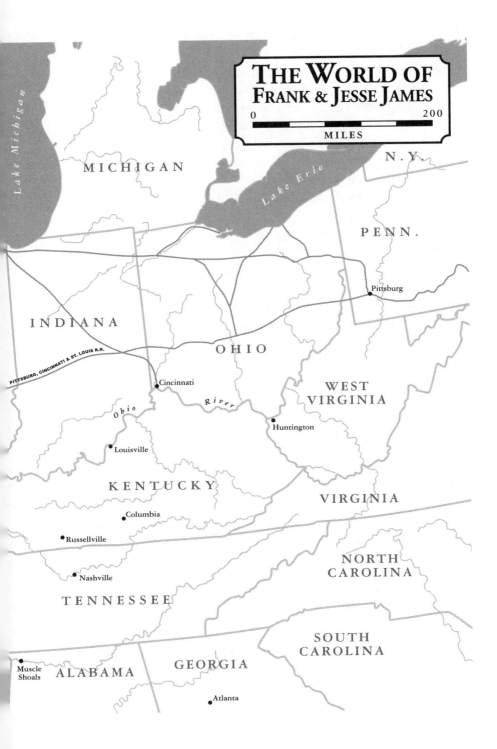

THE WORLD OF
FRANK & JESSE JAMES

0   200

MILES

Lake Michigan

MICHIGAN

Lake Erie

N. Y.

PENN.

Pittsburg

INDIANA

OHIO

PITTSBURG, CINCINNATI & ST. LOUIS R.R.

Cincinnati

River

WEST
VIRGINIA

Ohio

Huntington

Louisville

KENTUCKY

VIRGINIA

Columbia

Russellville

NORTH
CAROLINA

Nashville

TENNESSEE

SOUTH
CAROLINA

Muscle
Shoals

ALABAMA

GEORGIA

Atlanta

scanned the streets. The four men entered the bank, pulled Colt revolvers, and ordered the cashier to hand over the bank's money. The robbers stuffed $4,000 into a wheat sack, but the large number of mounted strangers near the bank had attracted suspicion. Several citizens came running with pistols drawn, suspecting a robbery. The gunmen began shooting, killing three citizens. The robbers galloped west on fast horses toward Liberty and lost a pursuing posse near the Fishing River bottoms.

On the Sunday following the robbery and murders, a warrant was issued for the arrest of seven suspects, including Allen Parmer, who later married Frank and Jesse's sister, Susan James. Six of the men identified had ridden with Quantrill, including Dick Burns, Payne Jones, and James White, who had surrendered with Frank James in Kentucky. One of the alleged robbers, Thomas Little, a former Quantrill guerrilla, was arrested, but he was lynched by a mob before he could be put on trial. It was also suspected that Frank and Jesse James had joined the robbery. Shortly after the murder of Sheets, a newspaper reported that Jesse "was implicated at the robbery in Richmond." A man who had grown up with Frank and Jesse and who was in Richmond that day also identified the brothers as among the robbers.[10]

The last bank robbery before the murder of Sheets in which Frank and Jesse James were suspected of participating occurred on March 20, 1868, in Russellville, Kentucky. The robbers probably struck outside of their home counties because Clay and Jackson counties were crawling with posses and bounty hunters searching for them. During the first week of March 1868, the James brothers were thought to be staying in rooms in a hotel in Chaplin, Kentucky, along with at least four former bushwhackers: Cole Younger, Ole Shepherd and his cousin George, and Arthur McCoy.[11]

About ten days earlier, one of the men, probably Younger, posing as "Thomas Coleman" (Coleman was Younger's middle name), scouted the bank's interior by offering to sell the owner of the bank, Nimrod Long, a bond at par, although it would normally bring a 6 or 7 percent discount. Long wasn't interested. "Coleman" came back a week later and tried to get change for a one-hundred-dollar bill. Long refused, saying the bill appeared to be counterfeit. Finally, at about two on the afternoon of March 20, "Coleman" entered the bank with two other men, shoved a fifty-dollar bill at Long, and asked, "Is that good, sir?" "Looks counterfeit to me," said Long, prompting Younger to pull his Colt revolver and order Long to empty his vault.[12]

Long wheeled around and leaped for the back door of the bank, as the astonished Younger looked on. When Long pushed open the back door, another bandit stationed outside it pulled his revolver and fired a shot at Long's head, grazing his scalp and tearing away hair and flesh. While Long was making his spectacular escape, Younger was busy filling a grain sack with $3,000 in gold coins and $9,000 in currency. The bandits escaped on thoroughbreds.[13]

There were at least five bank robberies after Sheets's murder and before 1883 in which Frank and Jesse James were thought to have been involved and that provide additional information about their robbery techniques. As described in chapter 7, at about 1:00 p.m. on Saturday, June 3, 1871, five months before Henry McDougal obtained a judgment against Frank and Jesse, four men, thought to be the James brothers, Cole Younger, and Clell Miller, rode into the public square of Corydon, Iowa, a few miles north of the Missouri state line. Corydon was the seat of Wayne County, in the heart of the hog and corn belt.[14]

The four strangers dismounted in front of the Ocobock Brothers' Bank, located on a corner of the public square. One man held the horses and guarded the front door while another guarded the back door. Two others entered the bank and pointed their revolvers at the cashier. They forced the cashier to unlock the bank's vault, from which they took $5,242 in currency and stamps. A posse of as many as ninety men pursued, but their horses were no match for the robbers' thoroughbreds.

The second crime occurred about eleven months later, on April 29, 1872, when five men robbed the bank in Columbia, Kentucky, which is also discussed in chapter 7.[15]

The following year, late on the morning of May 29, 1873, four men robbed the Ste. Genevieve Savings Association. Ste. Genevieve was an old French trading post eighty miles south of St. Louis on the western banks of the Mississippi River. Three bandits went into the bank, pointed their pistols at the cashier, and ordered him to "open the safe door!" The cashier filled their wheat sack with about $4,000, much of which was in silver coin. The sack was so heavy that it dragged on the ground as they ran from the bank. The St. Louis police soon identified the James and Younger brothers as the robbers.[16]

The fourth robbery occurred on Monday, September 6, 1873, at 2:00 p.m., when four bandits rode into Huntington, West Virginia, a small town along the Ohio River, and tied their horses near a blacksmith shop. One of the men stayed with the horses. Two of the men, later identified as Cole Younger and Tom Webb, walked into the Bank of Huntington while the third man remained across the street from the bank. The two men pulled revolvers on the bank cashier and ordered him to empty the contents of the safe into a grain bag. Then, at gunpoint, they forced the cashier and another bank employee outside the bank and toward their horses. The four men galloped away, escaping from a posse.

The final crime during this period, also discussed in chapter 7, occurred on September 7, 1876—almost one year to the day after the Huntington crime—when an attempted bank robbery by at least eight men in Northfield, Minnesota, was foiled using deadly force.

The numbers of men involved in the James brothers' bank robberies, the careful planning, and the use of grain sacks or saddlebags to hold loot distinguish these crimes from the two-man operation at Gallatin. Prosecutor William Wallace likely realized that the evidence and eyewitness testimony strongly suggested that the motive for the execution-style murder of Captain Sheets was assassination, not robbery.

The next question Wallace would have considered was whether Frank James had the motive, opportunity, and means to kill Cox. Other than an October 1883 motion to dismiss the Sheets murder charges against Frank James, which cites an absence of witnesses, no written record has been located of the prosecutor's reasoning leading to the dismissal of the charges. An analysis of the murder, however, leads to the conclusion that Frank James may not have been at Gallatin on December 7, 1869. Certainly, the evidence was insufficient to obtain a conviction, as Wallace apparently concluded.

Although Frank and Jesse James were indicted for Sheets's murder, all of the evidence linking them to the crime was circumstantial and principally consisted of Kate, the mare left behind in Gallatin after the murder. No one was recognized or identified, no one was captured, and no one confessed. The eyewitnesses apparently did not know Frank or Jesse James. The eyewitnesses probably provided the estimated height of the gunmen that appeared in the reward notice, but the descriptions ("Jesse—about 6 feet in height, rather slender built, thin visage" and "Frank—about 5 foot 8 or 10 inches in height, heavy built, full in the face") did not match either man (Jesse was approximately five foot nine, and heavier than Frank, and Frank was about five foot eleven and more slender than Jesse). Frank was apparently named as a participant only because he was Jesse's brother and because two gunmen fled the Jameses' barn when Deputy Sheriff Thomason attempted his arrest on December 14, 1869. Because the murder had taken place in a bank, newspaper reporters assumed that the crime was the latest in a series of bank robberies.[17]

But once Wallace concluded that Sheets's murder was an attempt to assassinate Major Cox rather than a bank robbery, the pool of possible suspects narrowed considerably. Many had a motive to rob a bank, but far fewer had a reason to assassinate Cox. Frank James did not appear to have a motive to kill Cox. He was not a member of Bill Anderson's guerrilla band but rode with Quantrill, who had no love for Anderson. In 1864, while wintering in Texas, Anderson and Quantrill had skirmishes between themselves and their bands. Anderson thereafter rode and operated separately from Quantrill's band.[18]

In addition, one of the eyewitnesses who saw the two gunmen before they went into the Daviess County Savings Association building, William Ewing, said that the taller of the two men "was taller than Frank James" and that "he had a full, light beard and mustache," while the other gunman was shorter than Frank James. Based upon witnesses such as this, Wallace could not have persuaded a jury to convict Frank James for Sheets's murder.[19]

Wallace also would have had a difficult time convincing a jury that an experienced gunman and former guerrilla like Frank James allowed a bank clerk to knock his gun away, and then missed shooting the clerk three times at close range. It was also implausible that Frank would have gotten "lost" and needed a guide around Kidder to make his escape, less than a day's ride from his boyhood home.

It had been assumed that Frank was the other rider who fled the barn in response to Thomason's purported arrest attempt at the James-Samuel farm a week after Sheets's murder. But neither the Thomasons nor anyone else in the posse positively identified Frank James as one of the riders. Moreover, given that it was apparently snowing and the riders were wearing coats with collars turned up and hats pulled down low, an identification of the riders' faces would be difficult, if not impossible.

It was later claimed in Jesse's purported letter to the newspaper that he had not recognized Oscar Thomason because Thomason's face was so "muffled with furs." In the same letter another assertion is made: it "was not my brother with me when we had the fight." In other words, the author of the letter admits that Jesse was one of the riders but not Frank. Why would the writer of the letter have gone out of his way to deny that Frank also shot at Thomason? After all, Frank could have used the same excuse as Jesse in explaining why he had fled—that he had not recognized Thomason.

If, on the other hand, Frank had not been with Jesse when the two riders fled, then Jesse may have been motivated by a concern for maintaining good relations with his older brother, if nothing else, to tell John Edwards to make it clear in the newspaper that Frank was not involved. Moreover, in the six alibis/affidavits submitted by Jesse's stepfather, mother, sister, and three Kearney residents, no mention was made of Frank. Perhaps Frank's family members and friends saw no need to include Frank in their sworn affidavits because he was not involved in the murder. The June 1870 letter to Governor Joseph W. McClurg contains only two references to Frank—as though Frank had not been charged with the murder of Sheets. The second letter to the governor does not mention Frank at all.

If not Frank, who entered the Gallatin bank with Jesse James? Cox said after the murder that Jim Anderson had sent him a letter before the murder demanding that he send Anderson his deceased brother's revolvers. Cox believed that Anderson had traveled to Gallatin to kill him. Cox also said that Clell Miller told him Anderson was plotting against him.

The affidavits printed in the newspapers in July 1870 also implicate Jim Anderson. According to Dr. Samuel, Jesse's stepfather, "I came home from my father's late Sunday evening, December 5, 1869, and my step-son, [Jesse James] told me that he had sold Kate to a man from Kansas . . . and got $500 for her." Jesse's sister, Susie, said that the man who purchased the horse "was from Topeka, Kansas." Jesse's mother gave a similar statement: "my son sold my daughters bay mare the Sunday previous to the bank robbery at Gallatin, and the man who bought the mare said he was from Topeka, Kansas. He paid my son five one hundred dollar bills." Jim Anderson was from that area of Kansas.

Does Jim Anderson fit the description of one of the two murderers given in the reward notices? Historian Paul

Peterson believes that Jim Anderson was about five foot eleven. In one of the few known photographs of Anderson, worn as a mourning pin by his sister Molly after his death, he has a narrow face with a high forehead, generally matching Frank James's appearance around that time. Both men were also approximately the same age. Accordingly, Anderson may have been the taller and more slender of the two gunmen whose physical description was provided in the reward notice.

The only reason given by historians for ruling out Jim Anderson as one of the gunmen is the unsupported assertion by former guerrilla George Shepherd, years after the fact, that Shepherd had killed Jim Anderson in 1868. It has been recently pointed out, however, that Jim Anderson was living in Sherman, Texas, in November 1869, the month before Sheets's murder. In fact, Jim Anderson and his wife apparently conceived a daughter in November 1869, who was born on August 21, 1870. Historian Peterson concludes that "Jim Anderson was slain sometime after November 1869." Another historian has concluded that Anderson may not have been killed until 1875. Intriguing evidence therefore suggests that Jim Anderson, not Frank James, may have been the taller of the two gunmen at Gallatin.[20]

Because of these and other evidentiary problems, Wallace and McDougal turned their attention to trying Frank James for another crime for which the evidence was much stronger: the October 1879 murder of passenger and stonemason Frank McMillen on a Rock Island train outside of Winston, Missouri, just a few miles west of Gallatin. And so Wallace began preparing for the Frank James trial—the "Trial of the Century"—which began on a sweltering Friday, August 24, 1883, in Gallatin, Missouri.

ELEVEN

THE TRIAL OF THE CENTURY

BEFORE AMERICANS BECAME ACCUSTOMED to Hollywood spectacles of triumph and tragedy in movie theaters, we witnessed the real thing in the form of criminal trials and hangings. Particularly in the West, these were often the most widely attended events in society. Celebrity participants and sensational facts generated great public interest, and when combined with skilled advocacy, these trials could capture or transform the views or prejudices of the times.[1]

In the Midwest, no nineteenth-century trial was more famous, reported on, and discussed than the August–September 1883 trial of Alexander Franklin "Frank" James. It was among the first to claim daily multimedia coverage—from newspaper journalists and from one of the greatest inventions of the times, "the voice of God," the telegraph. At the time, Frank and his late brother Jesse were the two most celebrated outlaws in American history. The crime for which Frank was tried—the 1879 murder of Frank McMillen during the Winston, Missouri, train robbery—was sensational, and virtually all knew that the crime was just one of many similar crimes the brothers had committed. The criminal careers of Frank and Jesse James also presented conflicting narratives. Their supporters claimed that they were defenders of a Southern tradition of honor and their Northern pursuers merely cowardly profiteers. To those not accepting this myth, the brothers were common criminals. The James brothers were therefore emblematic of the cultural war fought after the Civil War. In some ways, the trial of Frank James was the last event of the Civil War in Missouri, and a test of the power of the Lost Cause myth.[2]

It was somehow fitting that Frank James's very public outlaw career would end in the same place it had so sensationally begun thirteen years earlier. Gallatin had changed significantly since 1869: its population had swelled to about three thousand, thanks in large part to Henry McDougal's success in bringing two great railroads—the Wabash, St. Louis and Pacific, and the Chicago, Rock Island and Pacific—to the town, which was the junction of the lines. Trains now chuffed and snorted on the outskirts of town, creating a world of soot and clanking, screeching iron. The Wabash depot was on the east side of town. The Rock Island train from Kansas City to Gallatin took about five hours in 1883, and it dropped passengers off in the wood-sheltered little depot located in a hollow about a half mile north of town.

McDougal was now one of the most respected and influential lawyers in Gallatin. (The esteemed Samuel Richardson, Frank and Jesse James's lawyer in McDougal's 1870–71 lawsuit, died the year before the Frank James trial.) McDougal's railroad clients had provided him and his family a comfortable living. Eight years earlier, McDougal, Emma, and their three children had moved into a new, two-story, brick, Italian Renaissance-style home they had built in Gallatin, said to be the finest home in the county.

All of Missouri's newspapers sent reporters to the trial. As it unfolded, national newspapers began sending their own reporters to cover the dramatic events. Judge Charles A. Goodman, from neighboring Gentry County, presided. Governor Crittenden had asked Goodman to be the trial judge because of his no-nonsense demeanor and reputation for following the law. Goodman had been in the Union army during the Civil War, and after his discharge he studied law. He was prosecuting attorney for Gentry County for four years before being elected to the bench. He was forty, had a mustache and beard as black as his robe, and he ran a tight courtroom.[3]

Frank James's seven defense lawyers were the most accomplished and famous in Missouri. John F. Philips of Kansas City, a former Union colonel and past president of the Missouri Bar Association, was chief counsel. The forty-eight-year-old Philips sported a thick black mustache and beard, He was also a commissioner of the Missouri Supreme Court, and as such, he could one day be asked to pass judgment on the very case he was now involved in as counsel. A former congressman, Philips was one of the most respected lawyers in the state. Also representing Frank James were forty-seven-year-old former lieutenant governor Charles P. Johnson of St. Louis, the most noted criminal lawyer in the state; US representative John M. Glover of St. Louis; William H. Rush, a former Daviess County prosecutor; James H. Slover, former mayor of Independence who had assisted in jury selection for the defense in the John Bugler trial; Joshua W. Alexander of Gallatin; and prominent Ray County attorney Christopher T. Garner. Philips's and Johnson's distinguished service as Union officers in the Civil War was mentioned repeatedly during the trial. Rush and Alexander assisted in jury selection for the defense.[4]

In addition to William Wallace and Henry McDougal, the prosecutors were William D. Hamilton, the prosecuting attorney of Daviess County; and McDougal's law partners, Marcus A. Low and John H. Shanklin. Low had met with Governor Crittenden a little over two years earlier and had authorized, on behalf of his railroad client, a cash contribution of $10,000 reward each (for a total of $20,000) for

Frank and Jesse James's capture. Low had also drafted the reward proclamation, although these facts were not publicly known at the time of Frank James's trial. Low and Shanklin operated in the background and apparently assisted the prosecution in selecting the jury and reported on the proceedings to their railroad clients.

The process of selecting a jury in 1883 in Gallatin bore little resemblance to the slow, painstaking process that occurs today, particularly in a major criminal case. There were no detailed, written questionnaires filled out in advance by prospective jurors, no professional consultants to help the lawyers find favorable jurors, and no lengthy examinations by the lawyers or the judge in an effort to discover hidden biases. Instead, the potential jurors for Frank James's trial were asked a few questions about their age, address, occupation, and political party. They were then asked if they could be fair and make a decision based on the facts of the case. If they said "Yes," they qualified. For this reason, it was critical that the process of selecting the group of citizens from which the jury would be drawn was fair and impartial. Wallace and McDougal knew it would be difficult to seat a jury in Gallatin that would not already have its mind made up about the legendary outlaw.

On Monday morning, August 20, 1883, the streets surrounding the courthouse were lined for blocks with wagons, buggies, and saddle horses that had carried spectators to the trial. At 10 a.m., Judge Goodman called the case of *State of Missouri v. Frank James* and asked the clerk to read the indictment. Because the attorneys for both sides were still collecting their witnesses, however, Goodman adjourned the case until two o'clock that afternoon.

By two o'clock, such a large crowd had gathered that the small courtroom was packed almost to suffocation. Spectators spilled into the courtyard, standing five deep outside of the open windows of the courtroom, hoping to be able to catch a glimpse of Frank James and hear the proceedings. James was dressed in a black suit and looked more like a clergyman than a notorious, long-haired, Colt-revolver-slinging outlaw. His wife, Annie, and the couple's six-year-old son also attended as part of the defense strategy to exhibit his loving family to prospective jurors. Judge Goodman asked the state if it was ready to proceed. "We are ready," Hamilton replied. But defense counsel William Rush asked for additional time to get a jury seated and summon absent witnesses. The state objected, but the judge continued the case until one o'clock the next afternoon.[5]

Before adjourning, Goodman ordered Daviess County sheriff George T. Crozier to impanel one hundred citizens as potential jurors, and he told the lawyers to be ready the next day to begin questioning them. He also ordered that any person in the courtroom found with a weapon would be fined and possibly jailed. And because of the large number of spectators, he ordered that the trial would be moved across the street from the courthouse to the opera house.

Frank James was a fan of Shakespeare's, whom he quoted often. One of his favorite quotes was, "All life is merely a stage, and we are but actors upon it." It was therefore fitting that his trial was held in the wooden Gallatin Opera Hall, a theatrical setting that, although rickety, could seat four hundred people. Still, approximately three thousand people traveled to Gallatin to attend the trial, doubling the town's population. Demand for seats was so great that Sheriff Crozier was forced to issue tickets of admission for the hundreds who wanted to see the trial each day.[6]

The opera house was across the street to the west of the courthouse on the public square and was simple and unassuming. It was the old city hall and had been purchased a few years earlier by Joshua Alexander, one of Frank James's lawyers. Tables were set up on the little stage for the judge and newspaper reporters. In front of the stage a platform was built to the same level of the stage to seat the jury and witnesses. The lawyers sat with their backs to the spectators.[7] Although Goodman said this would prevent the noise of a packed courtroom and people coming and going, the opera house would also be more secure, as it had fewer windows through which a gun could be fired.

The judge had reason to be concerned about violence. Emotions still ran high about the murder of Sheets. Of those who had descended upon Gallatin for the trial, at least half supported James. Many of these men, such as Dave Pool and Bill Gregg, had ridden with Quantrill's guerrillas or had been young soldiers under Confederate generals Price and Shelby. In fact, the trial became a Confederate reunion. Most of the men still carried their sidearms from the war and were walking arsenals. For this reason, Judge Goodman intended to keep the trial moving as quickly as possible. It was reported that the sheriff collected over one hundred weapons during the proceedings.[8]

Dick Liddil caused the greatest uproar among the James supporters. Threats against his life could be heard in the city saloon, hotel lobbies, and stores throughout Gallatin. Although Liddil had not fought in the War Between the States (as it was referred to at the time by Lost Cause proponents), he had violated the guerrilla's code by turning on one of his own and testifying against Frank James. Liddil was compared to Jesse's murderer, Robert Ford. To make matters worse, Robert Ford also showed up in Gallatin for the trial.

Liddil had been transported to Gallatin from Jackson County in the custody of Marshal Maurice Langhorne, the deputy marshal of Jackson County who had guarded Tucker Bassham and Bill Ryan during Ryan's trial two years earlier. Upon reaching Gallatin, Langhorne enlisted the assistance of former Daviess County sheriff John Ballinger in guarding Liddil. Ballinger had captured the notorious John Reno of the Reno Gang sixteen years earlier. In an extraordinary display of how dangerous things were for Liddil, Langhorne and Ballinger allowed Liddil to wear a pair of Colt Navy revolvers strapped to his waist and thighs under his long coat.[9]

It didn't help that Gallatin was scorching hot the last week of August 1883. Oddsmakers felt it likely that there would be bloodshed before the end of the week. Both McDougal and Wallace went to the extraordinary lengths of carrying pistols in their pockets for protection as well.[10]

After court on the first Monday afternoon of the proceedings, Wallace was sitting in Hamilton's office. Through the open window, which provided a slight breeze, Wallace could see that the courthouse yard and square were full of people anticipating the trial. He then noticed Sheriff Crozier in the yard. The sheriff pulled a paper out of his pocket, looked at it, crossed the street, talked with someone on the boardwalk, came back into the courthouse yard, and repeated the process.[11]

Wallace walked outside and up to Crozier. "It looks as if we'll have a packed [unfair] jury," Wallace told him. The sheriff asked Wallace why he said such a thing. Wallace told him that he had been watching him, and that it appeared that the sheriff had a list of men's names in his pocket. (The jurors were supposed to include men from rural areas of the county, not just townspeople.) The sheriff blurted out that he was "merely getting a good jury." Wallace reminded the sheriff that he had promised to get an honest jury chosen from the entire county. The sheriff replied that he would get a "good jury without going outside Gallatin."[12]

Wallace strode back to Hamilton's office to draft a motion alleging improper conduct by Crozier and requesting that the county coroner, a Dr. D. M. Claggett, replace Crozier. McDougal objected to Wallace's plan because Claggett was a former Confederate soldier. Wallace asked McDougal if Claggett was honest; McDougal replied that Claggett had been honest in his dealings with him. Wallace explained that he had been fighting the James brothers for three years and he knew that many ex-Confederates were tired of the way they flouted the law. "Let's let the ex-Confederate Claggett pick the jury," Wallace said.[13]

Judge Goodman, hearing of the situation, hurried to Hamilton's office and asked if Wallace intended to file a motion to replace Crozier in the selection of the jury. Wallace replied that he did. The judge became angry and said that Frank James's friends, who had crowded the town and were well armed, had threatened violence if the jury selection was thrown out. "I am not in the habit of announcing my decisions beforehand, but if you file such a motion, I will overrule it to prevent bloodshed."[14]

Wallace was furious and stormed to his hotel to pack his belongings and go home. Hamilton and McDougal begged him to reconsider, as Hamilton and the other prosecutors knew only a part of the evidence. Wallace finally relented, but said the "verdict of the jury is already written."[15]

On Tuesday, August 21, jury selection began. Groups of eight men from Crozier's list were called in one at a time and questioned by the judge and the lawyers. Most of the few Republican businessmen on the panel, who were generally favored by the prosecution, gave various excuses, and an unusual amount of "sickness" developed, preventing them from serving. No doubt, prospective jurors were concerned about their personal safety should they be selected on a jury that might vote to convict the notorious outlaw. In those days, the names and identities of jurors was public knowledge. In fact, the names of the jurors were printed in the newspapers after they were selected, along with their ages and occupations.[16]

On Wednesday, August 22, as jury selection continued, Harfield Davis and Judge Alex Irving, both of whom had been listed as witnesses for the state, received threatening letters that read, "You had better be careful about your evidence against Frank James. A Friend." Both men had been in the posse that had pursued the two gunmen out of Gallatin after Sheets's murder. Irving had also been one of the Gallatin men in Deputy Sheriff Thomason's posse that had ridden to the James farm the week after the murder to arrest Frank and Jesse. Irving was now a judge and one of the most respected men in Gallatin. Harfield Davis was the publisher of the *Gallatin Weekly Democrat*, which had published notice of McDougal's lawsuit against Frank and Jesse James in 1870.[17] Both groups of opposing lawyers met that evening and denounced the letters. The prosecutors blamed the defendant for the letters, and the defense lawyers argued that neither they nor Frank James had anything to do with the letters.

On Thursday, the lawyers used up their objections to the remaining prospective jurors, whittling the group down to twelve. All of the jurors were Democrats, which boded ill for the prosecution. Two were Confederate army veterans. Judge Goodman told the lawyers that the trial would start the next day. Eighty-nine witnesses for the state and thirty-nine witnesses for the defense were sworn at the same time, the day before the trial started, standing together to take the oath collectively. After being sworn, all witnesses were excluded from the courtroom so their testimony would not be influenced by other testimony. Only one witness—Frank James—would be sworn just before taking the stand.[18]

On Friday morning, August 24, a deputy sheriff stationed at the door to the opera house told the men that had been gathered there for most of the night that no guns could be taken inside. Arguments began because men who had packed guns since the Civil War said they'd be damned if they would give them up: a gun was a man's private property, and he could do what he wanted with it. Many of the men were finally talked out of their guns, however, and went into the makeshift courthouse feeling undressed. Most of those who attended the trial were supporters of Frank James's. The men who were turned away at the door grumbled and milled about the public square or went into nearby saloons to drink.

Meanwhile, Frank James was in court sitting with his lawyers, dressed in a black suit and wearing a black tie pierced by a gold stickpin that held a large pearl. His long, thin face was weather worn and unsmiling. There were deep lines about his thin-lipped mouth and furrows on his face. Newspaper reporters said his gray eyes were ever watchful with suspicion and anxiety. His long, large nose dominated his face.

Wallace made a one-hour opening statement for the prosecution. In a detailed, no-nonsense presentation, he told the jurors that the evidence would show that Frank James, Jesse James, their cousins Wood and Clarence Hite, and Dick Liddil robbed the train at Winston, during the course of which Frank McMillen, a passenger and stonemason, was shot and killed. Liddil, he said, would testify that the Jameses and Wood Hite entered the passenger cars while Liddil and Clarence Hite guarded the engine crew. Liddil, an admitted member of the gang, would be the state's key witness.

The defense announced that it would not make an opening statement, reserving its opening comments for after the close of the prosecution's case. The court then adjourned for lunch.[19]

Wallace began the testimony with dramatic effect by calling witnesses who were on the train to describe the frightening robbery and cold-blooded murder. The witnesses were kept outside the courtroom in the shady courthouse yard until summoned for their testimony by the sheriff. Because Wallace was a guest prosecutor in Gallatin, he allowed Daviess County prosecutor William Hamilton the honor of calling the first witness, John L. Penn, a sandy-haired stonemason with large, callused hands. Penn testified that at about 9:00 p.m. on July 15, 1881, he, McMillen, and McMillen's father had boarded the train at Winston, where they were building a railroad trestle. Several other men, wearing long dusters and slouch hats pulled down over their faces, with collars turned up and white handkerchiefs about their necks, also boarded the train at Winston.[20]

Penn described how three of these men pulled revolvers, one in each hand, as conductor William Westfall was taking the passenger's tickets. The three robbers, who had entered the car from the front, followed Westfall to the back, shooting and yelling, "Down!" at the passengers. The robbers then rushed back to the front of the car, and after they passed Penn, he and McMillen rushed out the back door of the car and sat on the platform steps to get out of the line of fire. The robbers continued to fire shots and yell,

"Down, down!" Penn and McMillen heard a voice call out, as if in distress. McMillen said, "It's father!" He jumped up to look in the passenger-door window, and one of the robbers, "a big man" (Frank James was rather tall for that time, when most men were five feet seven or shorter), shot him above the eye, sending him tumbling backward off the platform. Penn tried to catch him but couldn't. The train had been moving slowly all this time, but now it stopped. The three robbers jumped off the train, and Penn could see them run past him as he crouched on the rear platform. They disappeared into the woods next to the tracks.

Charles Johnson conducted an effective cross-examination of Penn. The defense needed to prove that none of the train passengers could identify Frank James as one of the robbers. Johnson forced Penn to admit that, with the murderers' hats pulled down and collars turned up, he was unable to see their faces. Penn also admitted that the robbers appeared to fire their shots in an effort to scare the passengers and keep them from interfering, not to kill. Penn also admitted he wasn't sure which of the three men fired the shot that killed McMillen.

It did not matter, however, whether Frank James pulled the trigger of the murder weapon. Under the felony murder rule then and now, if someone is killed during the commission of a felony, all participants are guilty of the murder, regardless of who pulled the trigger. Practically, however, James's lawyers no doubt hoped that the jury might ignore this instruction of law if they concluded that he participated in the robbery but that he did not pull the trigger of the murder weapon.[21]

Wallace then called other witnesses to testify about the vicious nature of the robbery. Addison E. Wollcott, the train engineer, said the train left Winston at 9:30 p.m. He received a signal to stop shortly after leaving the station. Two men with revolvers jumped off the coal in the tender and into the cab. One of them ordered him to keep the train moving or "I will shoot you." The man told him to stop the train at the water tank in a hollow. After Wollcott stopped the train, the two men jumped off. Under cross-examination by Johnson, Wolcott admitted that it was so dark that he could not see the men's faces.[22]

Governor Crittenden caused a stir as he entered the makeshift courtroom just as Charles M. Murray, the express agent on the train, began his testimony. Murray told the jurors that after the train left the Winston depot, he heard shots fired, and a robber entered the express car, pointed a revolver at him, and ordered him to open the safe. The robber asked Murray repeatedly, "Is this all the money?" The robber seemed angry and told Murray they had killed the conductor, and he was going to kill him. The robber ordered Murray to get down on his knees; when Murray refused, the man clubbed him over the head with his revolver, knocking him unconscious. Murray didn't awaken until after the robber had left. He didn't know how much money had been taken.

Dr. Claggett, the coroner, testified briefly that he had examined McMillen's body and had found a bullet hole above the right eye, which was the cause of death. The judge then ordered the luncheon recess.[23]

After lunch Wallace called William L. Earthman, the Tennessee justice of the peace who had captured Bill Ryan outside of Nashville. Wallace knew from the Ryan trial that Earthman was a good witness. Earthman had met Frank James in 1879 at a horse race in Nashville. Earthman knew James as "B. J. Woodson." Earthman last saw him in 1880 in Nashville. Earthman said he had not seen him again until a few months before the trial in the Gallatin courtyard, where James had asked Earthman if, "I had come up here to hang him."

The day ended with the testimony of an express agent regarding the shipping of a box to the Fords, which Wallace had told the jury in his opening statement contained a shotgun shipped by Frank and Jesse James from Tennessee.[24]

Many of the spectators got their weapons back from the deputy sheriff as they left the opera house and slept in the courthouse yard that night. When court opened the next morning, Saturday, they again checked their weapons at the door before entering. Now Wallace, having established the day before that Frank James used an alias and was present in Tennessee in 1879–80, called his star witness, Dick Liddil. Defense attorney Glover immediately objected and argued that Liddil, as a convicted felon for horse theft, was not competent to testify under Missouri law. Wallace had anticipated the objection and produced a written pardon. He argued that the governor had the power to pardon Liddil, and that Liddil should therefore be allowed to testify. After lengthy arguments outside the presence of the jury and a recess, the judge agreed with Wallace.

Liddil was a thin, handsome man, about five foot ten, with dark sideburns and a mustache. Clad in a dark business suit, he told the jury that he was thirty-one and had been born and raised in Jackson County, Missouri. He had met Frank and Jesse James in 1870 at Robert Hudspeth's farm in Jackson County, where Liddil worked as a farmhand. He saw the James brothers probably a dozen times between 1870 and 1875. Cole and John Younger were often with them. They were always armed and on horseback. They would stay somewhere one or two days and then leave.

Liddil eventually joined the gang. At that time, Bill Ryan, Ed Miller, Tucker Bassham, and Wood Hite were also members. The James brothers and Miller then moved to Tennessee. Liddil joined them in Nashville in the summer of 1880. At Nashville, Frank went by the name B. J. Woodson, and Jesse called himself J. D. Howard.

When Bill Ryan was captured in March 1881, "we took a skeer [scare] and lit out," Liddil testified. Ryan had been traveling to "old man Hite's" (Wood Hite's father's home) in Kentucky when he got drunk and was arrested. Liddil read about it in a paper the next day, and he and the James brothers packed up and left Nashville at dark. They rode forty miles to old man Hite's and got there at sunup. They were armed with pistols and Winchester rifles.[25]

In May 1881, Liddil and Jesse took the train to Kearney, Missouri, and from there they rode to Jesse's mother's house. Frank joined them a week later. Two months later, in July, Liddil, the James brothers, and Clarence and Wood Hite rode off from the James-Samuel's farm toward Gallatin. They stopped in some timber about a mile outside of Winston. After hitching their horses in the woods, they walked to the Winston train depot. The five men got on the train with some passengers, including stonemasons. After the train pulled out of the depot, Liddil and Clarence Hite climbed onto the tender and then dropped down into the engine room. They fired their revolvers to scare the engineer and fireman. They heard firing back in the passenger car. Jesse and Frank James broke into the express car. Frank came out of the car and shut down the engine. As the train slowed, Frank, Clarence, and Liddil jumped off. They had stolen seven or eight hundred dollars.

Frank talked to Liddil after the robbery and said he thought they had killed two men. Jesse shot one, and Frank thought he shot and killed someone who had peeked into the passenger car door window. They rode to a pasture by the Crooked River, and Jesse divided the money, giving each about $130. The last time Liddil saw Frank James was at widow Mattie Bolton's house in September or October 1881.[26]

John Philips, with obvious disdain, cross-examined Liddil. He asked whether Liddil remembered telling Governor Crittenden that Frank James had told Liddil that he yelled at Jesse for the killing on the train and reminded him of their agreement before the robbery that no one would be hurt or killed. Liddil said he did not remember making these statements. At this point, Philips caused a stir in the courtroom by calling Governor Crittenden as a witness.

The lawyers had agreed that Crittenden could be called out of turn in order to save him the trouble of staying in Gallatin another day while he waited to testify. Crittenden and Philips knew each other well, as both had fought at the October 23, 1864, battle of Westport, Missouri. In fact, Philips was Crittenden's commander in the battle. Philips perhaps used their former relationship to his advantage, as he immediately got Crittenden to contradict Liddil: Crittenden testified that Liddil told him that Frank James had said there "was to be no bloodshed," and that after the robbery was over Frank had said, "Jesse, why did you shoot that man? I thought the understanding was that no one was to be killed, and I would not have gone into it if I had known or thought that there was to be anything of that sort done." Liddil said Jesse had responded, "By God, I thought that the boys were pulling from me, and I wanted to make them a common band of murderers to hold them to me."

It was a damaging blow to Wallace and the prosecution to have the governor contradict the testimony of Liddil, the state's star witness. For perhaps one of the few times in his prosecutorial career, Wallace seemed unprepared for the testimony. Of course, under the felony murder rule it did not matter that there was an agreement before the robbery that no one was to be killed—all participants in the robbery were equally accountable for any murder committed during robbery. Practically, however, Crittenden's testimony on behalf of Frank James no doubt severely undermined Liddil's credibility with the jury.

The third day of the trial, Monday, August 27, began at 8:00 a.m. Philips continued to grill Dick Liddil. He asked Liddil to confirm for the jury that he had been convicted of horse theft, for which he had spent thirty-one months in the state penitentiary. After his release from prison, he went to work for the Hudspeths in Jackson County.

Philips questioned Liddil as to his travels with Frank and Jesse James in 1879 and 1880. Liddil was in Tennessee with them when Bill Ryan was arrested on March 26, 1881. The gang left the night they heard of the arrest. They "borrowed" the horses they rode during the trip. Liddil said they didn't ask the horses' owners for permission to take them, as "the folks were asleep." This drew a chuckle from the spectators. The cross-examination lasted all morning, but Liddil did not waver in his story in any substantial respect. He admitted, however, that Wallace had given him passes to travel on the railroads and had paid his meal and hotel expenses. In a somewhat weak redirect examination by Wallace, Liddil said the Jameses each carried two revolvers during the train robbery.[27]

Wallace then called witnesses to place Frank James near Gallatin at the time of the robbery. Thomas Ford, the father of Bob and Charles Ford, who lived in Ray County, north of Richmond, Missouri, testified that he saw Frank James a short time before the Winston robbery. Mattie Bolton, sister to Bob and Charlie Ford, testified she also saw Frank James at her brother's house in May 1881, reading Shakespeare in his room. On cross-examination, she stubbornly insisted that Frank James was in the area just before and after the Winston robbery, which directly contradicted the defense's strident assertions that he had not stepped foot in Missouri for four years. Wallace's case seemed to be getting back on track.

Bolton then acknowledged that Wood Hite died on December 5, 1881. The court sustained Wallace's objections to testimony as to how Hite had died, or what was done with his body. Glover argued outside the presence of the jury that he intended to show that Liddil had killed Wood Hite and then gave himself up and agreed to testify against Frank James to obtain immunity from prosecution for Hite's murder. The court ruled that Liddil's credibility might be attacked, but not in that manner.

The next morning, Philips argued that the circumstances as to Wood Hite's death were relevant as to Liddil's credibility. He argued that any person who allowed a guest and friend to die without medical attention and then dragged his body out and dumped him in a shallow trench and covered him with stones "like a hog" was so morally bankrupt as to make him unworthy of belief in a case in which Frank James was on trial for his life. Wallace vehemently argued that the circumstances of Hite's death were not relevant to the case. The court ruled, however, that Mrs. Bolton could be recalled and examined as to the disposal of Wood Hite's body. In dramatic testimony, Bolton testified that Hite was shot and killed in her dining room. His body was then taken upstairs. She didn't know when the body was taken out, but he was buried about two hundred yards from the house. Fearing retribution by Jesse James, she moved out of the house in February, "as I understood that Wood Hite and Jesse James were cousins." Judge Goodman then allowed the defense to recall Elias Ford, Bob Ford's brother, who said Wood Hite was killed about 9:00 a.m. on December 5, 1881, about ten minutes before he arrived. The body lay upstairs until about 9:00 p.m., when four people carried it outside. Hite's body was buried in a horse blanket about one-quarter of a mile east of the house in a hole under some rocks. Dick Liddil was shot and wounded about this time and "was a long time recovering" from his wounds.

The gruesome testimony concerning Wood Hite's murder and burial caused a sensation in the courtroom and in the newspapers. After lunch, Wallace continued with a parade of witnesses who placed Frank James near Gallatin at the time of the robbery. Joseph Mallory was a farmer who saw Frank James at Potts's blacksmith shop outside of Winston before the robbery, where Frank was getting his horse shod. Jonas Potts, a blacksmith who lived four miles northeast of Winston, also testified that he shod a horse for James before the Winston robbery.[28]

Perhaps the most entertaining witness was the Reverend Benjamin Matchett, a Methodist clergyman. He testified that on the day before the train robbery, two men had stopped at his home near Winston for dinner. The two men said their names were Willard and Scott. Matchett said Willard was the defendant, Frank James, who quoted Shakespeare to Matchett after eating. Matchett said he was so confident that James was the man who stopped at his house that if James hadn't paid for his dinner, he would say right there in court, "Mr. Willard, I would be pleased to have the amount of that . . . bill," which caused the courtroom to erupt in laughter. Wallace was beginning to feel good about his case again.[29]

The trial of Frank James was a long one, and to get a little fresh air to help him bear the strain of the proceedings, Wallace took a horseback ride in the country after court each evening. Just as he was starting out one evening, a Gallatin citizen told him that not two minutes earlier, "a noted shooter said he intended to kill you on sight," and he told Wallace to stable his horse and go back to his hotel room. Wallace replied, "The surest plan for me to get shot is to run." Wallace took his ride that evening and did so until the case ended, but he continued to carry a pistol in his pocket for protection.[30]

On Thursday morning, August 30, the defense began its case. Before the trial began, Wallace believed that the defense would seek to prove mistaken identity, that the fifth robber was a gang member named Jim Cummins, not Frank James. Accordingly, James's lawyers had repeatedly questioned prosecution witnesses about Cummins and his whereabouts. By the time the defense began its case, however, it was clear that Frank James could not be mistaken for Cummins. Wallace had effectively countered the defense strategy by asking witnesses to describe and imitate Cummins' peculiar drawl, which could not have described Frank. Shifting strategy, William Rush now announced in his opening statement to the jury that there were really only four robbers, and that Liddil and other prosecution witnesses had conjured up the fifth robber and Frank James's presence on the train.

Rush spent much of his presentation describing Frank's efforts to get away from the gang. He was not part of the gang when it robbed the Winston train, and Dick Liddil's testimony was not to be believed, he said. Mattie Bolton's and her brothers' character was also questionable, as they had, with "the ghost of recent death in their house," entertained guests and could not be trusted. The other witnesses were mistaken in their identification of Frank James at the blacksmith's shop and elsewhere.

The defense strategy mirrored that of the Clell Miller trial: demonize the chief accuser (Liddil) and make the defendant appear to be a decent, law-abiding citizen. Frank James wanted nothing to do with the outlaw life. He had lived honorably and peaceably in Nashville from 1879 to March 1881. He had been refused amnesty and clemency. His mother had been maimed and his infant brother killed by those in league with the prosecution. Frank James was not in Missouri in 1881, nor at the Winston robbery. There was a conspiracy between the railroads, Liddil, the Fords, the Boltons, and the prosecutors to hang Frank James.[31]

The key witness for the defense's four-robber theory was Samuel T. Brosius, a thirty-six-year-old Gallatin attorney. Brosius had been a passenger on the train and said he had gotten a good look at the men who had come on board and started shooting. The defendant was not one of them. He said there were only two gunmen on the train, not three.

Wallace cross-examined Brosius. In response to Wallace's questioning, Brosius said he did not recall telling people after the robbery that he had been so afraid that he had hid under his seat, and that he was so scared that the robbers "appeared fifteen feet high with revolvers that appeared to be three or four feet long." Wallace forced Brosius to admit that he had gone to Nashville before the trial with a note from Frank James that read:

> Mr. Brosius, go to see Mr. Clint Cantwell by all
> means. He lives in sight of the Jeff Hyde property.
> Remember me kindly to all the family.
> Respectfully,
> B. J. Woodson
> May 3, 1883

Despite the letter, Brosius implausibly denied going to Nashville on Frank James's behalf in order to locate support for an alibi.[32]

The defense then began calling its character witnesses. Fletcher Horn, a detective from Nashville, testified that he knew the defendant as B. J. Woodson from summer 1877 until March 1881, and that Woodson was a hard-working and respectable farmer. During cross-examination, Wallace was unable to make any headway in his efforts to call into question Frank's character.

During the noon hour, the town gossip swirled around a group of cattlemen who had just rode into town: Allen Parmer, Frank James's brother-in-law; Dave Pool, a former Quantrill guerrilla and now a stockman in Texas; and several strangers. The rumor was that these men would help provide an alibi for Frank James.

The defense's star witness, fifty-two-year-old former general Joseph O. Shelby, testified after lunch. The rail-thin Shelby sported a waxed mustache, chin whiskers, and long hair streaked with gray that touched his shoulders. He was the most popular man in Missouri at the time. What Robert E. Lee was to the South, Jo Shelby was to Missouri—at least to the southern part of Missouri. Shelby, born in Kentucky, made his fortune as a Missouri slave owner and planter. When the Civil War started, he joined the cavalry of General Sterling Price and soon rose to command his own regiment and brigade. He strode into the courtroom with a glare and looked around before asking where the judge was located.[33]

Shelby attempted to shake hands with Judge Goodman. The judge fidgeted as a twitter ran through the courtroom, and, with a quizzical expression, he suggested that the witness should defer formalities and answer questions. Shelby then asked where the jury might be; when it was pointed out to him he bowed, and then sat down. Even the gaily dressed ladies in attendance noticed that Shelby had been drinking.

Shelby told the jury (although it needed no telling) that he had lived in Lafayette County for thirty-four years, nine miles from Lexington. Shelby said he knew Frank James because "he was with me in the Confederate Army." Shelby asked the judge if he could shake hands with his fellow soldier. Goodman, attempting to keep control of the courtroom, replied, "No sir, not now." Shelby testified that in fall 1880, he came back from his fields and found Jesse James and Dick Liddil on horseback in his yard. He asked them whether they knew anything about a recent bank robbery, telling them that he believed that the men who had been arrested were innocent. He said James turned to Liddil and pointed at him, saying, "there's the man who hit the cashier." Shelby explained that James's wife later came to him asking if he could assist in Frank's surrender. As an aside, Shelby mentioned that he told her to leave an order with a shipping agent for the shipment of her sewing machine.[34]

Wallace had his hands full during his cross-examination of the cantankerous and alcohol-fueled Shelby. When Wallace began, Shelby turned his chair toward him and glared at him. Wallace immediately placed the old general's credibility at issue by asking him if he was sure he had nothing to do with, and never saw, Mrs. James's sewing machine (in order to prove that Frank James and his wife had moved back to Missouri from Tennessee and were in Missouri during the time of the Winston train robbery). Shelby pulled his chair even closer to Wallace and said, in a loud voice, "Yes, as sure as I am about you."

The judge banged his gavel. "No more of that talk, or I shall enter a fine of $50 against you," Goodman told Shelby.

"Is the judge going to permit him [Wallace] to insult an unarmed man, who is a witness?" Shelby asked.

"Every witness comes in here unarmed, sir," the judge replied.

Wallace continued: "What are your initials?

"If you are desirous of knowing, go to this bank here and you will find out," Shelby snapped.

Judge Goodman ordered Shelby to answer the question. Shelby said, "J. O. S."

Wallace then presented the express bill for the sewing machine, initialed as received by "J. O. S." Shelby denied it was him, telling Wallace, "There may be a great many people in Lafayette with those initials." Shelby then told Wallace that perhaps they should step outside if Wallace was challenging his testimony. Philips interrupted and suggested that the cross-examination be deferred, under the circumstances.

"Not at all. Now is the time for it to go on," Shelby replied.

In an effort to demonstrate that Shelby had never seen Dick Liddil before the trial, Wallace asked Shelby if the defendants' lawyers had not subpoenaed Shelby to appear at Ballinger's home so that Shelby could get a look at Liddil. Philips indignantly objected at the insinuation, and Shelby shouted, "I saw him like a viper, curled up in a rocking chair."

Shelby also admitted that Jesse James, Jim Cummins, and Bill Ryan had eaten at Shelby's home. Wallace asked whether Shelby notified anyone that these wanted men were at his home. Shelby warned, "Wallace, if you don't want to make this a personal matter don't go any further." Shelby took out one of his cards for presentation (challenging Wallace to a duel) and told Wallace, "I'll face you anywhere," which drew another rebuke from the judge. As Shelby left the witness stand and walked by Frank James, he said, in a voice loud enough to be heard by the jury, "God bless you, old fellow."[35]

The defense then played its sympathy card by calling Zerelda James, the gray-haired, one-armed, fifty-five-year-old mother of Frank James, as a witness. Wearing a black dress, black bonnet, and mourning veil, she said she had lived in Clay County near Kearney for forty years and was the mother of Frank James, who was forty years old. She sobbed and choked as she told of Jesse's death two years earlier. Jesse was at her house in May or June 1881. Frank was not there, and she did not see him until after he turned himself in and was jailed at Independence.

When cross-examined, she told Wallace that she did not see Frank in 1881 and thought he was dead. She admitted she provided a dress, apron, and bonnet in August after the train robbery to Jesse, Liddil, and the Hites.

"Why did you do that?" asked Wallace.

"Because they wanted to pass one of the gentlemen off as a lady, so you folks could not catch them," was her smug reply.[36]

The defense then called its alibi witnesses. Allen Parmer, Frank James's brother-in-law and a cattleman from Wichita Falls, Texas, testified that he had lived in Texas for almost twenty years. He was away from home the summer of 1881, hauling cattle on a railroad, and returned home on August 1 and found Frank James there. Upon cross-examination, Parmer could not remember much about the places he allegedly worked that summer, or for whom he worked.[37]

The prosecutors and others at the trial believed that the testimony of Frank James's family members and friends in an effort to establish an alibi had not been convincing. Accordingly, the defense lawyers decided to put Frank James on the stand, an unusual and desperate strategy for any criminal defendant. The trial occurred during a time of transition in the development of modern cross-examination. As strange as it may seem, it was once the law in every US jurisdiction that interested parties, including criminal defendants, were disqualified as witnesses in their own cases. A defendant could not by his own testimony provide his own alibi, or raise any other defense. Accordingly, lawyers had little reason to develop the short, leading questions that are now considered essential in order to cross-examine a hostile defendant. Cross-examination instead was generally used to fill in gaps in the direct testimony. In 1864, Maine became the first state to abolish the prohibition against interested party testimony. Missouri followed in 1877, just five years before Frank James's trial, so James was allowed to testify in his own behalf.[38]

At about three in the afternoon, Frank James strode to the witness stand, causing a stir in the courtroom. Everyone knew that the trial would likely be won or lost on his testimony. Frank was cool, collected, and matter-of-fact. He said he moved to the Nashville area in July 1876. He raised wheat and corn, and did some logging. In spring 1879, he ran into Jesse in a store, where both men were buying grain. Jesse told him he was living in Humphrey County, about one hundred miles west of Nashville.[39]

Frank tried to persuade Jesse not to go to Missouri, but Jesse went anyway. Frank left Jesse and went to Texas. He visited his sister in the summer of 1881. When Frank left Tennessee, he told his wife to go to General Shelby and see if arrangements could be made for his surrender. He returned to Missouri on October 5, 1881, and surrendered to the governor.

Wallace now faced perhaps the toughest cross-examination of his life. It may also have been the first time he had ever cross-examined a criminal defendant. He painstakingly questioned James about his travels in Kentucky and Tennessee, which Frank recalled in detail. But when it came to James's alleged travels in Texas, his testimony fell apart and he could not recall where he had stayed or whom he met. James blamed his lack of recall on being "alone and anxious" at the time. Although Wallace scored points because of James's inexplicable inability to provide key details about his alleged travels in Texas, James did not wilt under Wallace's lengthy and blistering cross-examination. The defense then rested, and the judge adjourned court for the day.[40]

At the close of the evidence, the consensus was that the prosecution had put on a reasonably strong case and that while victory was not certain, it was not out of the question. It was now up to the lawyers to argue to the jury why the testimony and evidence the jurors had heard and considered led to the conclusion that Frank James was guilty or innocent. John Philips gave the defense's most crucial and persuasive speech, which was described as "the event of the trial" and "the greatest forensic display ever heard," and was cited by observers as the pivotal event of the trial. His argument was a masterful weaving of the myths of the Lost Cause and the noble robber.[41]

Giving the jury an avenue to reach a not guilty verdict without overtly disregarding the law, Philips argued that the evidence failed to demonstrate guilt beyond a reasonable doubt. The basis for his argument was grounded in his view of the trial witnesses' honor and dishonor. Philips argued that Frank James, his family, and friends exemplified Southern honor. They were intensely loyal to each other. They used violence, but for noble ends. They represented honor and therefore truth. On the other hand, the prosecution witnesses were motivated by money, not honor. They were treacherous, not loyal; cowardly, not brave. The prosecutors should have been ashamed to have brought these witnesses to testify against this last soldier of the "War Between the States."

Philips superbly played the war card, but he did so as a former Union soldier rather than a Confederate, thus appealing to all members of the jury:

> In that fierce . . . strife, which swept the land like a tornado, dividing families, brother against brother, in deadliest contention, Frank James and I stood in mortal antagonism. . . . The episode of the James brothers was the bitter fruit of that dire strife. . . . And when I saw [Frank James seeking] reconciliation—with but one aspiration and one hope, to devote, if allowed, the remainder of his life and energies to the duties of a husband, father and good citizenship, my whole heart went out in congratulation.[42]

Depicting James as a combatant rather than a thief meant Philips argued that James was entitled to use force until his surrender. Thus, while not supporting robbery and murder, Philips attempted to portray James as acting in the tradition of Robert E. Lee. Philips also sought to appeal to the jurors' emotions by demonizing efforts to bring James to justice. He reminded the jurors of the Pinkerton raid in discussing James's mother:

> Day unto day . . . this old mother Samuel, never lifts up in prayer, or moves in her daily round of domestic duty, her right arm that its missing hand does not remind her of persecution and suffering endured because she was a mother. And if, as often as her

children have looked upon that handless arm, they have felt the beatings of the tiger's heart within them, as they thought of the mercenary vandals who, to slake their thirst for gold . . . threw hand grenades into a mother's home, tearing muscle from muscle and bone from bone, and murdering her innocent helpless child, is it too much . . . to say the world ought to forgive them!

Another theme Philips emphasized was Frank James's love of family and their love of him. Philips insisted that James's love of family was important because honorable men act to support and protect their families. James's surrender was honorable because of its motivation: to allow James to return to his family. His love of family caused him to move to Tennessee because

the miseries and ghosts of the war hung around his footsteps in Missouri. Weary and heartsick of it all he determined to turn his back upon it, and seek a new home, under an assumed name, in the hope that he might find a new life of peace and humble, honest industry. He had just taken to his bosom and confidence a young, trusting sweet woman. That itself was highest proof that he was no longer seeking adventure, but the pleasure and happiness which comes surest from domestic life and retirement.

The soldier had become the honest farmer, his "hands hardened with honest toil."[43]

Family loyalty was another theme Philips stressed. Family loyalty is often problematic for defense attorneys because it is a reason why individuals may lie for one another. According to Philips, however, family loyalty is not a reason for disbelief, but rather a virtue and reason for belief:

If Frank James was not in Texas, as he testified, Palmer and wife were perjurers. . . . Is Mrs. Palmer unworthy of belief because she is a sister? Is it the unwritten law of a Christian land that where blood

runs thick and sisterly love is quick, perjury breeds?
You, gentlemen of the jury, beheld her on the witness stand. You looked into her calm, sweet face, all
over which God has written innocence, purity and
truth. Will you stamp it with perjury?"[44]

Philips was even more forceful in arguing for the truth-
fulness of Frank James's wife and mother. His mother testified that he was not in Missouri at the time of the robbery.
Philips argued that her testimony was believable because of
her love:

> Mrs. Samuel, it is true, is the prisoner's mother. I
> know how the unfeeling world and a sensational
> press have chided her—even making her the subject
> of ribald jest. But whatever else she may be to the
> world, she is to this prisoner a mother. Whatever he
> may be to the jaundiced public eye, to her he is a
> son—her boy Buck. Oh how much of divinity and
> consecration are wrapped up in those two words—
> mother and child! How the one stirs our youth;
> while the other quickens the pulse and gladdens the
> heart of old age.

Perhaps more effective was Philips's sanctification of
James's wife, Annie. Philips argued that she turned him
from an "adventurer" into an individual seeking the pleasure and happiness of domestic life. The woman who could
produce such an effect was a trusting, sweet woman. Philips
argued that it was obvious that such a woman must be
telling the truth when she said that she had gone to
Missouri in 1881 to arrange Frank's surrender. Philips
closed his speech by citing Annie's virtue as he explained
why Frank James turned away from his "war": she was
"spotless as the fallen snow," "gave the bold rider her virgin
heart . . . and like a good angel she has attended him . . .
and drawn the cords of affection about him."

Philips argued that loyalty explained the obvious holes
in James's testimony about his visit to Texas and people he

visited there. The one friend James was willing to describe
he nevertheless refused to name. Philips explained:

> But why don't you give up the name of the friend,
> as required by the state's counsel? I'll tell you
> frankly: it is because Frank James, unlike your pet
> Dick Liddil, never betrays a friend or foe. Situated as
> Frank James was, with the royal posse of the state
> after him, with a swarm of detectives and spies
> scenting his footsteps like sleuth-hounds, stimulat-
> ed to assassination by large rewards, it was perilous
> for any citizen to give this hunted man shelter,
> bread, or to be even the medium of a word of love
> from his far-away wife. Whatever the world may
> think of Frank James he is made of that stuff, before
> he would expose to public criticism, with his con-
> sent, the name of the man who assisted him, he
> would march to the deadfall on the scaffold.[45]

As much as Philips lionized James and his family as
embodiments of virtue, he portrayed Liddil as its opposite:

> Dick Liddil is so morally dead that like Lazarus he
> stinketh in the nostrils. . . . [He] is a coward because
> to save himself he would, through perjury, destroy
> his alleged confederate; a traitor he is to friendship,
> confidence and honor, even among thieves. He
> comes, just before this trial, to this State, crawling
> vampire-like, from jail, to drink the lifeblood of this
> defendant; to taint the sanctuary of justice with his
> false breath.[46]

Philips argued that the prosecution's witnesses were
unworthy of belief. Not only were they dishonorable, so,
too, was the prosecution, which should never have brought
a case against James, at least on such thin evidence.
Philips's speech moved members of the audience to tears.

Philips's oratory did not go unanswered. The final and
most notable prosecution rebuttal argument was made by
William Wallace. His closing argument to the jury was also

widely proclaimed as one of the finest ever delivered. Unlike Philips's discussion of themes of Southern honor, love of family, and loyalty, Wallace engaged in a detailed recitation, without notes, of the evidence and the court's instructions on the law. Wallace appealed to the jurors' reason; Philips appealed to their emotion. Even so, Wallace's speech contains several emotional appeals, in an effort to counteract Philips's:

> So the ill-fated Rock Island train departed on July 15, 1881; so it sped on like a meteor through the darkness until it reached the prairies of your own county. . . . Frank James was there to meet that train, gentlemen. . . . Let us look a moment at . . . the remarkable "hero" now on trial. . . . I am going now by the evidence—no fancy. Dick Liddil and Clarence Hite climb upon the tender to take charge of the engineer and fireman. Jesse James, Frank James, and Wood Hite rush into the smoking car from the front door. . . . The two tall men come right up to Conductor Westfall. . . . Just at that instant Jesse James—quick as a tiger for his victim, pulls the cruel trigger, and Westfall goes reeling down the aisle to the rear end of the car; as he goes the firing at him is continued. He opens the door, struggles out and falls dead from the train; dead in the harness! Dead on duty!
>
> Westfall has fallen, but the murderous fire still continues. Now it is contended "it was not intentional, do not know the particular man who did it," and so on. It makes no difference, you know from the evidence Frank James did it; but if you did not, you would know one of the band he belonged to— bent on robbery and murder—did it, and that is enough. . . . Penn and Frank McMillan now get up, and in search of a safer place, go to the rear platform of the "smoker" and take seats on the steps. . . .

Frank McMillan, sitting on the rear steps, says, "That's father's voice," . . . and he bounded to the door, and death met him as he came. The whizzing ball of the idle, roving assassin meets the sweated brow of hard-working Frank McMillan, he falls dead from the train, and the soil of free Missouri drinks up his honest blood. "Oh, he is but a poor laborer," I hear the [defense lawyers] say; "What is his life when measured with the precious existence of a daring, chivalric hero?" . . . Here is Mrs. Westfall to my right, clad in mourning, with a thick black veil hiding the saddened face; and Mrs. McMillan here to my left, similarly attired; and the little children hiding their faces in the folds of their mother's dresses—these, Colonel Philips, are the trophies of your kind of chivalry.

Some members of the audience erupted in applause, which the judge ordered the sheriff to put an end to, threatening to "clear the room" if it was repeated. Wallace then argued that Frank James was a criminal, not a legend. He ridiculed the idea that, having evaded capture until his brother had been killed and the rest of the gang captured or disbanded, he was entitled to be released when he turned himself in. He argued that the notion that James should be acquitted because of his war service was an insult to those Southern soldiers who did not devolve after the war into "pillage, plunder, train robbery and murder." Wallace concluded: "No matter who the defendant is, or was, or who his friends may be, we ask and implore you to stand bravely by your duty and your oaths given to your country and your God. Gentlemen, my task has ended. May the God . . . of the widow and the fatherless—of McMillan's wife and child—come into your hearts and guide you to a righteous verdict in this case. I thank you for your kind attention." The spectators erupted in applause, which was again quashed by the judge. The jury then adjourned to decide the fate of Frank James.[47]

◆◇◆◇◆

Despite Wallace's eloquence, the jury soon rendered a verdict of not guilty, and the Opera Hall erupted in applause, as some threw their hats into the air. After a dramatic, sixteen-day trial, Frank James had been acquitted. The defense themes that had been used in both the Clell Miller and Bill Ryan trials had been perfected: the prosecution had charged the wrong man, a family farmer who was nowhere near the scene of the crime, and the prosecution's chief witness was a liar. Frank James was the embodiment of the Lost Cause myth, and perhaps the first example of the potential power of the myth, at least when carefully directed at a select audience.[48]

Outside of rural Missouri and certain of the Southern states, the verdict resulted in disgust and outrage. Journalists argued that an acquittal by a jury from which Republicans had been excluded and to whom the Civil War card had been played had been an act of nullification. Even those not outraged believed that the verdict was the product of sympathy for the outlaw rather than a lack of evidence. Years later Wallace said that the jury was so sympathetic to Frank James and indignant at the state for prosecuting a man they regarded as the last returning soldier of the Confederate cause that no amount of evidence would have convinced them to convict him.[49]

After Frank James's acquittal in Gallatin, Wallace continued to pursue the former outlaw and brought him back to Jackson County, had him placed in jail in Independence, and intended to try him for robbing the train at Blue Cut in Jackson County on September 7, 1881. Wallace believed it would be impossible for James to escape that charge because Wallace had a strong case and because Jackson County marshal Cornelius Murphy, who summoned the jury that convicted Bill Ryan, would have summoned the jury to try Frank James and would have made sure that the jurors were fair and impartial. But there was still doubt as to the admissibility of Dick Liddil's testimony, since he had been convicted of a felony, and placed in the penitentiary before he joined the James Gang. His pardon may not have been enough to convince another judge to disregard the Missouri law at the time prohibiting testimony by convicted felons.

While Frank James was in jail at Independence awaiting trial, the Missouri Supreme Court handed down an opinion in the case of *State v. Grant* that said a witness convicted of larceny was not competent to testify. Every lawyer who read the opinion concluded, "That disqualifies Wallace's witness, Dick Liddil," and it did, just as if it had been written in the Frank James case. Without Liddil's testimony, Wallace could not proceed, and he dismissed the charges.[50]

But Frank James would have to face one more jury before he could return to something resembling a normal life.

TWELVE

AFTERMATH AND REVELATIONS

REVERBERATIONS OF THE FRANK JAMES not guilty verdict continued long after the jury was dismissed. A number of newspapers were distressed at the political influence they believed was brought to bear on James's behalf, including Governor Thomas Crittenden's testimony for the defense and the participation of former Union colonel Thomas Philips in his legal defense. With Philips having represented himself to the jury as a member of Missouri's Supreme Court Commission, his presence indicated to the jury that even though the nominal representative of the state was the prosecuting attorney, the real power of the state was there for the defense, in the person of a representative of the Supreme Court. According to the *St. Louis Post-Dispatch*, Philips took the case in exchange for a promised higher office. Sure enough, following the verdict, Philips was appointed to the Missouri Court of Appeals. The newspaper demanded an investigation by the state legislature.[1]

None of the jurors ever gave a formal interview, so it is difficult to know how they reached their verdict. In one newspaper account, one of the jurors said the jury's verdict was a result of its unwillingness to believe Dick Liddil. Shortly after the verdict, Kansas City police commissioner Henry Craig released Liddil's written confession and the confession of Clarence Hite. Both confessions described James's role in the Winston train robbery. The confession of Hite, James's cousin, shortly before his death in prison, when there seemed to be no reason to implicate Frank, was particularly powerful.[2]

Many believed that James got away with murder, and the years after the verdict were kind to him and his lawyers. Joshua Alexander served as a representative in the Missouri House, including a year as speaker. In 1901, he was appointed a circuit judge, and in 1907, he was elected to the US House. John Glover was elected a state representative one year after the trial. James Slover became a judge of the Jackson County Circuit Court. William Rush became an assistant US attorney. And former general Joseph Shelby, who had testified on James's behalf, was appointed a US marshal.

During the Civil War, Missouri was a western border state, divided between North and South. After the war, the victors sought to ally the state politically with the Union and emancipation. But those Missourians defeated in the war resisted fiercely and, in the end, achieved a form of nullification of their own. The 1884 Missouri state elections completed a transformation in Missouri politics. Former Confederate general John Marmaduke was elected governor. Like the Confederacy itself, the mythology of Confederate Missouri centered on the Lost Cause and a lost way of life. Southern sympathizers celebrated the legend of the noble guerrilla, a farm boy forced to fight to protect friend and family from Northern domination. Having been a symbol of this myth, it is perhaps fitting that Frank James became its beneficiary during his trial. Throughout the 1880s, Missouri continued to heal, with its rapidly developing Northern industry.[3]

◆-◇◆◇◆

Henry McDougal remained active in politics throughout his life, although he declined requests that he run for Congress. He continued to perform legal work and lobbying for the Rock Island and Wabash railroads, spending much of his time in Washington, DC. As a result of his connections to the railroads, his role in prosecuting Frank and Jesse James, and perhaps in part due to his connections as a result of membership in the Masonic Lodge, McDougal was personally acquainted with each of the ten US presidents who held office from 1866 through 1910—Andrew Johnson to William Howard Taft.[4]

In the 1880s, McDougal's law firm of Shanklin, Low & McDougal had more cases before the Missouri Supreme Court and won a higher percentage of them than any other law firm in the state. Shortly after the September 1883 trial of Frank James, McDougal decided to leave Gallatin for a larger city where he could pursue his profession and remain at home a bit more. Legal work was increasing rapidly in Kansas City, Missouri, in part because of the city's role as the regional railroad center. When McDougal had first visited there in 1867, Kansas City was a small village.

The railroads had transformed Kansas City into a leading American city. When the Civil War ended, the four thousand residents of the muddy Town of Kansas (which became Kansas City, Missouri) found that they occupied the right spot at the right time. The war had decimated Southern herds of cattle and depleted Northern cities of meat needed to feed Union troops. When the guns fell silent, the Northern beef-craving cities looked to the vast grasslands of Texas to supply their dinner tables.[5]

In 1867, the investors for the Hannibal & St. Joseph Railroad decided to build the first bridge over the Missouri River at Kansas City, Missouri, which jump-started the city's growth, connecting it by rail to Chicago and points east. The decision caused the town's population to explode, lined the pockets of railroad men who bought land in the West Bottoms (which became stockyards and meatpacking plants), and provided a rail link to Chicago, a meatpacking center. At the time, the Kansas Pacific Railroad out of Kansas City, Missouri, reached as far as Abilene, Kansas, 150 miles to the west. Stockyards and pens were built in Abilene, and Texas cattlemen were coaxed to drive their animals there by going north along the Chisholm Trail. Then the cattle were sent east by railroad to Kansas City. Driving their cattle north to Abilene was quicker than driving them to the railhead at Sedalia, Missouri, and also allowed the Texans to avoid the roving gangs of thieves and outlaws that plagued Missouri after the war.

In 1871, in the bridge's initial year of operations, thirteen thousand cattle and fifteen thousand hogs were slaughtered in the Kansas City West Bottoms and the meat sent east to Chicago. Kansas City quickly surpassed in population and importance its neighboring cities of Leavenworth, Kansas, and St. Joseph, Missouri.[6]

On arriving in Kansas City in January 1885, McDougal entered into a law partnership with Crittenden, known as Crittenden, McDougal and Stiles, which was located in the Brisbane Building at Seventh and Delaware streets. Crittenden considered McDougal a "first class lawyer, learned in the black letter wisdom of the books, and as pleasant a social companion as ever a man had or could wish to have." McDougal became the city counselor of Kansas City and wrote the city's charter. In 1885, McDougal successfully represented Kansas City before the US Supreme Court in the city's acquisition of the National Water Works plant, paving the way for the city's future growth.[7]

In September 1891, needing a young lawyer to travel and try railroad cases, McDougal entered into a law partnership with Frank Payne Sebree, which they called McDougal & Sebree. Their office was in the newest "skyscraper" in Kansas City, the ten-story New York Life Building at 20 West Ninth Street. Their primary clients were McDougal's clients, the Rock Island and Wabash railroads. In 1902, Governor Alexander Dockery appointed McDougal and Sebree to the Kansas City Board of Election Commissioners. Sebree went on to associate with Edgar Shook, David R. Hardy, and Charlie Bacon, leading to the eventual formation of the internationally known firm of Shook, Hardy & Bacon LLP.[8]

McDougal was unanimously elected president of the Kansas City and Missouri Bar Associations before he retired from active practice in 1902. On September 7, 1908, McDougal's daughter Florence married Ralph M. Roosevelt, a relation to President Teddy Roosevelt. McDougal died on December 17, 1915, at age seventy-one.[9]

●◆◇◆●

On June 14, 1887, William H. Wallace married Elizabeth G. Chiles of Independence. After the Frank James trial, Wallace went on to successfully prosecute many more cases, and he was narrowly defeated in 1906 for the Democratic nomination for Congress for the district including Jackson County. On April 3, 1907, Wallace became a Kansas City Criminal Court judge. In 1908, he ran unsuccessfully for governor. Wallace believed that his role as prosecutor in the James trial was a primary reason he lost his races to be Missouri governor, a US representative, and a US senator. Although McDougal left Gallatin for the growing railroad town of Kansas City, he and Wallace remained close friends until the end. On the inside cover of his 1914 book, *Speeches and Writings,* Wallace wrote, "To my friend Judge H. C. McDougal." Wallace wished Frank James well and told him when they met after his 1882 trial in Gallatin that he had "tried to hang him but could not, and hoped he would make of himself a good citizen." Wallace died on October 21, 1937, at age eighty-nine.[10]

◆◇◆◇◆

Jesse James's wife, Zee James, in an effort to raise money, contracted to endorse Frank Triplett's effort to further the James mythology in the form of his book *The Life, Times and Treacherous Death of Jesse James*. Zee and her mother-in-law also supplied some items that were associated with the story—photographs, guns, and a piece of the "bomb" thrown by the Pinkertons in the 1875 raid on the James farm—for engravings used in the book. The book attacked Governor Crittenden, saying he should be tried for murder.[11]

◆◇◆◇◆

Shortly after the dismissal of the Blue Cut train robbery charges, Frank James was arrested and charged with the March 11, 1881, robbery of $5,200 from an army paymaster on the banks of the Tennessee River near Muscle Shoals, Alabama. Because a federal employee was robbed of a federal payroll, James was tried in federal court in Huntsville, Alabama. A large, cheering crowd greeted his train as it arrived at the city depot. Newspaper reporters from far and wide descended on the tiny town, filling the boarding rooms and hotels.

This time the prosecutor was William H. Smith, a former Reconstruction governor of Alabama who, through the patronage system, had managed to get himself appointed US attorney. Smith proved to be no match for the formidable legal team assembled on behalf of Frank James. He was represented by Leroy Pope Walker, who happened to be the former secretary of war for the Confederacy. Joining Walker was Raymond F. Sloan, a Nashville attorney who had known James as Ben Woodson and who had testified for him at Gallatin. Sloan had the benefit of having watched a good part, if not all, of the Gallatin trial, which proved to be a dress rehearsal for the Huntsville trial. Rounding out the legal team was James Newman of Winchester, Tennessee.

The defense team made sure the jury was made up largely of Confederate veterans. Walker, who was well known and respected as a former Confederate cabinet officer, emphasized in his opening statement that Frank James had fought for the "Cause," having served with the Missouri "irregulars" under William Quantrill. Prosecutor Smith countered with the facts of the case. He put witnesses on the stand who identified James as one of the three robbers, but the witnesses could not withstand Walker's withering cross-examination. The witnesses were forced to admit that the robbers had been masked, making any identification of Frank James speculative at best. The witnesses also contradicted themselves in their descriptions of the robbers.

As in Gallatin, Dick Liddil was the state's star witness, and, as in Gallatin, he was subjected to a brutal cross-examination. The Alabama federal court held that Alabama law did not exclude the testimony of a convicted felon when a governor had pardoned the witness, so Liddil was allowed to testify. During his cross-examination, Walker effectively made Liddil out to be a liar and career criminal, intent on destroying the character of an upright and honorable man like Frank James so Liddil could avoid going to the gallows for murder. The defense then called a parade of witnesses who swore that they saw Frank James in Nashville on the day of the robbery.

Walker was brilliant in his closing argument. At the end of the ten-day trial, on April 26, 1882, the jury, after six hours of deliberating, announced a verdict of not guilty to rousing cheers and applause from the spectators. Frank James was immediately arrested by the sheriff of Cooper County, Missouri, for the train robbery of July 7, 1876, at Rocky Cut near Otterville, but in February 1885, charges were dropped because the state's main witness had died. Frank James was now a free man.[12]

After the Gallatin and Huntsville juries found him not guilty, Frank James had a long career in the horse-racing business. On May 9, 1889, he attended the Kentucky Derby, one of the most memorable and controversial derbies of all time because of its disputed finish. The largest derby crowd up to that point, twenty-five thousand people, attended. The race was one of the major upsets in the history of the derby. Proctor Knott was the 1-2 favorite, while Spokane, a chestnut colt, trailed the field at 10-1. At that time there were no charts, newspaper handicapping, or printed information on the horses and their records. It was up to the bettor to get his information on his own as best he could. After studying Spokane's gait and physique, Frank James bet $5,000 on the long shot. He won.[13]

Frank James's reputation as a keen judge of horseflesh spread quickly throughout the racing world. He and Annie moved to St. Louis in about 1883. By October 1895, he was starting races at the St. Louis Fair Grounds Race Course. He earned a reputation as being one of the most profitable starters in the country for the tracks. His appearances at the races sometimes attracted more spectators than the horses.

◆◇◆◇◆

Frank James was lucky indeed. Most of the other members of the gang were either dead or behind bars. Several months earlier, Bill Ryan, who was dying of tuberculosis, had been released by the governor. On May 4, 1884, Charlie Ford, terminally ill with the same disease and addicted to morphine, shot himself. Bob Younger died of tuberculosis at the Stillwater Penitentiary on September 16, 1889. On June 18, 1892, Bob Ford was gunned down in Creed, Colorado. Dick Liddil had a more peaceful end, dying of a heart attack at a racetrack in July 1901. Jim Younger committed suicide in 1902.

And on May 4, 1889, newspaperman John Newman Edwards died of a heart attack in Jefferson City.

Frank James moved to Oklahoma in 1909, where he raised horses. When his mother died in 1911, he and Annie returned to the Clay County family farm, where he greeted visitors and charged admission for tours of the farm. He died on February 18, 1915, at age seventy-two. As mourners came to pay their respects, the sputtering of automobile engines caused nervous horses to snort and stomp their hooves.

Jesse James's son, Jesse Edwards James (named in honor of John Edwards), became a lawyer.

EPILOGUE

It has been over forty years since British historian Eric J. Hobsbawm explored the concept of the social or "noble" robber. Hobsbawm explained that social bandits are "peasant outlaws, whom the lord and state regard as criminals, but who remain within peasant society, and are considered by their people as heroes, as champions, avengers, fighters for justice, perhaps even leaders of liberty and, in any case, as men to be admired, helped and supported." He cites England's Robin Hood, a character of dubious historical authenticity, as the archetypal "noble robber." Hobsbawm also admits, however, that "such is the need for heroes and champions, that if there are no real ones, then suitable candidates are pressed into service. In real life, most Robin Hoods were far from noble."[1]

In real life, Jesse James, too, was "far from noble." His Robin Hood story was crafted by John Newman Edwards, his chief propagandist. Frank and Jesse James were not the only outlaws to be compared to Robin Hood by journalists seeking to sell newspapers. The same sort of overblown claims were later made about the Doolin-Dalton Gang: "Bill Doolin . . . is as fully a romantic figure as Robin Hood ever cut." William Quantrill was also compared to a noble robber/Robin Hood in a popular folk ballad.[2]

Viewing Frank and Jesse James and their gang members through the eyes of the prosecutors who put them on trial allows us to see them more clearly as little more than murderers and robbers who shot down unarmed men in cold blood, leaving widows and orphans; robbed women; and beat senseless unarmed train and express car employees. Jesse James didn't steal because he was poor and hungry, or to give to the poor. He stole because he wanted more, and he wanted it without paying or working for it. He stole to live high, ride thoroughbred horses, wear nice clothes, buy drinks in saloons, and do some high-stakes gambling. He wanted the rewards without the labor and, to get them, took from others what they had worked hard to gain.

After Frank's trials and Jesse's death, facts began to emerge as to how they spent their stolen money. During August 1876, in the course of scouting targets for his next bank robbery in Minneapolis, Jesse visited a bordello kept by Molly Ellsworth. She recognized him from the days she kept a similar establishment in St. Louis. "I used to know him well," she said.[3] The James brothers had been frequent visitors to the health resorts and horse tracks frequented by the sporting crowd of their day, such as Monegaw Springs, Missouri, Hot Springs, Arkansas, and Long Branch, New Jersey. The outlaws were seen at Hot Springs shortly before the January 15, 1874, stagecoach robbery between Hot Springs and Malvern, Arkansas. Jim Cummins, a Quantrill veteran who was a friend of the Miller family's, said that Ed Miller and Jesse James "gambled frequently and lost considerable money. After one of his racehorses lost, Jesse was broke. He finally had to sell his horse to get back home."[4]

Given Jesse's fondness for cards, gambling, and fast horses, it is possible, if not likely, that some of his crimes were committed with a view toward paying off his gambling debts and providing a bankroll for the late-June-through-October racing season. In fact, many of his robberies were committed just before, during, or just after the racing season.[5]

Frank also enjoyed horse racing. While living in Nashville, he entered his horse Jewel Maxey for the gents' riding stakes at Nashville two successive years, winning first prize the first time and second money the second year. The Jameses also raced their horses at the Nashville Blood-

Horse Association track, in Nashville near the Cumberland River. On October 4, 1879, four days before the Glendale train robbery, Jewel Maxey finished second in the Tennessee State Fair.[6]

William H. Wallace, who studied the men and their crimes for years, perhaps more closely than anyone else, came to the conclusion that "they robbed for money, not for revenge."[7] But for the pen of Edwards and Jesse James's alliterative name, he might be no more famous today than one of the Dalton or Younger brothers. Jesse James's most dangerous weapon was not his politics—it was his pistol. He was not the cavalier of Confederate legend—he was a murderer with a press agent. He was not the last rebel of the Civil War—he was one of the most successful robbers following the Civil War.

How did law enforcement deal with Frank and Jesse James? Not very effectively. In fact, it was their inability to turn themselves in and be assured of a fair trial without fear of a lynching, a fact accepted by their Southern sympathizers, that gave them an excuse for their fugitive status. The failure of the rule of law also generated sympathy and support for the James brothers by Missouri's Southerners, who were familiar with the injustices of some of the state's post-Civil War laws.

The trials of the James-Younger Gang members demonstrate the truism that the facts are not always as they first appear. Gallatin authorities rushed to judgment and concluded that Frank James was one of the gunmen responsible for John Sheets's murder based primarily on the physical evidence—the horse—left behind after the murder. In fact, however, Frank James was most likely not at Gallatin. If he had been captured after Sheets's murder, he may have been hanged for a crime he did not commit.

In a society based on the rule of law, American citizens must be treated equally, including those suspected of criminal actions. Governor Crittenden based his apparent violations of the law and due process in sanctioning state-sponsored assassination on his assertion that the James brothers and their gang members were wartime enemies, not criminal defendants. If the rule of law can be suspended based solely on a declaration that a society is at war, however, then that society risks abdicating its citizens' basic protections to government officials who may not be elected or known, and to whom is left the decision as to whether an individual is an enemy and therefore undeserving of the basic protections of the law and due process.

Due process of law is the foundation of the freedom of the individual against the arbitrary authority of government. The concept originates in the celebrated Clause 39 of the English Magna Carta, which states, "No free man shall be taken or imprisoned . . . except by the lawful judgment of his peers or by the law of the land." The Magna Carta became one of the touchstones of the American Declaration of Independence and Constitution. The concept of due process of law can be found in the Fifth Amendment of the Constitution: "No person shall be . . . deprived of life, liberty, or property, without due process of law." In 1868, the phrase entered the Constitution again, in the Fourteenth Amendment: "No State shall deprive any person of life, liberty, or property without due process of law." Recent presidential administrations have been criticized for bending the rule of law in efforts to combat terrorism, albeit primarily regarding non-US citizens.

The state-sponsored assassination of Jesse James caused a similar public outcry. In fact, the assassination may have been largely responsible for his enduring legend as a martyr for the Lost Cause. John Edwards published an obituary raging against his murder, saying James "refused to be banished from his birthright, and when he was hunted he turned savagely about and hunted his hunters." Edwards described the murder as cowardly and unnecessary, saying "this so-called law is an outlaw."[8]

Even though law enforcement had the latest technology available—the railroads, the telegraph, and a nationwide police force in the Pinkerton Detective Agency—technology did not prevail over indigenous criminals familiar with the terrain and supported by a sympathetic community. In fact, the collateral damage caused by Pinkerton's use of nineteenth century technology (incendiary devices) on the James cabin, killing a child and mangling Mrs. Samuel's right arm, provoked outrage and became a rallying point in Missouri against law enforcement.

The Gallatin trial of Frank James demonstrates the power of myth, even in the face of stark facts. The trial also reflects that trials are not just about truth, they are also about clarity. The most convincing case usually wins, not necessarily the truer one. As we've seen, the prosecutors in the Clell Miller and Frank James trials seemed at times to have formidable cases, but the defense teams constructed coherent, unified theories and stories that successfully exploited flaws in the prosecutions' cases.

The defense lawyers in the trials discussed here learned from one trial to the next. They were perhaps overconfident in defending Bill Ryan, given the location of the trial in the heart of Jackson County and the home of Ryan and other gang members and their supporters. They did not repeat their mistakes in successfully defending Frank James in Gallatin in 1883. That trial was not merely an episode in the story of the James-Younger Gang, as most historians have tended to treat it. The verdict was also the first, and perhaps the most important, victory for those committed to the Lost Cause myth, a myth that continues to be propagated today.[9]

The Civil War was about slavery and the definition of human liberty: are all people created equal? The war was about our obligation to live up to the best part of ourselves. Slavery was evil, and it had to be defeated.

Today, a new battle for history is being waged, with some arguing that noble Southern aristocrats fought because of states' rights, not slavery. Journalists, pulp-fiction writers, and Hollywood have fed the public appetite for the noble outlaw myth by perpetuating the legend, rather than realistically portraying the James-Younger Gang as selfish bank robbers and cold-blooded bushwhackers.[10]

Abraham Lincoln hoped that we may be guided by the better angels of our nature, even when the darker angels beat their wings all around us. That's a prayer worth repeating. Despite the noble robber myth, little evidence exists that Frank and Jesse James were guided in their robberies and murders by their better angels.

TIMELINE

December 28, 1841	Reverend Robert James marries Zerelda Cole
Spring 1842	Robert and Zerelda James move to Centerville (now Kearney), Missouri
January 10, 1843	Birth of Frank James, son of Robert and Zerelda
December 9, 1844	Birth of Henry C. McDougal
September 5, 1847	Birth of Jesse James, son of Robert and Zerelda
July 16, 1848	Birth of Emma Chapdu, future wife of Henry McDougal
November 25, 1849	Birth of Susan James, daughter of Robert and Zerelda
August 1850	Death of Robert James
May 1854	Kansas-Nebraska bill becomes law
May 21, 1854	Missourians sack Lawrence, Kansas
March 14, 1861	Abraham Lincoln's inauguration
April 12, 1861	Fort Sumter fired on
April 17, 1861	Virginia State Convention adopts ordinance of secession
May 1861	McDougal's brother John enlists in Confederate army
July 21, 1861	First Battle of Bull Run
July 27, 1861	McDougal enlists in Union army
August 10, 1861	Frank James at Battle of Wilson's Creek, Missouri
August 21, 1863	Frank James and Cole Younger with William Quantrill at Lawrence, Kansas, massacre
May 1864	Jesse James joins William "Bloody Bill" Anderson's guerrillas
August 7, 1864	McDougal musters out of Union army, becomes a clerk in the Quartermaster's Depot at Gallipolis, Ohio
August 13, 1864	Jesse James is wounded
September 27, 1864	Centralia, Missouri, massacre
October 26, 1864	Captain Samuel Cox kills Bloody Bill Anderson; Clell Miller captured

April 9, 1865	General Robert E. Lee surrenders to General Ulysses S. Grant at Appomattox Court House, Virginia
May 15, 1865	Jesse James is shot on Salt Pond Road
July 6, 1865	Quantrill dies
July 26, 1865	Frank James surrenders at Samuel's Depot, Kentucky
February 13, 1866	Clay County Savings Association Bank robbed at Liberty, Missouri
June 1866	McDougal meets with President Andrew Johnson
October 25, 1866	McDougal arrives in Missouri
October 30, 1866	Lexington, Missouri, bank (Alexander Mitchell & Co.) robbery
December 13, 1866	Arch Clement killed
May 22, 1867	Richmond, Missouri, bank (Hughes & Wasson) robbery
September 3, 1867	Death of US senator James A. McDougall
November 17, 1867	Reno Gang robs Gallatin, Missouri, treasurer's office
1868	McDougal becomes city clerk in Gallatin
March 17, 1868	Mob takes Andy McGuire and James M. Devers from Richmond, Missouri, jail and hangs them because of their suspected role in the May 22, 1867, Richmond bank robbery
March 20,1868	Russellville, Kentucky, bank robbery
November 6, 1868	McDougal licensed as lawyer
1869	McFerran & McDougal law firm established
November 2, 1869	McDougal marries Emma Chapdu
December 7, 1869	Murder of John Sheets, cashier of Daviess County Savings Association and former Union army captain, and theft of Daniel Smoote's horse
December 14, 1869	Deputy Sheriff John S. Thomason attempts to arrest Frank and Jesse James for Sheets murder
January 1870	Reward notices published for James brothers for Sheets murder
January 10, 1870	McDougal files *Daniel Smoote v. Frank and Jesse James* Petition, Affidavit, Writ of Attachment, and Attachment Bond
February 4, 1870	Return of Service on Writ of Attachment on one bay mare by Sheriff William F. Flint
March 12, 1870	Sheriff's Return filed with court regarding left writ and petition "with a white person a member

	of the family where the within named Jesse James and Frank James usually reside over the age of 15 years"
April 1870	McDougal elected mayor of Gallatin
April 11, 1870	Attorney Samuel Richardson files Motion to Quash Return of Sheriff on behalf of Frank and Jesse James
May 1870	Murder indictment filed against Frank and Jesse James for Sheets murder
May 1870	Grand larceny indictment filed against Frank and Jesse James for theft of Daniel Smoote's horse
June 14, 1870	Writ of Attachment on Jesse James's horse issued to Clay County sheriff
June 16, 1870	Sheriff's Return: Clay County sheriff O. P. Moss states "Jesse James and Frank James cannot be found in my County"
July 12, 1870	Smoote affidavit that "Jesse James and Frank James have absconded or absented themselves from usual place of abode in this state so that the ordinary process of law cannot be served upon them"
July 1870	Jesse James's alibi affidavits published in *Kansas City Times* newspaper
July 14, 1870	Continuance granted by the court in *Smoote v. Frank and Jesse James*
August 28– September 15, 1870	Notice of Smoote lawsuit published in *Gallatin Weekly Democrat*
September 1870	Southwestern branch of Chicago, Rock Island & Pacific Railroad comes to Gallatin
October 10, 1870	Affidavit of Publication of notice of lawsuit filed with court
October 11, 1870	Plaintiff's Proof of publication approved by court
October 14, 1870	Court Order: "Defendants [Frank and Jesse James] have 45 days in which to Plead" in response to Smoote petition
November 21, 1870	Sheriff Moss states Jesse James not found in Clay County on murder warrant and grand larceny warrant
December 14, 1870	*Smoote v. Frank and Jesse James* case continued by agreement
April 11, 1871	Frank and Jesse James, by their attorney, file answer to plaintiff's petition

April 21, 1871	Continuance granted by court
June 3, 1871	Robbery of Ocobock Brothers Bank in Corydon, Iowa
July 18, 1871	Continuance of trial date by agreement
October 30, 1871	Defendants withdraw answer by their attorney
October 30, 1871	Court judgment: "This cause coming on for trial, the defendants come not but make default, the court finds for the plaintiff in the sum of $223.50, and that the property of the defendants attached be sold to satisfy."
November 4, 1871	Susan James marries Allen Parmer in Kentucky
February 29, 1872	Undercover detective R. W. Westfall meets with Clell Miller at his home in Liberty
March 1872	Miller's arrest and indictment for bank robbery
April 29, 1872	Bank of Columbia, Kentucky, robbery
May 9, 1872	Former Daviess County sheriff William Flint, for Daviess County sheriff Thomas Flint, states Jesse James not found in Daviess County
September 26, 1872	Kansas City Exposition robbery
September 29, 1872	*Kansas City Times* editor John Edwards's "The Chivalry of Crime" editorial published
October 22–26, 1872	Miller's trial for Corydon, Iowa, bank robbery
November 1872	McDougal elected judge of Probate Court
May 27, 1873	Ste. Genevieve, Missouri, bank robbery
July 21, 1873	Council Bluffs, Iowa, train robbery
January 31, 1874	Gads Hill, Missouri, train robbery
March 5, 1874	Pinkerton Detective Joseph Whicher murdered
April 24, 1874	Jesse James marries Zerelda "Zee" Mimms
June 1874	Frank James marries Annie Ralston
August 30, 1874	North Lexington, Missouri, stagecoach robbery
December 8, 1874	Muncie, Kansas, train robbery
December 1874	McDougal forms law partnership with Marcus Low
January 25, 1875	Pinkerton raid on James farm cabin
March 17, 1875	Missouri General Assembly proposes resolution granting amnesty to James brothers
April 12, 1875	Jesse James's neighbor, Daniel Askew, murdered for his alleged complicity in the Pinkerton attack on James cabin
September 5, 1875	Huntington, West Virginia, bank robbery
January 1876	Shanklin, Low and McDougal law firm formed
July 6, 1876	Rocky Cut, Missouri, train robbery

September 7, 1876	First National Bank of Northfield, Minnesota, bank robbery; Clell Miller killed
October 8, 1879	Glendale, Missouri, train robbery
July 9, 1880	Tucker Bassham arrested for Glendale robbery
July 15, 1880	Bassham's preliminary hearing
September 3, 1880	Robbery near Mammoth Cave, Kentucky
March 11, 1881	Muscle Shoals, Alabama, government payroll robbery
March 25, 1881	James Gang member William Ryan arrested in Tennessee for Glendale, Missouri, train robbery
July 15, 1881	Winston, Missouri, train robbery; conductor William Westfall and passenger murdered
September 7, 1881	Blue Cut, Missouri, train robbery
September 22–27, 1881	Ryan trial and conviction in Independence, Missouri, for Glendale, Missouri, train robbery
First week of November 1881	Jesse James moves from Kansas City to St. Joseph, Missouri
December 5, 1881	James Gang members Dick Liddil and Bob Ford kill gang member and James brothers cousin Wood Hite
January 13, 1882	Ford meets secretly with Missouri governor Thomas Crittenden and Clay County sheriff Henry Timberlake and offers to provide information leading to arrest of Frank and Jesse James in exchange for a reward and pardon
January 24, 1882	Liddil surrenders to authorities and offers to provide information leading to arrest of Frank and Jesse James in exchange for a pardon
February 11, 1882	Clarence Hite, brother of Wood Hite and cousin of James brothers, arrested based on information as to his whereabouts provided by Liddil
February 20, 1882	Murder indictment filed against Frank James in killing of Westfall in Winston, Missouri, train robbery; robbery indictment filed against Frank James, Jesse James, and Clarence Hite in Winston train robbery
March 30–April 5, 1882	Wallace prosecutes, then drops robbery charges against John Bugler for the Blue Cut, Missouri, train robbery
April 3, 1882	Jesse James killed by Robert Ford in St. Joseph
April 4, 1882	Wallace goes to St. Joseph to view Jesse James's body

April 17, 1882	Ford brothers plead guilty to murdering Jesse James and are convicted, then pardoned
October 4, 1882	Frank James surrenders to Governor Crittenden
October 20–27, 1882	Ford brothers trial for murder of Wood Hite
February 6, 1883	Jackson County marshal G. W. Page states he cannot find Frank James in Jackson County on murder warrant
February 8, 1883	Grand jury indictment for Sheets murder filed against Frank James
August 21– September 6, 1883	Frank James trial for Winston, Missouri, train robbery and murder
October 16, 1883	Dismissal of charges against Frank James in Sheets murder
April 26, 1884	Frank James found not guilty of the Muscle Shoals, Alabama, government payroll robbery
January 1, 1885	McDougal moves to Kansas City, Missouri
February 21, 1885	Charges against Frank James for Rocky Cut, Missouri, train robbery dismissed
1885–89	McDougal and Crittenden law firm
September 10, 1891	McDougal enters into partnership with Frank P. Sebree
1894	McDougal unanimously elected president of Missouri Bar
1896	McDougal serves as Kansas City counselor
1902	McDougal retires, ends law partnership with Sebree
February 18, 1915	Death of Frank James
December 17, 1915	Death of Henry McDougal

NOTES

PROLOGUE

1. Kenneth M. Stampp, ed., *The Causes of the Civil War* (New York: Simon & Schuster, 1991), 152–53; Paul Finkelman, "The End of War and Slavery Yields a New Racial Order," *American Bar Journal* (April 2011), 45–46; Abraham Lincoln, Second Inaugural Address, March 4, 1865.

2. William B. Hassletine, ed., *A Tragic Conflict: The Civil War and Reconstruction* (New York: George Braziller, 1962), 5 ("fiery crucible"); Gary W. Gallagher and John T. Noland, eds., *The Myth of the Lost Cause and Civil War History* (Bloomington: Indiana University Press, 2000); James Oliver Horton and Lois E. Horton, eds., *Slavery and Public History: The Tough Stuff of American Memory* (Chapel Hill: University of North Carolina Press, 2006), 170–71; Harold Holzer, "An Inescapable Conflict," *American Bar Journal* (April 2011), 38–40. Many historians also reject "states' rights" as the reason for secession particularly since the Confederate Constitution provided little in the way of additional states' rights from those in the U.S. Constitution. In fact, there was one key difference—states in the Confederacy did not have the right to outlaw slavery. "Southern Discomfort," *Kansas City Star*, June 12, 2011, A-1, 12. However, "if slavery is the reason secession came," that does not mean that it was the reason one million Southern men later fought. Perhaps 90 percent of the men who wore gray did not own slaves; they may have "fought and died because they felt their Southern homeland had been invaded and their natural instinct was to protect home and hearth." William C. Davis, *The Lost Cause: Myths and Realities of the Confederacy* (Lawrence: University Press of Kansas, 1996), 182–83.

3. This was cultivated during the war. In his memoir, *Co. Aytch*, Confederate soldier Sam Watkins recalls how in a sermon delivered to the troops before the battle of Chickamauga, the regimental reverend, "began to pitch in on the Yankee nation, and gave them particlar fits as to their geneology. He said that we of the South had descended from the royal and aristocratic blood of the Huguenots of France, and the Cavaliers of England, etc.; but that the Yankees were the descendents of the crop-eared Puritans and witch burners, who came over in the Mayflower, and settled at Plymouth Rock." Sam Watkins, *Co. Aytch, or a Side Show of the Big Show. A New Edition Introduced and Annotated by Philip Leigh* (Yardley, PA: Westholme, 2013), 103–4.

4. Gallagher and Nolan, *Myth of the Lost Cause*, 1, 16.

CHAPTER ONE: THE GRAND RIVER COUNTRY

1. Colonel Joseph Hamilton Daviess of Kentucky was the first lawyer west of the Appalachian Mountains to argue a case before the US Supreme Court. Daviess was also the US district attorney for Kentucky who, in his official capacity, wrote letters to President Thomas Jefferson warning him of conspiratorial activities by Aaron Burr. Daviess was killed while he commanded the dragoons of the Indiana Militia at the 1811 Battle of Tippecanoe. *The History of Daviess County, Missouri* (Kansas City: Birdsall & Dean, 1882), 498.

2. Gallatin was named after Albert Gallatin, who was appointed secretary of the treasury in 1801 by President Thomas Jefferson. Walter Williams, ed., *A History of Northwest Missouri* (Chicago: Lewis, 1915), 459–60; Darryl Wilkerson, "First Settlers Found a Hunter's Delight," *Daviess County Historical Society*, June 24, 2004; "An Account of the 1869 James Gang Robbery," *Gallatin Democrat*, December 7, 1913; Robert J. Wybrow, "Gallatin," unpublished manuscript; Joseph H. McGee, *Story of the Grand River Country: Memoirs of Major Joseph H. McGee, 1821–1905* (Gallatin: North Missourian Press, 1909), 11–13.

3. Mayna Milstead, "Murder in the Streets of Gallatin," *Gallatin North Missourian*, September 15, 1993; David Stark, "Who Was Capt. John Sheets?" *Daviess County Historical Society*, March 24, 2004.

4. McGee, *Story of the Grand River Country*, 11–13; "What's the Mormon War?" *Gallatin North Missourian*, June 9, 1993; Brandon G. Kinney, *The Mormon War: Zion and the Missouri Extermination Order of 1838* (Yardley: PA, Westholme, 2011), 133–40, 158–59.

5. National Archives Veterans Records for John W. Sheets, including Company Muster Roll, Muster-in Roll, and Muster-out Roll (in author's possession); John Taylor Hughes, *Doniphan's Expedition: An Account of the U.S. Army Operations in the Great American Southwest* (Chicago: Rio Grande Press, 1962); *History of Daviess County*, 498; Stark, "Who Was Capt. John Sheets?"

6. John C. Leopard and R. M. McCammon, *History of Daviess and Gentry Counties, Missouri* (Topeka, KS: Historical Publishing, 1922), 102–3; David Stark, "Deadly Skirmish in Daviess County," *Daviess County Historical Society*, March 6, 2004.

7. David Stark, "Bad Luck Seemed to Be Lot in Life of Capt. John Sheets," *Gallatin North Missourian*, August 18, 2004. The murdered men were relatives of John Sheets's first wife, Martha R. Casey, who married Sheets on November 4, 1850. The couple had two children: Earnest, born in 1852, and Mary, born in 1855. Sadly, Martha died on November 2, 1856. In September 1861, Sheets married Mary G. Clingan, the daughter of a Gallatin hotel owner, Major Thomas Clingan.

8. David Stark, "Argument Over 50-Cents Leads to Murder," *Gallatin North Missourian*, March 17, 2004; *History of Daviess County*, 497–98.

9. Milstead, "Murder in the Streets."

10. "Capt. John W. Sheets," *Weekly Western Register*, December 16, 1869. In his highly acclaimed biography, *Jesse James: Last Rebel of the Civil War* (New York: Random House, 2002), T. J. Stiles misidentifies McDowell as "a lawyer who kept his office in the bank building" (203). McDowell arrived in Gallatin in early 1869. On March 6, 1869, he was sponsored by Sheets and Harfield Davis to be a notary public, a useful certification for a bank clerk at the time. It would have taken approximately a year of study to become licensed as an attorney in Missouri at the time. After Sheets's murder, McDowell became an attorney, before moving back to Alleghany City, Pennsylvania. *History of Daviess County*, 860. See also Williams, *History of Northwest Missouri*, 457, describing McDowell as "an assistant in the bank"; *Gallatin Democrat*, November 2, 1899; *History of Daviess and Gentry Counties*, 176–77; Darryl Wilkinson, "Samuel Cox—A Daviess County Hero," *Daviess County Historical Society*, March 17, 2004.

11. "Sensational Surprises," *St. Louis Republican*, August 23, 1883. Jesse James had kin in Gallatin. Philip Wirt, who had been there almost as long as Sheets, owned a small dry-goods store on the southeast corner of the town square. Wirt's store was the primary meeting place in the county and was called "Secessionist Corner" during the Civil War. Wirt was Jesse James's uncle by marriage. Wirt had a son, William, about Jesse's age, and the boys likely played together in Gallatin when they were young. David Stark, "In-Laws of Old West Outlaws Tied to Daviess County," *Gallatin North Missourian*, February 22, 1995. Wirt's mother, Mary Simms, was a sister-in-law of Zerelda James's, Jesse's mother.

12. "Sensational Surprises," *St. Louis Republican*, August 23, 1883.

13. *Kansas City Journal*, January 10, 1923; Milstead, "Murder in the Streets."

CHAPTER TWO: THE MURDER OF CAPTAIN JOHN W. SHEETS

1. "Sensational Surprises," *St. Louis Republican*; *History of Daviess County*, 498, 550–51.

2. "A Most Horrible Murder," *St. Joseph Daily Gazette*, December 8, 1869; "Terrible Tragedy," *St. Joseph Gazette*, December 9, 1869; "Bank Robbery at Gallatin Mo.," *Kansas City Daily Journal of Commerce*, December 9, 1869, 4, col. 3; *History of Daviess County*, 498. Banknotes were issued by banks, stamped with their identity, and made redeemable in the recently created national paper currency, nicknamed the greenback.

3. *History of Daviess County*, 498; "The Only Living Witness Tells How Jesse James Held Up a Bank in Gallatin, Mo. 73 Years Ago," *St. Louis Globe-Democrat*, October 17, 1942, 1, col. 3.

4. Henry Clay McDougal, *Recollections: 1844–1909* (Kansas City, MO: Franklin Hudson, 1910), 498; "Only Living Witness," *St. Louis Globe-Democrat*, October 17, 1942. Some modern accounts of the crime have Sheets

sitting down and writing when he was shot. William A. Settle, *Jesse James Was His Name, or, Fact and Fiction Concerning the Careers of the Notorious James Brothers of Missouri* (Lincoln: University of Nebraska Press, 1977), 38. I lean toward the 1882 *History of Daviess County* description of the crime because it was written closer to the events described and appears to be more accurate.

5. "Only Living Witness," *St. Louis Globe-Democrat*.

6. Ibid.

7. Ibid. Seventy-three years later, Edward Clingan misidentified the building across the street from the bank as the post office and the building next to the bank as a drugstore. Gallatin records and the town plan indicate that the dance hall was across the street from the bank in 1869, and a hotel stood south of the bank. The bank moved one block east in the 1870s, across the street from the post office and next to a drugstore.

8. January 10, 1870, affidavit of Daniel Smoote filed in *Daniel Smoote v. Frank and Jesse James,* Daviess County, Missouri Court of Common Pleas. William Settle spells Smoote's last name "Smoot." Settle, *Jesse James Was His Name*, 39. T. J. Stiles spells it "Smoots." Stiles, *Jesse James*, 204. Smoote's affidavit spells it "Smoote."

9. "Terrible Tragedy," *St. Joseph Daily Gazette*. A warrant was a promise to pay, often issued by local governments.

"Most Horrible Murder," *St. Joseph Daily Gazette*.

10. "The Gallatin Tragedy. The Murderers Closely Pursued," *St. Joseph Daily Gazette*, December 10, 1869; "The Gallatin Murderers," *Weekly Western Register*, December 16, 1869; *History of Daviess County*, 498.

11. Jesse was accused, probably for the first time, of being involved in one of the earlier robberies when it was said "he was implicated in the robbery at Richmond." "The Gallatin Bank Robbers," *St. Joseph Daily Gazette*, December 17, 1869.

12. "The Gallatin Bank Robbers: They are Surprised in Clay County and Fired Upon," *Kansas City Times*, December 16, 1869.

13. Ted P. Yeatman, *Frank and Jesse James: The Story Behind the Legend* (Nashville: Cumberland House, 2001), 95.

14. *History of Daviess County,* 466–67, 542; McDougal, *Recollections*, 194; "Only Living Witness," *St. Louis Globe-Democrat*. Barnum was paid $19.95 for his expenses incurred "in pursuing murderers of Capt. Sheets." Minutes of Daviess County Court of Common Pleas, August 1, 1870, Book D, 272.

15. "Frank James on Old Days," *Washington Post*, March 7, 1915.

16. "The Gallatin Bank Robbers," *Kansas City Times*, December 16, 1869; "The Gallatin Bank Robbers," *St. Joseph Daily Gazette*; "The Gallatin, Daviess County, Murder," *Liberty Tribune*, December 17, 1869.

17. Smoote was 53 at the time of Captain Sheets's murder, married, and had seven children. He had been a well-to-do farmer before the war, primarily

because of the seven slaves he owned, who helped him farm 540 acres of land west of Gallatin. After the war and the loss of his slaves, Smoote was in financial difficulty, and he would be a defendant in at least three lawsuits filed by his creditors. Daviess County Civil Court records located in Gallatin, file drawer numbers 145–47.

18. This is not to say that all of America's frontier was devoid of law and order. As Mark Ellis notes in *Law and Order in Buffalo Bill's Country*, many of America's early settlers brought a respect for law and justice to the frontier with them. Mark Ellis, *Law and Order in Buffalo Bill's Country: Legal Culture and Community on the Great Plains, 1867–1910* (Lincoln: University of Nebraska Press, 2007), xiii; David Stark, "Reno Gang Steals $23,000 from Daviess County," *Gallatin North Missourian*, March 24, 1993; James D. Horan, *The Pinkertons: The Detective Dynasty That Made History* (New York: Bonanza, 1967), 19–20.

19. *History of Daviess County*, 285–288; Stark, "Reno Gang Steals $23,000 from Daviess County," *Gallatin North Missourian*; John Reno, *John Reno, The World's First Train Robber and Self-Proclaimed Leader of the Infamous Reno Gang* (Seymour, IN: 1879, 1940, 1993); McDougal, *Recollections*, 193–94. The Reno Gang apparently committed the country's first train robbery. The Pinkerton version of Reno's arrest was that Pinkerton sent a gambler named Phil Oates to a Seymour, Indiana, saloon, where he began gambling with (and losing to) John Reno. Reno considered himself an expert on trains, and so Oates made a $20 bet that No. 31 would be the next train into Seymour. The bettors went to the train station, and as the train pulled in, Oates allegedly pulled a revolver on Reno as Pinkerton and four Daviess County law officers got off the train and carried Reno, bellowing for help and kicking, aboard the train, which quickly pulled out. Reno Gang members galloped after the wood-burning locomotive, but the train soon outdistanced them. McDougal, however, wrote that Reno told him in his jail cell that when he saw Ballinger in the hotel, he knew the jig was up and surrendered. The 1882 *History of Daviess County* also states that Reno was captured in Indianapolis, not Seymour. Because McDougal writes that Reno's arrest occurred "in the hotel," which is supported by the *History of Daviess County*, that is the version of the arrest I believe to be accurate. McDougal, *Recollections*, 194; *History of Daviess County*, 285–86, 546–48.

20. McDougal, *Recollections*, 30. At that time, no photographs of Jesse James were known to exist. See James P. Muehlberger, "Showdown with Jesse James," *Wild West Magazine* (February 2010), 50–53.

21. Daviess County Court Minutes, December 24, 1869, Book D, 165; *Liberty Tribune*, January 14, 1870. Reward notices were published in newspapers throughout Missouri in early January 1870, stating, "The murderers are believed to be Jesse and Frank James of Clay County, Missouri, and are

described as follows: Jesse—about 6 feet in height, rather slender built, thin visage, hair and complexion rather light and sandy. Frank—about 5 foot 8 or 10 inches in height, heavy built, full in the face and hair and complexion." The descriptions given of Jesse and Frank in the notices did not match the brothers—Jesse was about five foot nine, and Frank was approximately five foot eleven. John N. Edwards, "A Terrible Quintet," special supplement, *St. Louis Dispatch*, November 22, 1873, 4; "Frank James on Old Days," *Washington Post*; "The Story of Frank and Jesse James," *St. Louis Republican*, October 17, 1897; "Profile of Jesse Woodson James," Professor James Starrs, 1, located at the James Farm and Museum, Kearney, Missouri.

22. In May 1870, the Daviess County grand jury, sitting in Gallatin, issued a murder indictment against Frank and Jesse. The grand jury issued another indictment against them for the theft of Smoote's horse. May 1870 Daviess County Murder Indictment against Frank and Jesse James, Daviess County Clerk's Office, Gallatin, Missouri.

CHAPTER THREE: RIVERS OF BLOOD AND IRON

1. Louis C. Hunter, *Steamboats on the Western Rivers: An Economic and Technological History* (New York: Dover, 1949), 226–28; G. E. Moulton, ed., *The Journals of the Lewis and Clark Expedition* (Lincoln: University of Nebraska Press, 1983–2001).

2. Ibid.

3. Mark Twain, *Roughing It* (New York: American Publishing, 1984), 21; Perry McCandless, *A History of Missouri*, vol. 2, 1820–1860 (Columbia: University of Missouri Press, 1972), 139; Suzanne P. Cole, "Steaming through History," *Kansas City Star Magazine*, January 16, 2011, 22.

4. David McCullough, *Truman* (New York: Simon & Schuster, 1992), 17–20.

5. Stiles, *Jesse James*, 16–17.

6. Stiles, 19–20; R. Douglas Hurt, *Agriculture and Slavery in Missouri's Little Dixie* (Columbia: University of Missouri Press, 1992), 170–71.

7. See Stiles, *Jesse James*, 37–55, for an excellent discussion of slavery in western Missouri in general, and on the James farm in particular.

8. The 260-mile railroad line was traversed in just more than four hours; the route had taken twelve hours by horse. The little steam engines that rolled over the Missouri lines in 1859 were much different than those today. The engine had a tall, bulbous smokestack, pouring forth pungent clouds of pine smoke. It had a large cow catcher in front, an oversize smokestack, a decorative headlight/oil lamp, square cab, and small boiler. In addition to the smoke, the wood-burning engine often generated live sparks, many of which descended on the passengers. Passenger cars were made of wood, and passengers sat on straight-backed benches that pained the back, buttocks, and knees. Poorly laid tracks gave a bruising bump-bump-bump to the cars as they chugged along. Kansans owe a debt of gratitude to their Missouri neigh-

bors: but for the existence of this new railroad line, Abraham Lincoln might never have visited Kansas. James P. Muehlberger, "Reflections on Lincoln's Kansas Campaign," *Journal of the Kansas Bar Association* 78, no. 10 (November/December 2009), 24, 28–29; *Weekly Register*, April 7, 1870.

9. Stiles, 38–39; James M. McPherson, *Battle Cry of Freedom: The Civil War Era* (New York: Oxford University Press, 1988), 8, 51, 57. Senator Henry Clay of Kentucky initiated the 1820 Missouri Compromise, then hammered and charmed it through a reluctant Congress.

10. Jay Monaghan, *Civil War on the Western Border, 1854–1865* (Lincoln: University of Nebraska Press, 1955), 3–4.

11. Ibid., 5.

12. Ibid., 7-8.

13. Patricia A. Duncan, *Tallgrass Prairie: The Inland Sea* (Kansas City, MO: Lowell Press, 1978), 5–8.

14. Richard Cordley, *A History of Lawrence, Kansas* (Lawrence: Lawrence Journal Press, 1895), 3–5.

15. McPherson, *Battle Cry*, 119–20.

16. Lincoln speech at Peoria, Illinois, on October 16, 1854, in Roy P. Basler, ed., *The Collected Works of Abraham Lincoln*, 8 vols. (New Brunswick, NJ: Rutgers University Press, 1953), 2:271–72 .

17. Michael J. Klein, *The Baltimore Plot: The First Conspiracy to Assassinate Abraham Lincoln* (Yardley, PA: Westholme, 2011), 7.

18. McPherson, *Battle Cry*, 146.

19. From below, Lane's fort looked like a giant hawk's nest. James P. Muehlberger, "The Kansas Lawyer Who Saved Lincoln's Life," *Journal of the Kansas Bar Association* 80, no. 2 (February 2011), 34, 36–37; Frank Baron, "German Republicans and Radicals in the Struggle for a Slave-Free Kansas: Charles F. Kob and August Bondi," *Yearbook for German-American Studies* 40 (2005): 3–26, 12. There is a myth that the Free State men were all abolitionists, who opposed slavery on ethical principles. While abolitionists certainly played a leading role in the struggle to make Kansas a free state, there may have been just as many farmers and laborers who opposed slavery because it undermined the wages of free laborers. Rita G. Napier, "Origin Stories and Bleeding Kansas," *Kansas History: A Journal of the Central Plains* 34, no. 1 (Spring 2011), 33n12.

20. Muehlberger, "The Kansas Lawyer,", 37; D. W. Wilder, *The Annals of Kansas* (Topeka: Kansas Publishing House, 1886), 99, 122.

21. Stephen B. Oates, *To Purge This Land with Blood: A Biography of John Brown* (Amherst: University of Massachusetts Press, 1970), 119, 134–36. See generally, Stephen Puleo, *The Caning: The Assault That Drove America to Civil War* (Yardley, PA: Westholme, 2012); Jeffrey S. Rossbach, *Ambivalent Conspirators: John Brown, The Secret Six, and a Theory of Slave Violence* (Philadelphia: University of Pennsylvania Press, 1982), 52, 77, 96.

22. Frank Baron, "James H. Lane and the Origins of the Kansas Jayhawk," *Kansas History: A Journal of the Central Plains* 34, no. 2 (Summer 2011), 115–117. The word "Jayhawk" evolved to become symbolic of those who worked to make Kansas slave free. The leader of the Seventh Kansas Calvary, Charles Jennison, gave his regiment the unofficial title of the "mounted Kansas Jayhawkers." Baron, "James H. Lane," 124. The name Jayhawker did not die with the Civil War. In 1886, the University of Kansas, located in Lawrence, selected the Jayhawk as its moniker and mascot. In the 1880s, the Civil War was still a fresh wound for Missourians who had lived during the border war and the Civil War, and they carried a gut-level dislike, even hatred, for Jayhawkers. Four years later, the University of Missouri, located in Columbia, reciprocated by choosing the Tiger as its moniker and mascot. Former Confederate officer, author, and newspaperman John Newman Edwards had praised the Missouri guerrillas fighting during the Civil War as bloodthirsty and pitiless "as Bengal tigers." Settle, *Jesse James*, 30. The militia that protected Columbia from attack during the Civil War had been named the Missouri Tigers. Edwards, *Kansas City Star*, February 25, 2012. By the time of the 1882 murder trial of Frank James, the image of the tiger as a metaphor for Missouri's Confederate guerrilla fighters was so established that one of Frank's lawyers described him as having a "tiger's heart," and the prosecutor described Jesse as "quick as a tiger for his victim" in his murder of an unarmed train conductor. See chapter 11 regarding the trial.

23. Oates, *Purge This Land*, 120; Craig Miner, *Seeding Civil War: Kansas in the National News 1854–58* (Lawrence: University Press of Kansas, 2008).

24. Hurt, *Agriculture and Slavery*, 54–55, 103–5; *Washington Post*, March 7, 1915.

25. An old poem written during the early days of the Kansas struggles noted:

Of all the states, but three will remain in story;
Massachusetts with its Plymouth Rock,
Virginia with its native stock;
and sunny Kansas with its woes and glory.

The poem refers to the fact that most states were formed for commercial reasons. Three states are exceptions to that general proposition: Massachusetts, which was founded for political liberty; Virginia, which was founded for religious liberty; and Kansas, which was founded to halt the spread of slavery. Michael H. Hoeflich, *Justice on the Prairie: 150 years of the Federal District Court of Kansas* (Kansas City, MO: Rockhill, 2011), viii.

CHAPTER FOUR: RAVENOUS MONSTERS OF SOCIETY

1. Shelby Foote, The Civil War: A Narrative (New York: Random House, 1957), 90 ("hold the country by the heart"); Wilder, *Annals of Kansas*, 45; W. H. Woodson, *History of Clay County, Missouri* (Topeka: Historical Publishing,

1920), 44, 123; Lawrence O. Christensen, *Dictionary of Missouri Biography* (Columbia: University of Missouri Press, 1999), 423–25 ("unholy war.").

2. *History of Clay County, Missouri*, 44; Stiles, *Jesse James*, 61–62; Yeatman, *Frank and Jesse James*, 30; W. M. Paxton, *Annals of Platte County, Missouri* (Kansas City, MO: Ramfre Press, 1965, repr.), 209.

3. McPherson, *Battle Cry*, 351–52; William Garrett Piston, *Wilson's Creek* (Chapel Hill: University of North Carolina Press, 2000), 45, 307.

4. Monaghan, *Civil War*, 182–83. In addition to other sources cited for this chapter, this section on Missouri draws extensively on Michael Fellman's *Inside War: The Guerrilla Conflict in Missouri During the American Civil War* (New York: Oxford University Press, 1989). See also Thomas Goodrich, *Black Flag: Guerrilla Warfare on the Western Border, 1861–1865* (Bloomington: Indiana University Press, 1995).

5. Yeatman, *Frank and Jesse James*, 32–33; Fellman, *Inside War*, 251n3. I use the terms "guerrilla," "bushwhacker," and "irregular" to mean the same thing.

6. Donald E. Fehrenbacher, ed., *Abraham Lincoln: Speeches and Writings* (Library of America, 1989), 2:523; Muehlberger, "Reflections," 25.

7. See generally Bruce Nichols, *Guerrilla Warfare in Civil War Missouri, 1862* (Jefferson, NC: McFarland, 2004). In Richmond, the Confederacy was watching these events carefully. In an effort to tap the discontent behind enemy lines, in April 1862, the Confederate government legitimized guerrilla organizations with the Partisan Ranger Act. Fellman, 6–7; Nichols, 60.

8. Donald E. Sutherland, *A Savage Conflict: The Decisive Role of Guerrillas in the American Civil War* (Chapel Hill: University of North Carolina Press, 2009), 122–25.

9. Stiles, *Jesse James*, 81, 87; Yeatman, *Frank and Jesse James*, 35–36.

10. Daniel E. Sutherland, "The Missouri Guerrilla Hunt," *America's Civil War* 22, no. 4. (September 2009), 55, 59; Yeatman, *Frank and Jesse James*, 38–40. The guerrillas' reliance on horses left them vulnerable in winter, when Missouri's cold weather debilitated both mount and rider, and horse feed was scarce. Winter also deprived the bushwhackers of another advantage: their concealment by foliage in the woods and brush. Nichols, *Guerrilla Warfare*, 59.

11. Albert Castel, *William Clarke Quantrill: His Life and Times* (New York: Frederick Fell, 1962), 119–20, 122; Richard S. Brownlee, *Gray Ghosts of the Confederacy: Guerrilla Warfare in the West, 1861–1865* (Baton Rouge: Louisiana State University Press, 1958); Yeatman, *Frank and Jesse James*, 35; *Kansas City Journal of Daily Commerce*, April 18, 1863.

12. *Kansas City Journal of Daily Commerce*, August 14, 1863; Yeatman, *Frank and Jesse James*, 44; Shelby Foote, *The Civil War: A Narrative* (New York: Random House, 1958), 1:704–6; Cordley, *History of Lawrence*, 239. Thomas

Goodrich's *Bloody Dawn: The Story of the Lawrence Massacre* (Kent, OH: Kent State University Press, 1991), gives one of the better accounts of the massacre.

13. Castel, *William Clarke Quantrill*, 144–49; Yeatman, *Frank and Jesse James*, 48.

14. Woodson, *History of Clay County*, 247; Brownlee, *Gray Ghosts*, 139–49; Yeatman, *Frank and Jesse James*, 50–51.

15. Woodson, *History of Clay County*, 250, 267; Nichols, *Guerrilla Warfare*, 52–55.

16. "Frank James Tells the Story of the Centralia Fight," *Columbia Missouri Herald*, September 24, 1897; Yeatman, *Frank and Jesse James*, 51–52.

17. Robert J. Wybrow, "'Ravenous Monsters of Society': The Early Exploits of the James Gang," *Brand Book* 27, no. 2 (Summer 1990), 4.

18. Albert E. Castel and Thomas Goodrich, *Bloody Bill Anderson: The Short, Savage Life of a Civil War Guerrilla* (Mechanicsburg, PA: Stackpole, 1998), 11; *History of Clay and Platte Counties, Missouri* (St. Louis: National Historical Co., 1885), 248, 251.

19. Cordley, 199.

20. Larry Wood, *The Civil War Story of Bloody Bill Anderson* (Austin, TX: Eakin Press, 2003), 11–12.

21. *Kansas City Post*, March 21, 1913; Brownlee, *Gray Ghosts*, 119–20.

22. *History of Carroll County, Missouri* (St. Louis: Missouri Historical Co., 1881), 343–45. By 1864, because of the atrocities committed by bushwhackers in Missouri, as well as the penchant for plunder that most guerrilla bands displayed, powerful Southern voices called for repeal of the Partisan Ranger Act. They argued that irregular warfare was barbaric and injurious to the cause. In early 1865, the Confederate Congress revoked the act. Jay Winik, *April 1865: The Month That Saved America* (New York: HarperCollins, 2001), 164.

23. Yeatman, *Frank and Jesse James*, 55–56; Davis, *The Cause Lost*, 90–91; Rick Montgomery, "Grim Legacy of Massacres Still Haunts the Region," *Kansas City Star*, July 24, 2011, A16; "Frank James Tells the Story of the Centralia Fight," *Columbia Missouri Herald*.

24. Woodson, *History of Clay County*, 252–53; *Columbia Missouri Herald*, September 24, 1897; Brownlee, *Gray Ghosts*, 211; *Columbia Missouri Statesman*, September 9, 1864.

25. Donald R. Hale, *They Call Him Bloody Bill* (Clinton, MO: The Printery, 1975), 79; "Major Samuel Porter Cox," *Gallatin Democrat*, August 21, 1913; report written by Samuel Cox to General Craig, October 31, 1864 (in the author's possession); "How Bill Anderson Was Killed," *Gallatin Democrat*, November 2, 1899; Edwards, "Terrible Quintet."

26. McDougal, *Recollections*, 31.

27. Stiles, *Jesse James*, 153–54; Edwards, "Terrible Quintet."

28. There appears to be little factual support for the myth that Jesse James was shot while trying to surrender to Union troops. Stiles, *Jesse James*, 153. Jesse's companion, Archie Clement, was one of the least likely of the guerrillas to surrender, given his notorious butchery of Union soldiers and civilians (which Clement had good grounds to suspect may lead to reprisals from Union soldiers and authorities). In fact, four days earlier, Clement had written a letter to the Union commander at Lexington, threatening to kill the soldiers there. Jim Cummins later said, "We had a fight with some federal troops at the Missouri River," never mentioning a possible surrender. Jesse's mother or wife recounted the "shot while surrendering" story to Frank Triplett, who printed it verbatim, without verification, in his *The Life, Times and Treacherous Death of Jesse James* (St. Louis: Chambers, 1882), which was slapped together in a couple of weeks. Yeatman, *Frank and Jesse James*, 74–75, 275. Unfortunately, some historians continue to accept the myth unquestioningly.

Chapter Five: A Private in Virginia

1. Henry Clay McDougal's maternal great-grandfather was Robert Boggess. Boggess was a planter and resident of Fairfax County, Virginia, and a neighbor and contemporary of George Washington's. In 1760, Boggess was indicted at the county courthouse, along with Washington and other planters of the county, for failing to pay taxes on carriages. Robert Boggess had a son named Henry Boggess, born May 7, 1736. Reared near Mt. Vernon, he often saw Washington, and for many years his grandfather was the only person McDougal knew who had attended the 1799 funeral of the father of his country. McDougal, *Recollections*, 293–95.

Boggess married Mary Ann Lindsay in approximately 1840. One of Mary Anne's ancestors was named by King James in his second charter to the Virginia Colony in 1609 as "Capt. Richard Lindsay," and soon thereafter he settled on the James River. McDougal was, therefore, a lineal descendent of the first American Lindsay, and of blood kin to Zerelda James, the mother of Frank and Jesse James. Henry Boggess was a staunch Union man during the Civil War. McDougal, *Recollections*, 289–90; *History of Daviess County*, 546–47; Joanne Smith, *Baugus, Boggus & Boggess: Footprints in the Sand of Time* (Drakesboro, KY: 1993), 67.

2. Henry C. McDougal, "Knew and Loved Him," *Kansas City Journal*, March 25, 1899.

3. Charles Bracelen Flood, *Grant and Sherman* (New York: Farrar, Straus and Giroux, 2005) 118–19; McPherson, *Battle Cry*, 281, 299, 340–48.

4. McDougal, "Knew Him," *Kansas City Journal*.

5. McDougal, *Recollections*, 215.

6. Boyd Stutler, *West Virginia in the Civil War* (Charlotte, NC: Educational

Foundation, 1966); McDougal, *Recollections,* 221. Some historians have concluded that West Virginia suffered from guerrilla warfare much like Missouri. McPherson, *Battle Cry,* 303. McDougal, however, did not experience it. He said that in the six months his company battled the Moccasin Rangers, the group committed no murders, nor did they kill or mistreat any Union prisoner. Henry C. McDougal, "Story of Lys Morgan," *Kansas City Journal,* June 19, 1893.

7. McDougal, "Lys Morgan," *Kansas City Journal.*

8. Ibid.

9. McDougal, *Recollections,* 178.

10. Ibid.

11. David H. Donald, ed., *Why the North Won the Civil War* (New York: Simon & Schuster, 1960), 35; Gabor S. Boritt, ed., *Why the Confederacy Lost the Civil War* (New York: Oxford University Press, 1992), 20.

12. McDougal, *Recollections,* 247. Colonel Wilkerson was responsible for a habit that would stay with McDougal the rest of his life: a love of fine literature. When McDougal joined the army, he was an unlettered youth, but Wilkerson soon introduced him to the classic novels from his personal library. As a result, McDougal became a self-educated, self-made man, not unlike another lawyer and lover of literature whom McDougal greatly admired, Abraham Lincoln. By the time of his death, McDougal had amassed a personal library of over one thousand books.

13. Ibid., 387; *History of Daviess County,* 547.

14. McDougal, *Recollections,* 183–84. McDougal also spent a day near the Great Falls of the Potomac with his grandfather's old neighbor, Mr. Kankey, who was ninety-eight and had known Thomas Jefferson. Mr. Kankey had been on several juries in which Jefferson was a lawyer. He told McDougal, "Jefferson never exerted himself, nor made a big set speech; he didn't have to, for he was always on the right side." Ibid., 294.

15. James Farr, "Not Exactly a Hero: James Alexander McDougall in the United States Senate," *California Historical Society Quarterly* 65, no. 2 (June 1986), 104–113.

McDougall met Lincoln when Lincoln was a young state representative and lawyer as early as January 1843, when McDougall, as the Illinois attorney general, filed a legal proceeding against Thomas C. Browne, a client of Lincoln's. McDougall and Lincoln also rode the same circuit in and around Springfield, Illinois. McDougall and Lincoln were opponents in at least four other lawsuits between 1843 and 1846. The two men quickly became friends. Earl Schenck Miers, *Lincoln, Day by Day: A Chronology 1829-1865* (Washington, DC: Lincoln Sesquicentennial Commission, 1960), 1:216, 241, 246, 264; Russell Buchanan, "James A. McDougall: A Forgotten Senator," *California Historical Society Quarterly* 15, no. 3 (September 1926), 200–202.

About the same time, McDougall and Stephen Douglas were members of the same Masonic Lodge in Illinois. Douglas was the Grand Orator of the lodge, and he was replaced by McDougall when Douglas was unable to fulfill his duties. John C. Reynolds, *History of the M. W. Grand Masonic Lodge of Illinois, Ancient, Free, and Accepted Masons* (Springfield, IL: H. G. Reynolds Jr., 1869), 149. On March 14, 1862, President Lincoln laid out his economic arguments in a letter to then senator McDougall in trying to induce slave-state representatives to initiate gradual, compensated emancipation. Ida M. Tarbell, *Life of Abraham Lincoln* (New York: Lincoln Historical Society, 1900), 2:101; Stephen E. Ambrose, *Nothing Like It in the World: The Men Who Built the Transcontinental Railroad* (New York: Simon & Schuster, 2000), 77–79.

16. McDougal, *Recollections*, 92–93. Senator McDougall was drinking heavily at the time and disgraced himself with his drunken behavior in the capital before he drank himself to death in September 1867. Buchanan, "James A. McDougall," 199–212.

17. McDougal, *Recollections*, 94.

Chapter Six: Showdown with Frank and Jesse James

1. McDougal, *Recollections*, 421–22

2. Ibid., 18–19.

3. Ibid., 18.

4. Ibid.

5. Ibid., 421–422.

6. Ibid., 29. After nearly a year of searching, I found the 170-year-old lawsuit papers in the back of a dusty file drawer in the Daviess County Civil Court records vault. See Brian Burnes, "Jesse James, the Outlaw and Defendant," *Kansas City Star*, September 24, 2007, A-1, 4.

7. *Smoote v. Frank and Jesse James*, Petition; Yeatman, *Frank and Jesse James*, 195.

8. Steven Lubet, *Murder in Tombstone: The Forgotten Trial of Wyatt Earp* (New Haven, CT: Yale University Press, 2004), 148–49.

9. Ibid., Writ of Attachment, Attachment Bond.

10. Daviess County records, Daviess County Courthouse, Gallatin, February 12, 1870, Book D, 195.

11. Ibid., February 4, 1870, Affidavit of Service, Sheriff's Return.

12. McDougal, *Recollections*, 29–30.

13. Ibid., 29; Stiles, *Jesse James*, 277; Yeatman, *Frank and Jesse James*, 129, 140–41, 148–49. Hardwick sent telegrams to Chicago coded in a single-word substitution cipher, keeping Allan Pinkerton informed of the James brothers' movements. Hardwick gave McDougal the key to the cipher, so McDougal was able decipher the communications. Yeatman, *Frank and Jesse James*, 129, 140–41, 348–49; McDougal, *Recollections*, 29.

14. "Judge H. C. McDougal Dead," *Gallatin North Missourian*, December 23, 1915.

15. McDougal, *Recollections*, 92; Ambrose, *Nothing Like It*, 77–79. McDougal mentions Senator McDougall only once in his 460-page book. This may have been because the senator died of alcoholism shortly after passage of the Union Pacific Railroad bill and disgraced himself with his behavior before he drank himself to death. The Chicago, Rock Island & Pacific Railroad ran north into Iowa, where it connected to the Union Pacific Railroad at Council Bluffs. It also ran south and tied into the Hannibal & St. Joseph Railroad at Cameron, Missouri.

16. Leopard and McCammon, *History of Daviess and Gentry*, 82; McDougal, *Recollections*, 18.

17. Williams, *History of Northwest Missouri*, 1684–85. Until this author discovered the Smoote legal file, it was not known that Jesse and Frank James had ever retained the services of a Missouri lawyer in a civil lawsuit. They typically employed quicker, albeit violent and unlawful, means to settle their disputes.

18. Richardson was married and had five children. His daughter, Roe Ann, married Joshua W. Alexander, who later defended Frank James during his 1883 murder trial. Williams, *History of Northwest Missouri*, 1685. Alexander went on to become a congressman, and he served as secretary of commerce from 1919 to 1921 under President Woodrow Wilson. It is unknown how Frank and Jesse selected Richardson as their attorney.

19. *Smoote v. Frank and Jesse James*, Motion to Quash Sheriff's Return of Service.

20. May 1870 murder indictment against Frank and Jesse James.

21. Yeatman, *Frank and Jesse James*, 99, 104.

22. Leonard Pitts, "Postwar Lies to the Contrary, Civil War Was about Slavery," *Kansas City Star*, April 12, 2011, A13. The Lost Cause legend has been the subject of several books, including Gallagher and Nolan's *Myth of the Lost Cause*; Thomas L. Connolly, *Marble Man: Robert E. Lee and His Image in American Society* (New York: Knopf, 1977); Gaines M. Foster, *Ghosts of the Confederacy: Defeat, the Lost Cause, and the Emergence of the New South, 1865 to 1913* (New York: Oxford University Press, 1987); James M. McPherson, *Ordeal by Fire* (New York: Knopf, 1982).

23. *Kansas City Times* in the *Liberty Tribune*, June 24, 1870.

24. Ibid.; *Liberty Tribune*, October 20, 1876; Wybrow, "From the Pen," 19–20 (the letter appeared in the *Kansas City Evening Star*, November 2, 1881. The following letter, handwritten and dated May 18, 1879, was from Jesse James (as J. D. Howard) to H. E. Warren of Box Station, Tennessee:

> Dear Sir,
> I felt very bad all day yesterday after drinking so much beer, but I am ok today. I expect to attend the faul races at Nashville this week and invest on the Louisville events and hope you will attend. . . . if you

come up bring up those claims you had at the races against me and
first winnings I make I will pay you, also bring up the $40 note
Jackson holds against me and if I ever win I will pay them off, what
does old Morry say about getting his foot in for the cost of getting
beat? . . .
Nashville
Your friend,
J. D. Howard

Jill Knight Garrett, *A History of Humphreys County* (Columbia, TN: privately
printed, 1963), 163–65. It is obvious that this unsophisticated letter, lacking
basic punctuation and spelling, and the June 24, 1870, letter to Governor
Joseph McClurg were not written by the same hand. This is not an insignif-
icant issue, as some authors rely heavily upon "Jesse's" letters to the *Kansas
City Times* for their argument that his crimes were politically motivated. If
James did, indeed, write this and other letters to the *Kansas City Times*, why
have none of the originals survived? Certainly, Edwards would have prized
and preserved any such letters, if they had ever existed. Finally, if James had
written this letter and surrendered on May 15, 1865, having been shot in the
process, he likely would have mentioned the incident in support of his assertion that he could not turn himself in.

25. *Smoote v. Frank and Jesse James*, Sheriff's Return dated June 16, 1870;
Yeatman, *Frank and Jesse James*, 99.
26. *Kansas City Times* in the *Liberty Tribune*, July 15, 22, 1870.
27. *Kansas City Times* in the *Liberty Tribune*, July 22, 1870.
28. *Smoote v. Frank and Jesse James*, Smoote Affidavit; *Liberty Tribune*, August
5, 1870.
29. *Smoote v. Frank and Jesse James*, Clerk's Affidavit; Daniel M. Pence, *I Knew
Frank . . . I Wish I Had Known Jesse* (Independence, MO: Two Trails, 2007),
159–60.
30. *Smoote v. Frank and Jesse James*, Order of Publication dated August 9,
1870.
31. Ibid., October 10, 1870, Affidavit of Publication.
32. Ibid., October 11, 1870, Order Approving Proof of Publication; October
14, 1870, Order Allowing Defendants 45 Days Within Which to Respond to
the Petition; Yeatman, *Frank and Jesse James*, 99.
33. Frank James and Jesse James Answer to the Plaintiff's Petition; February
14, 1871, Order of Continuance.
34. *History of Daviess County* (reprinted 1984), 11; *Weekly Western Register*,
April 7, 1870.
35. *Weekly Western Register*, October 5, 1871.
36. McDougal, *Recollections*, 29–30; Herbert F. McDougal, "When James
Boys Were Sued," *Kansas City Star*, undated (in author's possession).
37. Stiles, *Jesse James*, 213. Horse racing was a keen interest of the James

brothers, no doubt because they survived their robberies and murders, in part, because of the speed and staying power of their mounts.

CHAPTER SEVEN: THE TRIAL OF CLELL MILLER

1. McDougal, *Recollections*, 31; Ruth Coder Fitzgerald, "The Trial of Clelland Miller for Bank Robbery," unpublished manuscript in the author's possession.
2. Ruth Coder Fitzgerald, "Clell and Ed Miller—Members of the James Gang," *Quarterly of the National Association for Outlaw and Lawman History* 15, no. 3 (July–September 1991), 29.
3. *Liberty Tribune*, February 5, 1875.
4. *Kansas City Evening Star*, July 21, 1871; *Liberty Tribune*, June 16, 1871.
5. David Starks, "Lesser Known Jesse James Gunfight at Civil Bend," *Gallatin North Missourian*, April 4, 1993.
6. Starks, "Jesse James Gunfight," *Gallatin North Missourian*, April 4, 1993.
7. *Kansas City World*, November 19, 1898; Yeatman, *Frank and Jesse James*, 100; Robert J. Wybrow, "From the Pen of a Noble Robber: The Letters of Jesse Woodson James 1847–1882," *Brand Book* 24, no. 2 (Summer 1987), 18.
8. *History of Wayne County*, 536; Wayne County, Iowa, District Court Record Book, October Term, October 22, 1872, file 178. *State of Iowa v. Clell Miller*. The trial transcript is no longer contained in the Wayne County court records. I located it in the Prairie Trails Museum in Corydon, Iowa.
9. State of Iowa trial transcript, 9.
10. Ibid., 10.
11. Ibid.; Yeatman, *Frank and Jesse James*, 120.
12. State of Iowa trial transcript, 1–2.
13. Ibid.; Stiles, *Jesse James*, 199.
14. *Louisville Courier-Journal*, May 1–5, 1872.
15. Ibid.
16. Yeatman, *Frank and Jesse James,* 103.
17. Yeatman, *Frank and Jesse James*, 104; Settle, *Jesse James*, 45; March 2, 2002 "Crackerneck [Road] History Goes Back to Days of James Gang," *Independence Missouri Examiner*; Milton Forrest Hughes, "Bygone Days: Recalling Places and Faces from the Past," unpublished manuscript, Jackson County Missouri Historical Society Archives, 51.
18. The Jesse James letters published by the *Kansas City Times* were not the only letters published by the newspaper that were not written by the purported author. Less than two years later, in August 1874, the *Times* published a letter purporting to be from a Texas deputy sheriff regarding the alleged deathbed confession of Jim Reed, an alleged James-Younger Gang member, in which Reed exonerated the James brothers from the Gads Hill and Ste. Genevieve robberies. About a month later, the real Texas deputy sheriff wrote the paper declaring that the earlier letter had not been authored by him and, although he had heard Reed's deathbed confession, Reed neither discussed the

robberies nor exonerated the James brothers. The *Times* apparently chose not to publish the second letter, which was published by the *Dallas Daily Herald*. At least one writer has concluded that the *Kansas City Times* "article sounds suspiciously like a fabrication that a person sympathetic to the James and Younger brothers might write, perhaps even an editor." Robert J. Wybrow, "Texas Wants 'Em: A Case of Mistaken Identity," *The Brand Book* 43, no. 2 (Spring 2010), 17-18 (quoting Kenneth W. Hobbes, Jr., "Jim Reed, Southwestern Outlaw and Husband of Belle Starr: A Study of the Watt Grayson and San Antonio Stage Robberies," Master's Thesis, Texas Christian University, Fort Worth, 1975), 31).

19. A few years later, Jesse James was not so loyal to Clell Miller. After the December 8, 1874, train robbery at Muncie, Kansas, and the robbery of a store on May 15, 1875, near Clinton, Missouri, James wrote a letter to "My Dear Friend," who apparently was a law officer, based on the contents of the letter (perhaps Sheriff John Groom of Clay County). In the letter, James states that he is tired of others committing crimes for which he is blamed (and for which he didn't share in the robbery proceeds), and tells the recipient of the letter that Clell Miller committed the robberies. Miller could likely be found at his father's home, he was riding his father's iron gray mare during the robbery, and the sheriff of Henry County could perhaps identify the mare as the mount of one of the robbers. James had apparently learned from Gallatin that the getaway horse could be used as evidence to identify the robbers. This letter shows what a scoundrel James was in giving away not only the name, but also the whereabouts, of his companion of long standing. Wybrow, "From the Pen," 10–12.

20. State of Iowa trial transcript, 1–2, 5–6.

21. Ibid., 9–16.

22. Ibid., 17–18.

23. Ibid., 20–23.

24. Ibid., 24–29.

25. Ibid., 31–32.

26. Ibid., 33–36.

27. Ibid., 37–42.

28. Ibid., 43–46.

29. Ibid., 47.

30. Ibid., 49–54.

31. Ibid., 60–72. The hearsay evidence was inadmissible because it was an out-of-court statement by someone not in the courtroom, offered for the truth of the matter asserted.

32. Ibid., 72; *History of Wayne County*, 536.

33. Yeatman, *Frank and Jesse James*, 114–15.

34. Settle, *Jesse James*, 47; Edwards, "Terrible Quintet," 7.

35. Stiles, *Jesse James*, 254–55.

36. Ibid., 280; *St. Louis Republican*, April 17–18, 1876; Yeatman, *Frank and Jesse James*, 135–140.

37. *Kansas City Times*, January 29, 1875.

38. Stiles, *Jesse James*, 279–90; Yeatman, *Frank and Jesse James*, 115.

39. David J. Gottlieb, "Criminal Trials as Culture Wars: Southern Honor and the Acquittal of Frank James," *University of Kansas Law Review* 51 (2003), 417–18.

40. Stiles, *Jesse James*, 292–94.

41. Ibid., 304.

42. Yeatman, *Frank and Jesse James*, 169–75. Stiles had apparently been a surveyor for Dodge County, adjacent to Rice County, where Northfield is located. Yeatman, *Frank and Jesse James*, 425n12. John Koblas, in *The Jesse James Northfield Raid* (St. Cloud, MN: North Star Press, 1999), suggests that Stiles and Chadwell were different men.

43. Yeatman, *Frank and Jesse James*, 175–77.

44. *Missouri Republican*, October 3, 1883.

45. Yeatman, *Frank and Jesse James*, 211–16, 238; Carl W. Breihan, "Whiskeyhead Bill Ryan," *Pioneer West* (September 1979), 60–61.

CHAPTER EIGHT: THE ARREST AND TRIAL OF BILL RYAN

1. *Nashville American*, April 1, 1881.

2. William H. Wallace, *Speeches and Writings of William H. Wallace, with Autobiography* (Kansas City: Western Baptist, 1914), 274, 277.

3. *Milan Republican*, October 17, 1979.

4. Gottlieb, "Criminal Trials," 418–19.

5. Wallace, *Speeches and Writings*, 132, 173.

6. Ibid., 247–48.

7. Ibid., 251.

8. Wallace, *Speeches and Writings*, 253; Joseph Kelley, "The Trials of William Wallace and the Strength of His Conviction," *Jackson County Historical Society Journal* (Spring 2000), 8; Monaghan, *Civil War*, 121.

9. Wallace, *Speeches and Writings*, 253–55.

10. Ibid., 225–58.

11. Ibid., 259–63.

12. Kelley, "Trials of William Wallace," 9.

13. *Kansas City Journal of Daily Commerce*, April 4, 1882; *Kansas City Evening Star*, April 4, 1882; Robert J. Wybrow, "Wash My Hands in Your Heart's Blood: The Many Faces of Mattie Collins," *James Farm Journal* (2008), 1–2.

14. Wallace, *Speeches and Writings*, 263–64.

15. Ibid., 264–65.

16. Ibid., 263–66.

17. Contrary to myth, the members of the James-Younger Gang were not America's first train robbers. The Reno Gang has that distinction, although

it is comparatively unknown today, perhaps in part because it did not have John Newman Edwards as its publicist.

18. Wallace, *Speeches and Writings*, 276.

19. *Kansas City Journal*, July 16, 1880.

20. Wallace, *Speeches and Writings*, 276.

21. *Kansas City Evening Star*, October 30, 1882 (publishing May 16, 1882, letter from William Wallace); "Jackson County and the Train Robbers," *St. Louis Republican*, October 14, 1881.

22. "Billy Ryan," *Kansas City Journal*, September 23, 1881, 8, col. 4; "Ryan's Trial," *Kansas City Journal*, September 25, 1881, 8, col. 2. No transcript has been located for the trial, but the *St. Louis Republican* of October 10, 11, and 13, 1881, reported on the trial testimony, and the issue of October 2, 1881, carried Bassham's testimony. The author also has relied on William Wallace's letters and writings, and other contemporaneous newspaper articles, to reconstruct the testimony.

23. "Ryan's Trial," *Kansas City Journal*; "Shall We Have Order?," *Kansas City Journal*, 4, col. 2.

24. "The Glendale Robbery," *Liberty Tribune,* September 30, 1881; Yeatman, *Frank and Jesse James*, 258.

25. *St. Louis Republican*, October 10, 11, and 13, 1881.

26. "Ryan's Trial," *Kansas City Journal of Daily Commerce*, September 25, 1881.

27. "Ryan's Trial," *Kansas City Journal*.

28. "Crowd from Cracker Neck," *St. Louis Republican*, September 29, 1881; "Bill Ryan and His Friends," *St. Louis Republican*, September 30, 1881; "Excitement at Independence," *Kansas City Journal*, September 28, 1881, 4, col. 2; Wallace, *Speeches and Writings*, 277–78. Wallace seemed to know and expect that Ryan's attorneys would attack Bassham's credibility and put witnesses on the stand claiming that Ryan was a mere farmer. Given Wallace's thorough preparation, it would be surprising if he had not spoken with the prosecutor who handled the Clell Miller trial and/or read the Miller trial transcript.

29. Wallace, *Speeches and Writings*, 134–36.

30. Wallace, *Speeches and Writings*, 283.

CHAPTER NINE: THE DEATH OF JESSE JAMES

1. "Gov. Crittenden's Views," *Chicago Daily Tribune*, April 7, 1882.

2. H. H. Crittenden, *The Crittenden Memoirs* (New York: G. P. Putnam and Sons, 1936), 108. Jesse James had perhaps singled out McDougal's client, the Rock Island Railroad, in his train robberies, as it was the only line robbed more than once by the James-Younger Gang at the time of the reward proclamation. It should be noted that, other than the train passengers who were robbed, the gang's primary victims were express companies, which

transported currency shipments by train. Of course, the robberies also discouraged train passengers from traveling in Missouri, which caused the railroads lost revenue.

3. "Robbed on the Rail," *Kansas City Times*, September 8, 1881. See generally Robert J. Wybrow, "Jesse's Juveniles," *Brand Book* 12, no. 1 (October 1969), 1–11.

4. Wybrow, "Jesse's Juveniles," 3.

5. Ibid.

6. Ibid.

7. "Jesse's Juveniles," *Kansas City Times*, September 9, 1881.

8. "The Train Robbers," *Kansas City Times*, September 10, 1881. John Bugler was the son of Henry Bugler, sheriff of Jackson County in 1867, who was killed while defending the jail from a lynch mob. *St. Louis Weekly Globe-Democrat*, September 15, 1881.

9. *Kansas City Evening Star*, March 27, 1882.

10. *Kansas City Evening Star*, March 30, 1882. I have been unable to locate the Bugler trial transcript and so have relied on contemporaneous witness interviews in Kansas City newspapers and Wallace's writings.

11. "The Bandits," *Kansas City Evening Star*, April 4, 1882.

12. Robert J. Wybrow, "Jesse Woodson James—A 'Noble Robber'?," *Brand Book* 31, no. 1 (Winter 1996), 1.

13. *Kansas City Evening Star*, April 13, 1882.

14. Crittenden, *The Crittenden Memoirs*, 200; "Land Lied," *Kansas City Journal*, April 6, 1882; *Detroit Free Press*, July 18, 1882, reported in the *Kansas City Evening Star*, October 30, 1882.

15. Wybrow, "Jesse's Juveniles," 9–10.

16. On April 17, 1882, Bob and Charlie Ford were indicted for first-degree murder. Both pleaded guilty and were sentenced to be hanged on May 19. Governor Crittenden immediately issued unconditional pardons for both men. Yeatman, *Frank and Jesse James*, 275.

17. Wybrow, "Jesse's Juveniles," 10. The public critics of Wallace caused Wallace to write a defensive letter to the editor of the *Southern Law Review*.

18. Robert Ford was arrested immediately following his pardon and tried in October 1882 for the murder of Wood Hite, but he was found not guilty by a jury. It was reported that an agreement was entered into between the attorneys for Bob Ford and those of Frank James before the trial that none of the James family would appear on behalf of the state to prosecute Bob, in exchange for Robert and Charlie Ford agreeing not to testify against Frank when he went on trial. *Liberty Weekly Tribune*, October 27, 1882.

19. Wallace, *Speeches and Writings*, 283.

20. Ibid., 283–84.

21. Ibid., 284.

22. *St. Louis Globe-Democrat*, October 6, 1882. It is said that the governor, apparently with some concealed amusement, took one of the revolvers by its butt end and said, "Not since 1861?" The pistol was an 1875 model Remington. Yeatman, *Frank and Jesse James*, 279.

23. Yeatman, *Frank and Jesse James*, 279–80.

24. Ibid., 279–81.

25. Ibid., 285.

26. Ibid., 283.

27. Ibid., 281–83.

28. Ibid., 285.

Chapter Ten: The Attempted Assassination of Major Samuel P. Cox

1. Gerald S. Petrone, *Judgment at Gallatin: The Trial of Frank James* (Lubbock: Texas Tech University Press, 1998), 8.

2. Stiles, *Jesse James*, 203.

3. *Kansas City Journal of Daily Commerce*, December 9, 1869; *Liberty Tribune*, December 17, 1869; *St. Louis Republican*, August 24, 1883. Anderson's revolvers were lost when Cox's home burned down. David Stark, sixth generation Gallatin resident, in an interview with the author on February 2, 2012.

4. *St. Louis Republican*, August 24, 1883; May 1870 murder indictment. Cox worked as a county recorder in the only other small brick building on the Gallatin town square at the time of the murder—the circuit clerk's office, on the northeast corner of the square. Sheets worked in the other brick building on the town square, albeit on the southwest corner—the Daviess County Savings Association. The killers likely rode into Gallatin from the south or west and saw the Gallatin Savings Association building first; the county office building where Cox worked would have been blocked from their view by the Gallatin courthouse, which was situated in the middle of the town square.

5. May 1870: *State of Missouri v. Frank James and Jesse James*, Larceny Indictment for the theft of Daniel Smoote's horse.

6. It could be argued that perhaps one other man had accompanied Frank and Jesse James to Gallatin, waited outside the bank, and fled before being noticed by Gallatin citizens. There is little evidence of this, however. "Only Living Witness," *St. Louis Globe-Democrat*.

7. "Horrid Murder and Heavy Robbery," *Liberty Tribune*, February 16, 1866; *Liberty Tribune*, February 16, 1939; *Kansas City Star*, August 2, 1925. See Wybrow, "'Ravenous Monsters,'" for an excellent description of this and the James brothers' other early robberies.

8. *History of Clay County*, 202; *Liberty Tribune*, February 16, 1866; *Lexington Caucasian*, May 2, 1866; *Liberty Tribune*, February 16, 1939. According to Jesse's great-grandson James R. Ross, the James brothers went inside the

bank and Archie Clement shot the bystander. James R. Ross, *I, Jesse James* (Thousand Oaks, CA: Dragon, 1988), 63–69.

9. "Daring Bank Robbery," *Lexington Weekly Caucasian*, October 3, 1866; "Fletcher's Rubble," *Missouri Valley Register*, December 27, 1866. Jesse's great-grandson names the two James brothers, Cole and Jim Younger, and John Jarrette as the armed robbers. Ross, *I, Jesse James*, 73.

10. "Murder and Robbery!," *Richmond Conservator*, May 24, 1867; *Kansas City Journal of Daily Commerce*, May 28, 1867; *St. Louis Post-Dispatch*, February 10, 1874; *St. Joseph Gazette*, December 17, 1869.

11. "Daring Robbery," *St. Louis Republican*, March 23, 1868; "Russellville Bank Robbery," *St. Louis Republican*, March 26, 1868; *Jefferson City People's Tribune*, April 15, 1868. On March 2, 1867, six bandits attempted to rob the bank in Savannah, Missouri. Robert Wybrow's careful review of the crime casts doubt on any link to Frank and Jesse James. Wybrow, "'Ravenous Monsters,'" 10–11.

12. Wybrow, "'Ravenous Monsters,'" 15–16; *Kansas City Star*, April 11, 1874; Yeatman, *Frank and Jesse James*, 95.

13. Wybrow, 17–18. On March 28, 1868, the *Louisville Daily Journal* described one of the robbers as "5 feet 7 inches in height, short, curly, sand hair, round bull-dog head, prominent eyes, red face, and weighs 160 pounds," which could have been a description of Jesse James.

14. *Kansas City Evening Star*, July 21, 1871; *History of Wayne County*, 535–36.

15. *Liberty Tribune*, June 16, 1872; David Stark, "Lesser-Known Jesse James Gunfight at Civil Band," *Gallatin North Missourian*, April 4, 1993.

16. *St. Louis Republican*, August 24, 1872, May 28, 1873; *Kansas City Journal of Daily Commerce*, May 30, 1873.

17. *Liberty Tribune*, January 14, 1870; *Missouri Republican*, October 3, 1883.

18. *Columbia Missouri Herald*, September 24, 1897.

19. *St. Louis Republican*, September 9, 1883: *State of Missouri v. Frank James*, 1883 motion to dismiss, located in the Daviess County clerk's vault.

20. Paul Peterson, *Quantrill in Texas* (Nashville: Cumberland House, 2007), 223; Yeatman, *Frank and Jesse James*, 409n7.

CHAPTER ELEVEN: THE TRIAL OF THE CENTURY

1. Gottlieb, "Criminal Trials," 409.

2. Ibid., 410.

3. *History of Daviess and Gentry Counties, Missouri* (Topeka, KS: Historical Publishing, 1922), 238.

4. McDougal, *Recollections*, 31. Alexander later served many years in Congress, and from 1919–21, he was President Woodrow Wilson's secretary of commerce. Henry Clay Dean, who had volunteered his services for the cause, was the eighth member of Frank James's legal team. Philips and the other defense lawyers did not approve of Dean's presence, however, and ignored him until he finally quit. Petrone, *Judgment at Gallatin*, 71.

5. "Frank James," *Gallatin Weekly Democrat*, August 25, 1883. It was well known in Gallatin, that McDougal represented the railroads. For this reason, McDougal probably did not want to take too active a role with the state's witnesses, lest the defense lawyers question them about the railroad providing free transportation and lodging, which might undermine their credibility. McDougal and Low had also been involved on behalf of their client, the Rock Island Railroad, in investigating the train robbery and murder immediately after the crime. *Kansas City Evening Star*, July 16, 1881. Despite his precautions, McDougal said after the trial that he never knew a case in which the prosecutors were subject to personal attacks, as happened in this case about their motives for trying Frank James. McDougal, *Recollections*, 31–32.

6. Wallace, *Speeches and Writings*, 287.

7. Daviess County Record of Deeds, Book 38, page 267; Petrone, *Judgment at Gallatin*, 69.

8. Wallace, *Speeches and Writings*, 292–93.

9. "The Train Robber's Trial," *St. Louis Republican*, August 26, 1883.

10. Wallace, *Speeches and Writings*, 292.

11. Ibid., 287.

12. Ibid.

13. Ibid., 288.

14. This is not to suggest that the judge was corrupt or the outcome of the trial predetermined. The judge appeared fair in his rulings, ruling for the prosecution more or less as often as for the defense.

15. McDougal, *Recollections*, 32.

16. "Not Guilty," *Gallatin Weekly Democrat*, September 8, 1883.

17. "James and the Jury," *St. Louis Republican*, August 24, 1883.

18. Ibid. Given the number of witnesses who testified at trial, I have not attempted to describe all of their testimony here, but only the more important. Wallace's nephew, George F. Miller, published an abridged transcript of the trial based on Wallace's trial notes, *The Trial of Frank James for Murder* (St. Louis: 1898; repr., New York: Jingle Bob/Crown, 1977), which contains a description of all of the testimony.

19. Miller, *Trial of Frank James*, 8–11. Newspapers spelled the victim's name "McMillan" and "McMillen." His tombstone carries the name "McMillen." Carl W. Breihan, *The Man Who Shot Jesse James* (London: A. S. Barnes, 1979), 35, opposite photo of McMillen's grave and marker.

20. Miller, *Trial of Frank James*, 12.

21. Miller, *Trial of Frank James*, 12–15; "The McMillan Murder," *St. Louis Republican*, August 25, 1883.

22. Miller, *Trial of Frank James*, 15–16; "The McMillan Murder," *St. Louis Republican*.

23. Miller, *Trial of Frank James*, 17–18; *St. Louis Republican*, August 25, 1883.

24. Miller, *Trial of Frank James*, 19–27; *St. Louis Republican*, August 25, 1883.

25. Miller, *Trial of Frank James*, 25–36; "Train Robber's Trial," *St. Louis Republican*, August 26, 1883.

26. Miller, *Trial of Frank James*, 37–45; *St. Louis Republican*, August 26, 1883.

27. Miller, *Trial of Frank James*, 46–57; "Dick and the Defense," *St. Louis Republican*, August 28, 1883.

28. Miller, *Trial of Frank James*, 58–72; "Frank's Foes and Friends," *St. Louis Republican,* August 29, 1883.

29. "The State's Case Rested," *St. Louis Republican*, August 30, 1883.

30. Miller, *Trial of Frank James*, 77–79; Wallace, *Speeches and Writings*, 289.

31. Miller, *Trial of Frank James*, 91–94; "Was It Wood Hite?," *St. Louis Republican*, August 31, 1883.

32. Miller, *Trial of Frank James*, 94–96, 139; "Was It Wood Hite?," *St. Louis Republican*.

33. Miller, *Trial of Frank James*, 96–98. Upon seeing Shelby, McDougal recalled a night seventeen years earlier, shortly after he arrived in Gallatin, when he heard one of General Shelby's former troopers singing "Shelby's Mule." Aided by whiskey, the roughrider threw his whole soul into the song with such enthusiasm that McDougal never forgot the chorus: "Hi boys! Make a noise; The Yankees are afraid; The river's up; Hell's to pay, Shelby's on a raid." McDougal, *Recollections,* 209.

34. Miller, *Trial of Frank James*, 102–4; "Was It Wood Hite?," *St. Louis Republican*. In fact, it is likely that Shelby did not meet Frank James for the first time until after the Civil War. Yeatman, *Frank and Jesse James*, 35. Frank James may have recuperated at Shelby's home after being hit with a shotgun blast after the Corydon, Iowa, bank robbery. See discussion of Corydon, Iowa, bank robbery in chapter 7.

35. Miller, *Trial of Frank James*, 105–9.

36. Ibid., 115–17; "James Trial Cont'd," *Gallatin Democrat*, September 1, 1883; "All for an Alibi," *St. Louis Republican*, September 1, 1883.

37. Miller, *Trial of Frank James*, 117–18.

38. Missouri Statutory Laws 1877, at section 356, subsection 1.

39. Miller, *Trial of Frank James*, 123–25.

40. Ibid., 126–37.

41. Petrone, *Judgment at Gallatin*, 146; "Oratorical Contest," *St. Louis Republican*, September 5, 1883; "Not Yet Concluded," *St. Louis Republican*, September 6, 1883.

42. Miller, *Trial of Frank James*, 151; Gottlieb, "Criminal Trials," 428.

43. Gottlieb, "Criminal Trials," 429–30; "Oratorical Contest," *St. Louis Republican*, September 5, 1883.

44. Gottlieb, "Criminal Trials," 430.

45. Ibid., 431–33.

46. Ibid., 435.

47. Ibid., 439–40.

48. "Not Yet Concluded," *St. Louis Republican*, September 6, 1883; "It Didn't Take Long," *St. Louis Republican*, September 7, 1883. After the not guilty verdict, Judge Goodman told McDougal in his office that night, "Well, it's over, and I suppose I am the only man living that has no right to swear about that acquittal," because he allowed Crozier to pick the slate of people from whom the jury was selected. Editor John Edwards wrote to Frank James after the verdict: "Remember me to Sheriff Crozier. He is a man that is everything." McDougal, *Recollections*, 32.

49. *New York Times*, September 7, 1883, 4 ("the acquittal of Frank James is a miscarriage of justice"); "A Villainous Verdict," *Kansas City Daily Journal*, September 7, 1883; "The Most Unpleasant Incidents of the Affair," *St. Louis Globe-Democrat*, September 8, 1883, 6; "How the Jesse James Gang Was Wiped off the Earth," *Kansas City World*, November 6, 1898.

50. Stiles, *Jesse James*, 380.

Chapter Twelve: Aftermath and Revelations

1. *St. Louis Post-Dispatch*, September 7–8, 1883.

2. *Kansas City Times*, September 8, 1883. "We just did not believe Dick Liddil. He was the only one that said Frank was on the train, and we just did not believe him." Yeatman, *Frank and Jesse James*, 285.

3. Gottlieb, "Criminal Trials," 446.

4. McDougal was also a close friend of General William Tecumseh Sherman's, whom he saw in Washington and elsewhere. With his large frame, tall, gaunt form, uncombed hair, restless hazel eyes, jutting nose, furrowed face, and beard, Sherman still looked the picture of grim-visaged war. McDougal and Sherman were Missouri delegates to the annual Grand Army of the Republic meetings, which Sherman attended religiously. McDougal, *Recollections*, 92–109, 365.

5. Rick Montgomery, "The Rise and Fall of a Cowtown," *Kansas City Star Magazine*, December 9, 2012.

6. Charles N. Glaab, *Kansas City and the Railroads* (Lawrence: University Press of Kansas, 1993); William M. Reddig, *Tom's Town* (Columbia: University of Missouri Press, 1986), 2.

7. McDougal, *Recollections*, 120–21; Crittenden, *Memoirs*, 61.

8. McDougal, *Recollections*, 129; John C. Dods, "*Shook, Hardy & Bacon LLP: A History of Excellence*," unpublished manuscript, 2002.

9. McDougal, *Recollections*, 11, 13, 74; *Gallatin North Missourian*, December 23, 1915.

10. Wallace, *Speeches and Writings*, 306; *Kansas City World*, November 6, 1898.

11. Yeatman, *Frank and Jesse James*, 275–76; "The Trial of Frank James," *Florence North Star*, April 24, 1882, 1; "The Frank James Case," *Florence Gazette*, April 26, 1882, 3.

12. Yeatman, *Frank and Jesse James*, 287–88.

13. Mangum, *Kingdom*, 159–61.

EPILOGUE

1. E. J. Hobsbawm, *Bandits* (New York: Pantheon, 1969); Wybrow, "Jesse Woodson James," 1.

2. Richard White, "Outlaw Gangs of the Middle Border: American Social Bandits," *Western Historical Quarterly* (October 1981), 405; Fellman, *Inside War*, 260.

3. *Kansas City Times*, September 24, 1876; *Lexington Caucasian*, August 30, 1873; Thomas Coleman Younger, *The Story of Cole Younger, by Himself* (Springfield, MO: Oak Hills, 1996, orig. publ. 1903), 86.

4. Philip W. Steele, *The Many Faces of Jesse James* (Gretna, LA: Pelican, 1995), 35–37; William Preston Mangum, "The James/Younger Gang and Their Circle of Friends," *Wild West Magazine* (August 2003), 26; Jim Cummins, *Jim Cummins' Book, Written by Himself* (Denver: Reed, 1903), 86–87.

5. Steele, *Many Faces*, 35–37; *Missouri Republican*, October 3, 1883. The racing season generally started in May and ran through August. Note the dates of the following robberies: Richmond, Missouri, bank robbery, May 22, 1867; Russellville, Kentucky, bank robbery, March 20, 1868; Corydon, Iowa, bank robbery, June 3, 1871; Columbia, Kentucky, bank robbery, April 29, 1872; Kansas City, Missouri, exposition robbery, September 26, 1872; Ste. Genevieve, Missouri, bank robbery, May 23, 1873; Adair, Iowa, train robbery, July 21, 1873; Rocky Cut, Missouri, train robbery, July 6, 1876; Northfield, Minnesota, bank robbery, September 7, 1876; Glendale, Missouri, train robbery, October 8, 1879; Winston, Missouri, train robbery, July 15, 1881; Blue Cut, Missouri, train robbery, September 7, 1881.

6. Mangum, *Kingdom*, 161; *Missouri Republican*, October 3, 1883.

7. Wallace, *Speeches and Writings*, 269.

8. Yeatman, *Frank and Jesse James*, 271.

9. See, e.g., Holzer, "Inescapable Conflict," 38–40.

10. Fellman, *Inside War*, 263.

BIBLIOGRAPHY

BOOKS

Ambler, Charles Henry. *A History of West Virginia.* New York: Prentice Hall, 1933.

Ambrose, Stephen E. *Nothing Like It in the World: The Men Who Built the Transcontinental Railroad.* New York: Simon & Schuster, 2000.

Ayers, Carol D. *Lincoln and Kansas: Partnership for Freedom.* Lawrence, KS: Sunflower University Press, 2001.

Basler, Roy P., ed. *The Collected Works of Abraham Lincoln.* 8 vols. New Brunswick, NJ: Rutgers University Press, 1953.

Bassett, John. *Union Men and Their Sufferings in North-Western Missouri: The Remedy: Secrets of Rebels Exposed.* New York: Press of Wynkoop, Hollenbeck & Thomas, 1864.

Black, Robert C. *The Railroads of the Confederacy.* Chapel Hill: University of North Carolina Press, 1952.

Boritt, Gabor S., ed. *Why the Confederacy Lost the Civil War.* New York: Oxford University Press, 1992.

Bradley, Hugh. *Such Was Saratoga.* Saratoga Springs, NY: E. P. Dutton, 1953.

Brant, Marley. *Jesse James: The Man and the Myth.* New York: Berkley, 1998.

———. *The Outlaw Youngers: A Confederate Brotherhood.* Lanham, MD: Madison, 1992.

Breihan, Carl W. *The Complete and Authentic Life of Jesse James.* New York: Frederick Fall, 1953.

———. *The Man Who Shot Jesse James.* London: A. S. Barnes, 1979.

Brownlee, Richard S. *Gray Ghosts of the Confederacy: Guerrilla Warfare in the West, 1861–1865.* Baton Rouge: Louisiana State University Press, 1958.

Buel, William J. *The Border Outlaws and the Border Bandits.* Chicago: Donahue, Henneberry, 1892.

Burlingame, Michael. *Abraham Lincoln: A Life.* Baltimore: Johns Hopkins University Press, 2008.

Castel, Albert E. *Civil War Kansas: Reaping the Whirlwind.* Lawrence: University Press of Kansas, 1997.

———. *A Frontier State at War: Kansas, 1861–1865.* Ithaca, NY: Cornell University Press, 1958.

―――. *William Clarke Quantrill: His Life and Times.* New York: Frederick Fell, 1962.

Castel, Albert E., and Thomas Goodrich. *Bloody Bill Anderson: The Short, Savage Life of a Civil War Guerrilla.* Mechanicsburg, PA: Stackpole, 1998.

Christensen, Lawrence O. *Dictionary of Missouri Biography.* Columbia: University of Missouri Press, 1999.

Collins, Robert. *Jim Lane: Scandal, Statesman, Kansan.* Gretna, LA: Pelican, 2007.

Connelly, William E. *James Henry Lane, the Grim Chieftain of Kansas.* Topeka, KS: Crane, 1899.

Connolly, Thomas L. *Marble Man: Robert E. Lee and His Image in American Society.* New York: Knopf, 1977.

Cordley, Richard. *History of Lawrence.* Lawrence, KS: Lawrence Journal Press, 1895.

Crickmore, Henry G. *Krick's Guide to the Turf, 1878–80.* New York: H. G. Crickmore, 1883.

Crittenden, H. H. *The Crittenden Memoirs.* New York: G. P. Putnam's Sons, 1936.

Crittenden, Lucius E. *Recollections of Abraham Lincoln and His Administration.* New York: Harper and Brothers, 1891.

Croy, Homer. *Jesse James Was My Neighbor.* New York: Duell, Sloan and Pierce, 1949.

Cummins, Jim. *Jim Cummins' Book, Written by Himself.* Denver: Reed, 1903.

Davis, William C. *The Cause Lost: Myths and Realities of the Confederacy.* Lawrence: University Press of Kansas, 1996.

Donald, David Herbert. *Lincoln.* New York: Simon & Schuster, 1995.

―――, ed. *Why the North Won the Civil War.* New York: Simon & Schuster, 1960, 1996.

Duncan, Patricia A. *Tallgrass Prairie: The Inland Sea.* Kansas City, MO: Lowell Press, 1978.

Edwards, John N. *Noted Guerrillas, or the Warfare of the Border.* St. Louis: H. W. Brand, 1879.

―――. *Shelby and His Men, the War in the West.* Cincinnati: Miami Printing and Publishing, 1867.

Ellis, Mark R. *Law and Order in Buffalo Bill's Country: Legal Culture and Community on the Great Plains, 1867–1910.* Lincoln: University of Nebraska Press, 2007.

Etcheson, Nicole. *Bleeding Kansas: Contested Liberty in the Civil War Era.* Lawrence: University Press of Kansas, 2004.

Fehrenbacher, Donald E., ed. *Abraham Lincoln: Speeches and Writings.* Library of America, 1989.

Fellman, Michael. *Citizen Sherman: A Life of William Tecumseh Sherman*. New York: Random House, 1995.

―――. *Inside War: The Guerrilla Conflict in Missouri During the American Civil War*. New York: Oxford University Press, 1989.

Ferguson, Robert A. *The Trial in American Life*. Chicago: University of Chicago Press, 2007.

Filbert, Preston. *The Half Not Told: The Civil War in a Frontier Town*. Mechanicsburg, PA: Stackpole, 2001.

Flood, Charles Bracelen. *Grant and Sherman*. New York: Farrar, Straus and Giroux, 2005.

Foote, Shelby. *The Civil War: A Narrative, Fort Sumter to Perryville*. New York: Random House, 1958.

Foster, Gaines M. *Ghosts of the Confederacy: Defeat, the Lost Cause, and the Emergence of the New South, 1865 to 1913*. New York: Oxford University Press, 1987.

Gallagher, Gary W., and John T. Nolan, eds. *The Myth of the Lost Cause and Civil War History*. Bloomington: Indiana University Press, 2000.

Galloway, John D. *The First Transcontinental Railroad*. New York: Dorset, 1889.

Garrett, Jill Knight. *A History of Humphreys County*. Columbia, TN: privately printed, 1963.

Gilmore, Donald L. *Civil War on the Missouri-Kansas Border*. Gretna, LA: Pelican, 2006.

Glaab, Charles N. *Kansas City and the Railroads*. Lawrence: University Press of Kansas, 1993.

Goodrich, Thomas. *Black Flag: Guerrilla Warfare on the Western Border, 1861–1865*. Bloomington: Indiana University Press, 1995.

―――. *Bloody Dawn: The Story of the Lawrence Massacre*. Kent, OH: Kent State University Press, 1991.

―――. *War to the Knife: Bleeding Kansas, 1854–1861*. Mechanicsburg, PA: Stackpole, 1998.

Goodwin, Doris K. *Team of Rivals*. New York: Simon & Schuster, 2005.

Grant, U. S. *Personal Memoirs*. New York: Penguin Putnam, 1999. Originally published 1885.

Gwynne, S. C. *Empire of the Summer Moon: Quanah Parker and the Rise and Fall of the Comanches, the Most Powerful Indian Tribe in American History*. New York: Scribner, 2010.

Hale, Donald R. *They Called Him Bloody Bill: The Life of William Anderson*. Clinton, MO: The Printery, 1975.

Hesseltine, William B., ed. *A Tragic Conflict: The Civil War and Reconstruction*. New York: George Braziller, 1962.

Hildreth, Samuel C. *The Spell of the Turf: The Story of American Racing.* Philadelphia: J. P. Lippincott, 1926.

History of Carroll County, Missouri. St. Louis: Missouri Historical Co., 1881.

History of Clay and Platte Counties, Missouri. St. Louis: National Historical Co., 1885.

The History of Daviess County, Missouri. Kansas City, MO: Birdsall and Dean, 1882.

History of Daviess and Gentry Counties, Missouri. Topeka, KS: Historical Publishing, 1922.

The History of Jackson County, Missouri. Kansas City, MO: Union Historical Co., 1881.

History of Johnson County, Missouri. Kansas City, MO: Kansas City Historical Co., 1887.

The History of Wayne County, Iowa.

Hobsbawm, E. J. *Bandits.* New York: Pantheon, 1969.

Hoeflich, Michael H. *Justice on the Prairie: 150 Years of the Federal District Court of Kansas.* Kansas City, MO: Rockhill, 2011.

Holzer, Harold. *Lincoln at Cooper Union: The Speech That Made Abraham Lincoln President.* New York: Simon & Schuster, 2004.

Horan, James D. *The Authentic Wild West: The Lawmen.* New York: Crown, 1980.

———. *The Dalton Brothers.* New York: Crown, 1977.

———. *The Pinkertons: The Detective Dynasty That Made History.* New York: Bonanza, 1967.

Horton, James Oliver, and Lois E. Horton, eds. *Slavery and Public History: The Tough Stuff of American Memory.* Chapel Hill: University of North Carolina Press, 2006.

Howe, Edgar Watson. *The Story of a Country Town.* Cambridge: Belknap Press of Harvard University Press, 1961.

Hughes, John Taylor. *Doniphan's Expedition: An Account of the U.S. Army Operations in the Great American Southwest.* Chicago: Rio Grande Press, 1962.

Hunter, Louis C. *Steamboats on the Western Rivers: An Economic and Technological History.* New York: Dover, 1949.

Huntington, George. *Robber and Hero: The Story of the Northfield Bank Raid.* Originally published 1895. St. Paul: Minnesota Historical Society Press, 1986.

Hurt, R. Douglas. *Agriculture and Slavery in Missouri's Little Dixie.* Columbia: University of Missouri Press, 1992.

Johnson, David D. *John Ringo.* Stillwater, OK: Barbed Wire Press, 1996.

Kagen, Neil, ed. *Eyewitness to the Civil War.* Washington, DC: National Geographic Society, 2007.

Kaplan, Fred. *Lincoln: The Biography of a Writer.* New York: Harper Collins, 2008.

Kinney, Brandon G. *The Mormon War: Zion and the Missouri Extermination Order of 1838.* Yardley: PA, Westholme Publishing, 2011.

Klein, Maury. *Union Pacific: The Birth of a Railroad.* New York: Doubleday, 1987.

Klein, Michael J. *The Baltimore Plot: The First Conspiracy to Assassinate Abraham Lincoln.* Yardley, PA: Westholme, 2011.

Koblas, John. *The Jesse James Northfield Raid.* St. Cloud, MN: North Star Press, 1999.

Leach, George B. *The Kentucky Derby Diamond Jubilee.* Louisville, KY: Dial Press, 1949.

Leopard, John C., and R. M. McCammon. *History of Daviess and Gentry Counties, Missouri.* Topeka, KS: Historical Publishing, 1922.

Leslie, Edward E. *The Devil Knows How to Ride: The True Story of William Clarke Quantrill and His Confederate Raiders.* New York: Random House, 1996.

Love, Robertus. *The Rise and Fall of Jesse James.* Lincoln: University of Nebraska Press, 1990. Originally published 1925.

Lubet, Steven. *Murder in Tombstone: The Forgotten Trial of Wyatt Earp.* New Haven, CT: Yale University Press, 2004.

Mackay, James A. *Allan Pinkerton: The First Private Eye.* New York: John Wiley & Sons, 1996.

Malin, James. *John Brown and the Legend of Fifty-Six.* Philadelphia: Haskell House, 1971.

Mangum, William P., II. *A Kingdom for the Horse.* Louisville, KY: Harmony House, 1999.

McCandless, Perry. *A History of Missouri.* Vol. 2. Columbia: University of Missouri Press, 1972.

McCullough, David. *Truman.* New York: Simon & Schuster, 1992.

McDougal, Henry Clay. *Recollections: 1844–1909.* Kansas City, MO: Franklin Hudson, 1910.

McDougall, Walter A. *Let the Sea Make a Noise.* New York: Harper Collins, 1993.

McGee, Joseph H. *Story of the Grand River Country: Memoirs of Major Joseph H. McGee, 1821–1905.* Gallatin: North Missourian Press, 1909.

McGrane, Martin Edward. *The James Farm: Its People, Their Lives and Their Times.* Pierre, SD: Caleb Perkins Press, 1982.

McPherson, James M. *Abraham Lincoln and the Second American Revolution.* New York: Oxford University Press, 1991.

————. *Battle Cry of Freedom: The Civil War Era*. New York: Oxford University Press, 1988.

————. *Ordeal by Fire*. New York: Knopf, 1982.

Miers, Earl Schenck. *Lincoln, Day by Day*. Washington, DC: Lincoln Sesquicentennial Commission, 1960.

Miller, George, Jr. *The Trial of Frank James for Murder*. St. Louis: self-published, 1898. Reprint, New York: Jingle Bob/Crown, 1977.

Miner, Craig. *Kansas: The History of the Sunflower State, 1854–2000*. Lawrence: University Press of Kansas, 2002.

————. *Seeding Civil War: Kansas in the National News 1854–58*. Lawrence: University Press of Kansas, 2008.

Monaghan, Jay. *Civil War on the Western Border, 1854–1865*. Boston: Little, Brown, 1955.

Morn, Frank. *The Eye That Never Sleeps: A History of the Pinkerton National Detective Agency*. Bloomington: Indiana University Press, 1982.

Moulton, G. E., ed. *The Journals of the Lewis and Clark Expedition*. Lincoln: University of Nebraska Press, 1983–2001.

Mountcastle, Clay. *Punitive War: Confederate Guerrillas and Union Reprisals*. Lawrence: University Press of Kansas, 2009.

Nash, Gerald D. *Creating the West: Historical Interpretations of 1890–1990*. Albuquerque: University of New Mexico Press, 1991.

Neely, Jeremy. *The Border between Them: Violence and Reconciliation on the Kansas-Missouri Line*. Columbia: University of Missouri Press, 2007.

Nichols, Bruce. *Guerrilla Warfare in Civil War Missouri, 1862*. Jefferson, NC: McFarland, 2004.

Oates, Stephen B. *To Purge This Land with Blood: A Biography of John Brown*. Amherst: University of Massachusetts Press, 1970.

Paxton, W. M. *Annals of Platte County, Missouri*. Kansas City, MO: Ramfre Press, 1965, reprint.

Pence, Daniel M. *I Knew Frank . . . I Wish I Had Known Jesse*. Independence, MO: Two Trails, 2007.

Peterson, Paul. *Quantrill in Texas*. Nashville: Cumberland House, 2007.

Petrone, Gerard S. *Judgment at Gallatin: The Trial of Frank James*. Lubbock: Texas Tech University Press, 1998.

Pinkerton, Allan. *The Expressman and the Detective*. Originally published 1874. New York: Arno Press, 1976.

Pinkerton, William A. *Train Robberies, Train Robbers, and the "Holdup" Men*. New York: Arno Press, 1974.

Piston, William Garrett. *Wilson's Creek*. Chapel Hill: University of North Carolina Press, 2000.

Puleo, Stephen. *The Caning: The Assault that Drove America to Civil War*. Yardley, PA: Westholme Publishing, 2012.

Quiett, Glenn Chesney. *They Built the West: An Epic of Rails and Cities*. New York: D. Appleton-Century, 1934.

Reddig, William M. *Tom's Town*. Columbia: University of Missouri Press, 1947.

Reno, John. *John Reno, the World's First Train Robber and Self-Proclaimed Leader of the Infamous Reno Gang*. Seymour, IN: 1879.

Rhodes, Joel. *A Missouri Railroad Pioneer: The Life of Louis Houck*. Columbia: University of Missouri Press, 2008.

Ross, James R. *I, Jesse James*. Thousand Oaks, CA: Dragon, 1988.

Rossbach, Jeffrey. *Ambivalent Conspirators: John Brown, the Secret Six, and a Theory of Slave Violence*. Philadelphia: University of Pennsylvania Press, 1982.

Settle, William A. *Jesse James Was His Name, or, Fact and Fiction Concerning the Careers of the Notorious James Brothers of Missouri*. Lincoln: University of Nebraska Press, 1977. Originally published 1966.

Sherman, William T. *Memoirs of General William T. Sherman*. New York: D. Appleton, 1875.

Slotkin, Richard. *Gunfighter Nation: The Myth of the Gunfighter in 20th Century America*. New York: Harper Perennial, 1993.

Smith, Joanna. *Baugus, Boggus & Boggess: Footprints on the Sands of Time*. Drakesboro, KY: n.p., 1993.

Smith, Ronald D. *Thomas Ewing Jr.: Frontier Lawyer and Civil War General*. Columbia: University of Missouri Press, 2008.

Speer, John. *Life of General James H. Lane: The Liberator of Kansas*. Garden City, KS: John Speer, 1896.

Stampp, Kenneth M., ed. *The Causes of the Civil War*. New York: Simon & Schuster, 1991.

Starr, Kevin. *California: A History*. New York: Random House, 2005.

Stauffer, John. *Giants: The Parallel Lives of Frederick Douglass and Abraham Lincoln*. New York: Grand Central, 2008.

Steele, Philip W. *Jesse and Frank James: The Family History*. Gretna, LA: Pelican, 1987.

Steele, Philip W., with George Warfel. *The Many Faces of Jesse James*. Gretna, LA: Pelican, 1995.

Steiner, Mark E. *An Honest Calling: The Law Practice of Abraham Lincoln*. DeKalb: Northern Illinois University Press, 2006.

Stephenson, Wendell H. *Publications of the Kansas State Historical Society Embracing the Political Career of General James H. Lane*. Vol. 3. Topeka: Kansas State Printing, 1930.

Stiles, T. J. *Jesse James: Last Rebel of the Civil War*. New York: Random House, 2002.

Stutler, Boyd. *West Virginia in the Civil War.* Charlotte, NC: Educational Foundation, 1966.

Sutherland, Daniel E. *A Savage Conflict: The Decisive Role of Guerrillas in the American Civil War.* Chapel Hill: University of North Carolina Press, 2009.

Tarbell, Ida M. *Life of Abraham Lincoln.* New York: Lincoln Historical Society, 1900.

Triplett, Frank. *The Life, Times and Treacherous Death of Jesse James.* St. Louis: Chambers, 1882.

Twain, Mark. *Roughing It.* Hartford, CT: American Publishing, 1872.

US Department of War. *The War of the Rebellion: A Compilation of the Official Records of the Union and Confederate Armies.* 127 vols. Washington, DC: Government Printing Office, 1880–1901.

Wallace, William H. *Speeches and Writings of William H. Wallace, with Autobiography.* Kansas City, MO: Western Baptist, 1914.

Watkins, Sam. *Co. Aytch, or a Side Show of the Big Show. A New Edition Introduced and Annotated by Philip Leigh.* Yardley, PA: Westholme Publishing, 2013.

Waugh, John C. *Reelecting Lincoln: The Battle for the 1864 Presidency.* New York: Crown, 1992.

Weber, Thomas. *The Northern Railroads in the Civil War, 1861–1865.* New York: King's Crown Press, Columbia University, 1952.

Wilder, D. W. The Annals of Kansas. Topeka: Kansas Publishing House, 1886.

Williams, Walter, ed. *A History of Northwest Missouri.* Chicago: Lewis, 1915.

Wilson, Douglas L. *Herndon's Informants: Letters, Interviews, and Statements about Abraham Lincoln.* Chicago: University of Illinois Press, 1998.

———. *Lincoln's Sword: The Presidency and the Power of Words.* New York: Knopf, 2006.

Winik, Jay. *April 1865: The Month That Saved America.* New York: HarperCollins, 2001.

Wood, Larry. *The Civil War Story of Bloody Bill Anderson.* Austin, TX: Eakin Press, 2003.

Woodson, W. H. *History of Clay County, Missouri.* Topeka, KS: Historical Publishing, 1920.

Wunder, John R. *Jesse James and Bill Ryan at Nashville.* Nashville: Depot Press, 1981.

———. *Law and the Great Plains: Essays on the Legal History of the Heartland.* Westport, CT: Greenwood Press, 1996.

———. *The Nebraska-Kansas Act of 1854.* Lincoln.: University of Nebraska Press, 2008.

Yeatman, Ted P. *Frank and Jesse James: The Story behind the Legend.* Nashville: Cumberland House, 2001.

Younger, Thomas Coleman. *The Story of Cole Younger, by Himself.* Lee's Summit, MO: n. p., 1903. Reprint, Springfield, MO: Oak Hills, 1996.

ARTICLES

Baron, Frank. "German Republicans and Radicals in the Struggle for a Slave-Free Kansas: Charles F. Kob and August Bondi." *Yearbook for German-American Studies* 40 (2005): 3–26.

————. "James H. Lane and the Origins of the Kansas Jayhawk." *Kansas History: A Journal of the Central Plains* 34, no. 2 (Summer 2011): 115–127.

Breihan, Carl W. "Jesse James and the Gallatin Bank Robbery." *Real West* 14, no. 97 (October 1997): 33–34, 48–50.

Brinckerhoff, Fred H. "The Kansas Tour of Lincoln the Candidate." *Kansas History: A Journal of the Central Plains* 31, no. 4 (Winter 2008–2009): 275–93.

Buchanan, Russell. "James A. McDougall: A Forgotten Senator." *California Historical Society Quarterly* 15, no. 3 (September 1926): 199–212.

Carlson, Becky. "Manumitted and Forever Set Free: The Children of Charles Lee Younger and Elizabeth." *Missouri Historical Review* 96, no. 1 (October 2001): 16–31.

Castel, Albert. "Kansas Jayhawking Raids into Western Missouri in 1861." *Missouri Historical Review* 54, no. 1 (October 1959): 1–11.

————. "Order No. 11 and the Civil War on the Border." *Missouri Historical Review* 57, no. 4 (October 1962): 357–68.

Clevenger, Homer. "Railroads in Missouri Politics, 1875–1887." *Missouri Historical Review* 43, no. 2 (January 1949): 220–36.

Dods, John C. "Shook Hardy & Bacon: A History of Excellence." Unpublished manuscript in author's possession.

Edwards, John N. "A Terrible Quintet." Special supplement, *St. Louis Dispatch*, November 23, 1873.

Farr, James. "Not Exactly a Hero: James Alexander McDougall in the United States Senate." *California Historical Quarterly* 65, no. 2 (June 1986): 104–13, 152–53.

Finkelman, Paul. "The End of War and Slavery Yields a New Racial Order." *American Bar Journal* (April 2011): 45–46.

Fitzgerald, Ruth Coder. "Clell and Ed Miller—Members of the James Gang." *Quarterly of the National Association and Center for Outlaw and Lawman History* 15, no. 3 (July–September 1991): 29.

————. "The Trial of Cleland Miller for Bank Robbery." Unpublished manuscript in author's possession.

Gates, Paul W. "The Railroads of Missouri, 1850–1870." *Missouri Historical Review* 26, no. 2 (January 1932): 126–41.

Gottlieb, David J. "Criminal Trials as Culture Wars: Southern Honor and the Acquittal of Frank James." *University of Kansas Law Review* 51 (2003): 409–48.

———. "Forensic Oratory in Antebellum America." *University of Kansas Law Review* 51 (2003): 449–71.

———. "Law in the Republican Classroom." *University of Kansas Law Review* 43 (1995): 711–34.

———. "Lawyers and Law Books in Nineteenth-Century Kansas." *University of Kansas Law Review* 50 (2002): 1051–74.

———. "Legal Fees in Nineteenth-Century Kansas." *University of Kansas Law Review* 48 (2000): 991–1003.

Holzer, Harold. "An Inescapable Conflict." *American Bar Journal* (April 2011): 38–40.

Kelley, Joseph. "The Trials of William Wallace and the Strength of His Conviction." *Jackson County Historical Society Journal* (Spring 2000): 8–9, 16–17.

Langsdorf, Erich. "Jim Lane and the Frontier Guard." *Kansas Historical Quarterly.* Vol. 9, no. 1 (1941): 13–25.

Lincoln, Abraham. Gettysburg Address, November 19, 1863.

———. Second Inaugural Address, March 4, 1865.

"Lincoln in Kansas." *Kansas Historical Collections* 7 (1902): 536–52.

Mangum, William P., II. "Frank and Jesse James Raced Horses between Their Holdups." *Quarterly of the National Association and Center for Outlaw and Lawman History* 13, no. 2 (Fall 1988): 8–13.

———. "The James/Younger Gang and Their Circle of Friends." *Wild West Magazine* (August 2003): 22–23, 26–31.

McDougal, Henry Clay. "A Decade of Missouri Politics—1860 to 1870." *Missouri Historical Review* 3, no. 2 (January 1909): 126–53.

Minor, Craig. "Lane and Lincoln: A Mysterious Connection." *Kansas History: A Journal of the Central Plains* 24, no. 3 (Autumn 2001): 186–99.

Montgomery, Rick. "The Rise and Fall of a Cowtown." *Kansas City Star Magazine* (December 9, 2012): 1, 6–11.

Muehlberger, James P. "The Kansas Lawyer Who Saved Lincoln's Life." *Journal of the Kansas Bar Association* 80, no. 2 (February 2011): 34–43.

———. "Lincoln's Mercy: A Confederate Spy and a Missouri Lawyer." *Journal of the Missouri Bar Association* 68, no. 6 (November–December 2012): 340–43.

———. "Reflections on Lincoln's Kansas Campaign. *Journal of the Kansas Bar Association* 78, no. 10 (November/December 2009): 24–36.

———. "Showdown with Jesse James." *Wild West Magazine* (February 2010): 50–53.

Napier, Rita G. "Origin Stories and Bleeding Kansas." *Kansas History: A Journal of the Central Plains* 34, no. 1 (Spring 2011).

Owens, Amy. "Mr. Howard's Horses." *Blood-Horse* (Jan. 1988): 54–55.

Settle, William A., Jr. "The James Boys and Missouri Politics." *Missouri Historical Review* 36, no. 4 (July 1942): 412–29.

Sutherland, Daniel E. "The Missouri Guerrilla Hunt." *America's Civil War* 22, no. 4 (September 2009): 55–62.

———. "Sideshows No Longer: A Historical Review of the Guerrilla War." *Civil War History* 46, no. 1 (March 2000): 5–23.

Weiss, Earl J. "Western Lawmen: Image and Reality." *Journal of the West* (January/Winter 1985): 23–32.

White, Richard. "Outlaw Gangs of the Middle Border: American Social Bandits." *Western Historical Quarterly* (October 1981): 387–408.

Wood, Larry. "The Other Anderson: Bloody Bill's Brother Jim." *Missouri Historical Review* 97, no. 2 (January 2003): 93–108.

Wybrow, Robert J. "From the Pen of a Noble Robber: The Letters of Jesse Woodson James, 1847–1882." *Brand Book* 24, no. 2 (Summer 1987): 1–22.

———. "Jesse's Juveniles." *Brand Book* 12, no. 1 (October 1969): 1–11.

———. "Jesse Woodson James—A 'Noble Robber'?" *Brand Book* 31, no. 1 (Winter 1996): 1–16.

———. "'Ravenous Monsters of Society': The Early Exploits of the James Gang." *Brand Book* 27, no. 2 (Summer 1990): 1–24.

———. "Texas Wants 'Em: A Case of Mistaken Identiry." *Brand Book* 43, no. 2 (Spring 2010): 3–30.

NEWSPAPERS
Boonville Weekly Advertiser
Chicago Daily Tribune
Columbia Missouri Herald
Columbia Missouri Statesman
Florence North Star Gazette
Gallatin North Missourian
Gallatin Weekly Democrat
Jefferson City People's Tribune
Kansas City Evening Star
Kansas City Journal
Kansas City Journal of Daily Commerce

Kansas City Star
Kansas City Times
Kansas City World
Lexington Caucasian
Liberty Weekly Tribune
Louisville Courier
Milan Republican
Missouri Valley Register
Missouri World
Nashville American
Nashville Republican Banner
New York Herald
New York Times
New York World
Richmond Conservator
Richmond Missourian
Sedalia Daily Democrat
Sioux City Journal
St. Joseph Daily Gazette
St. Joseph Herald & Tribune
St. Joseph Morning Herald
St. Louis Dispatch
St. Louis Globe (later *St. Louis Globe-Democrat*)
St. Louis Republican
Washington Post
Weekly Western Register

OTHER

Clay County, MO, Recorder's Office, Abstract of Deeds.

Daniel Smoote v. Frank and Jesse James. Legal proceedings filed January 10, 1870. Drawer no. 145. Daviess County, Missouri Court of Common Pleas.

Fitzgerald, Ruth Coder. "The Trial of Clelland Miller; Clell and Ed Miller, Members of the James Gang. Unpublished paper, 1989.

Henry McDougal's personal copy of William Wallace's *Speeches and Writings of William H. Wallace, with Autobiography*. Kansas City, MO: Western Baptist, 1914 (in author's possession).

McDougal family scrapbook, in possession of Daviess County Historical Society.

Minutes of Daviess County Court of Common Pleas, 1870–71.

Missouri State Archives Soldiers' Records: War of 1812–World War I.

Missouri's Union Provost Marshal Papers: 1861–1866.

Smoote, Daniel. Probate file and tax records (in author's possession).

State of Iowa v. Clelland Miller, Indicted by Name of Clell Miller. Wayne County, Iowa District Court Records, Case No. 178, March 20, 1872: 534 et seq.

Undated Gallatin, MO, postcard of former Daviess County Savings & Loan Association.

US Bureau of the Census. *A Census of the United States, 1860: Population.* Washington, DC: Government Printing Office, 1864.

ACKNOWLEDGMENTS

Many people contributed to this book. My wife, Jayme, and our children, Alexandra and Max, endured countless hours, then weeks, then months, then years of my inattention as I sat in my study while researching, writing, and rewriting this book. Jayme—you stole my heart eighteen years ago. I love you. You are my world and dream come true. Alexandra—my heart, my beautiful, smart, green-eyed angel. Stay tough and always be a warrior for your heart. I'm so proud of you and love you to the moon and back. You have the world ahead of you—go get 'em girl. Maximilian—my shadow, my love, you have what it takes to win the game of life. You are an incredible gift, and I love you with everything I have. Don't ever give up! Their patience and understanding has put me forever in their debt. Mom—thank you for reading and rereading my manuscript in your special spot. I love you.

Thanks to David Stark, sixth-generation Gallatin historian and author, who provided me with numerous source materials and invaluable guidance and information as to Gallatin's rich history. Darryl Wilkerson, president of Gallatin Publishing Company, provided primary source information on Henry Clay McDougal. Theresa Hamilton, deputy, Circuit Court of Daviess County, patiently assisted me in my efforts to locate the Smoote lawsuit. Georgia Maxwell, Daviess County recorder of deeds, allowed me access to the Daviess County criminal records as to Frank and Jesse James. Seth Smith, of the Missouri Historical Society, assisted me in locating copies of original newspaper accounts of the events discussed in this book.

Thanks to Robert J. Wybrow, who offered valuable suggestions regarding historical research on Frank and Jesse James, provided newspaper articles and source documents that were key to my research, and reviewed an early version of my manuscript and offered helpful suggestions. Elizabeth Murphy, research assistant at the James Farm, and Beth Beckett, Clay County Historic Sites director, provided me with valuable assistance and insights into researching the Jesse James materials located at the James Farm and Museum. Thanks to Tim Rues, Kansas Historical Society, for his insight and assistance with Kansas Territorial history, David W. Jackson, of the Jackson County, Missouri Historical Society for his assistance with 19th-century Jackson County history, Bruce Johnson for his information on Daniel Smoote's family history, Brenda DeVore, Manager, Prairie Trails Museum of Wayne County, Iowa, for her assistance in locating the Clell Miller trial transcript, and Michelle Pollard, English Westerners' Society, who provided research assistance on Jesse James. My friends Bill Colby and Matt Keenan assisted and encouraged me to publish my findings. Thanks to Peter J. Casagrande, who patiently reviewed an early version of this manuscript and made many helpful suggestions. Henry McDougal's granddaughter provided me with information about her grandfather and photographs. The staff of the Johnson County, Kansas and Kansas City, Missouri public libraries have been very helpful over the years in obtaining source materials.

Last, but certainly not least, thanks to my publisher, Bruce H. Franklin, at Westholme Publishing, who guided me through the process and made invaluable suggestions that made the book much better, Ron Silverman, my copy editor, for his comments, all of which improved the book considerably, and Trudi Gershenov for her striking jacket design. Any errors are mine.

INDEX

Wilkinson, Allen, 30
Williams, Jack, 116
Wilson, Woodrow, 219n18
Wirt, Philip, 208n11
Wock, Ted, 88-89
Wollcott, Addison E., 163-164
Woodson, Ben, 190
Woodson, B. J., 164-165, 171
Woodson, Blake L., 111

Yeager, R. L., 111
Yellowstone, 44
Younger, Bob, 72, 99-101, 192
Younger, Henry, 72
Younger, Jim, 72, 99-101, 192
Younger, John, 72, 165
Younger, Thomas Coleman "Cole"
  Clell Miller and, 82
  Columbia, Kentucky, bank robbery
      and, 83, 86, 148
  Dick Liddil and, 165
  Northfield bank robbery and, 99-
      101
  Ocobock Brothers' Bank robbery
      and, 79
  Russellville, Kentucky bank robbery
      and, 146-147
  William Quantrill and, 72, 200